REMARKABLE
TREES
of VIRGINIA

REMARKABLE TREES of VIRGINIA

BY NANCY ROSS HUGO AND JEFF KIRWAN
PHOTOGRAPHY BY ROBERT LLEWELLYN

Albemarle Books

REMARKABLE TREES
OF VIRGINIA

Published by Albemarle Books
885 Reas Ford Road, Earlysville, Virginia 22936
434.973.8000

Distributed by University of Virginia Press
Charlottesville and London
www.upress.virginia.edu

Book Design by Michael Fitts

Printed and bound in China

First Published 2008
10 9 8 7 6 5 4

We gratefully acknowledge the support of The Ballyshannon Fund and of Trees Virginia in making this second
edition possible.

Library of Congress Cataloging-in-Publication Data

Hugo, Nancy R.
  Remarkable trees of Virginia / by Nancy Ross Hugo and Jeff Kirwan ; photography by Robert Llewellyn. -- 1st ed.
    p. cm.
  Includes index.
  ISBN 978-0-9742707-2-2
  1. Trees--Virginia. I. Kirwan, Jeffrey Lynn. II. Title.

  QK191.H84 2008
  582.1609755--dc22
                         2008014269

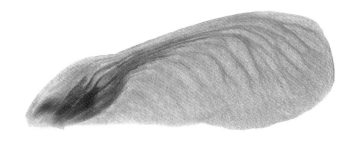

THIS BOOK

was created with the encouragement and support
of our sponsors who share our passion for
trees and who made our travels, our
research, and our opportunity
to tell tree stories possible.

TREES VIRGINIA (VIRGINIA URBAN FORESTS COUNCIL)

ROBERT H. SMITH FAMILY FOUNDATION

BARTLETT TREE EXPERTS

THE PECK FOUNDATION

VIRGINIA TECH DEPARTMENT OF FORESTRY

VIRGINIA FORESTRY EDUCATIONAL FOUNDATION

GWATHMEY MEMORIAL TRUST

BALLYSHANNON FUND

THE SEAY FOUNDATION

VIRGINIA FOUNDATION FOR THE HUMANITIES

VIRGINIA 4-H FOUNDATION
3NORTH ARCHITECTS
AMERICAN SOCIETY OF LANDSCAPE ARCHITECTS, VIRGINIA CHAPTER
GRACE STREET RESIDENTIAL DESIGN SYSTEMS
ANNE MCCRACKEN AND JIM ROGERS
JEANETTE AND DAVID MCKITTRICK
FRANK HARDY, INC., REALTORS
COLESVILLE NURSERY IN MEMORY OF AL GARDNER
VIRGINIA NURSERY & LANDSCAPE ASSOCIATION
ROBERT STRINI
TED AND SHEILA WESCHLER
ANNA LANE
MR. AND MRS. FREDERIC SCOTT BOCOCK
MID-ATLANTIC CHAPTER INTERNATIONAL SOCIETY OF ARBORICULTURE
PRECISION LANDSCAPING COMPANY
VIRGINIA TREE FARM COMMITTEE
VIRGINIA HORTICULTURAL FOUNDATION
THREE CHOPT GARDEN CLUB
VALLEY BEAUTIFUL FOUNDATION

Remarkable for its fall foliage, this blackgum (Nyssa sylvatica), also known as tupelo, grows in the city of Richmond's Hollywood Cemetery.

Contents

Baldcypress (Taxodium distichum)*, Lake Drummond, Chesapeake*

White oak (Quercus alba),
Cumberland County

INTRODUCTION

Trees aren't the only things that sometimes get bigger than you thought they would. When Jeff Kirwan and I launched the Remarkable Trees of Virginia Project in 2004, we conceived of a book that would celebrate some of Virginia's finest trees and a website through which people could nominate their favorite trees. Neither of us had any idea we would be sorting through over 1,000 tree nominations and traveling over 20,000 miles to see trees. (Jeff actually walked 300 miles, all the way across the state, to fulfill a lifelong dream and to experience trees and their habitats up close.) Our travels involved almost as many trips to visit trees we decided *not* to feature as to trees we decided *to* feature, but no trip seemed unproductive, because for Jeff and me, any day spent among trees is a good day.

We would like to report, however, that Virginia is a very big state with more than a few trees. It's sobering, for an eastern Virginia girl, to get to the Blacksburg area and realize you're still 3½ hours from the Lee County sassafras you're traveling to see. Our photographer, Robert Llewellyn, set up an impressive 4- by 6-foot table-top Virginia map in which he inserted color-coded flags indicating where all the trees he needed to photograph were, but of course, even when some of them looked close together, they weren't. "It's 30 miles and five mountains from the white pines to the sugar maples," Bob once reminded us, and even neighboring trees often had to be photographed in different seasons.

The travails of travel (which included only one wrecker and one Bates motel but more "I'll be late" calls home than we care to count) paled in comparison to the difficulty involved in choosing the trees and tree places we would feature. Not only did Jeff and I have different favorite trees, we each had more favorites than we could possibly include. Of the approximately 100 trees featured in this book, there are probably 20 that anyone on the trail of remarkable Virginia trees would have insisted on including; for the other 80, we could have made entirely different choices and still had a book filled with remarkable trees. Some of the factors influencing our choices were these: We wanted to include as many important native species as possible, we wanted as wide geographic distribution as possible, and we wanted trees that fit the criteria of our chapters (old trees, historic trees, community trees, etc.).

We soon learned that choosing remarkable trees is like choosing students for an Ivy League college: there are too many qualified applicants for the number of available spaces. We could have filled a book with fabulous white oaks alone—and hope that someday someone will—but that wasn't our mission. In the end, we came up with a selection of trees that both passed the "wow" test (turn a corner, see the tree, and go "wow") and that seemed reasonably representative of the kinds of remarkable trees in the state. Here, then, you will find not just trees remarkable for their size, but trees remarkable for their character, their history, their community significance, and other attributes that lift them out of the ordinary.

For those of us working on the project (whom we sometimes refer to as "the tree team"), the project involved more pleasant surprises than disappointments, but what challenges there were are worth noting, in case anyone else decides to launch a similar project. In one case—and only one—a tree we had hoped to feature was owned by someone who wouldn't give us permission to photograph it. That person was a developer who must have decided it was not in his interest to call attention to the tree. That was sad for more reasons than just depriving us of a tree we'd hoped to feature, because the tree is beloved in the community where it grows.

We also recognized early on—and this was really distressing—that, despite our best efforts, our writing and Bob's photography would never be able to capture the essence of the trees we were seeing. If you've ever tried to photograph a tree, you've seen it diminished the minute you view it through a viewfinder or LCD screen; photographs, even those as fine as Robert Llewellyn's, don't capture the "sense-around" experience of a tree. Words we found even less adequate. Author Primo Levi once noted that language wasn't up to the task of describing stars—adjectives designed to excite wonder often had the opposite effect, and trying to use language to describe stars was like "trying to plow with a feather."

He might have been describing the equally impossible task of describing trees. How we tried to avoid words like "great," "grand," "beautiful," and "majestic," but they slipped in, partly because there is such a huge gap between the tree you experience and the tree you can describe that it draws such adjectives in just to fill the void. It was frustrating not to find language equal to our trees, but we did the best we could and decided to "plow on" with our writing and photographing, knowing we would add this disclaimer: A tree on a page is not a tree in the woods, and if you find any tree featured here "great, grand, beautiful, or majestic," know that it is twice that outdoors.

The biggest surprise of our project was the quality of the tree nominations we received. We expected that anyone who cared enough about a tree to nominate it would go to some effort, but we did not expect to receive nominations that included poetry, elaborate photo CDs, extensive histories, heartfelt prose, and humor. Vicki Slonneger, for example, wrote her nomination of a black oak in King William County in ink made from black oak galls, and Kim Overstreet's

This American beech, which seems to be a special friend of sweethearts and woodcarvers, grows at Maymont in the city of Richmond. The carving isn't good for the tree, but it amazes visitors, who marvel at the initials engraved not only in the tree's trunk but also on its roots.

nomination of a white oak (growing in a parking lot at the Short Pump Towne Center in Henrico County) included this poem: "As I reach my limbs to heaven, I thank God they didn't turn me into a 7-11!"

We received nominations from old folks and children ("It's been there as long as we can remember," one group of kids standing in front of an enormous white oak wrote, with sweet irony); we received nominations from 4-H clubs and from a motorcycle club (the latter searches for champion trees as it rides); we received nominations from people celebrating births ("we planted this river birch in 1986 on the day the first grandchild was born into the Falkenstein family") and mourning losses ("It remains the steadfast reminder of the lasting quality of nature, through the turmoil of daily storms, and the difficulties of family life," wrote a Northumberland family that mourns the loss of a 6-year-old by gathering under a stately elm).

It was particularly heartening to receive nominations from people who didn't actually own the trees they were nominating—they just wanted them recognized as fine trees and were grateful for an opportunity to praise them. In fact, anyone who ever feels like a lone advocate for trees could renew his or her resolve just by perusing the Remarkable Tree website now and then. What's so uplifting about the website is that, in addition to conveying important information about Virginia trees, it conveys the voices of ordinary Virginians, each different but consistently emphatic in its appreciation of trees. A website is a temporary thing, of course, and we can't predict how long ours will endure, but in our experience it has proved to be an invaluable tool for gathering and sharing information about remarkable trees.

Four years of traveling the state visiting trees also showed us how hard many Virginians were working to take care of their trees. We were impressed by the big things—universities with arborists, cities with organized Tree Stewards and Tree Boards—and also by the small things, like a bell hung in the branch of a beloved oak beside a modest Gloucester home to warn the UPS truck not to proceed any farther or risk damaging a valued lower limb farther on. On Tuckahoe Plantation in Richmond, we found an old hackberry so well supported by wooden props we wanted to give the owner some sort of award for "best effort on behalf of an ancient tree," and at the University of Mary Washington, we wanted to tell everyone on campus you don't get those nice, sweeping branches close to the ground without someone like Joni Wilson, Director of Landscape and Grounds, training the mowers to avoid them.

In short, we discovered that what we had conceived of as a mission to educate the public about Virginia's finest trees and their importance had also become a mission to collect and share what Virginians already knew about their trees, because that knowledge and appreciation was vast. Here, then, you will find not just the thoughts of two writers and a photographer who spent four years visiting some of Virginia's finest trees, but the accumulated wisdom of all the tree nominators, arborists, foresters, botanists, landscapers, city planners, homeowners, hikers, naturalists, and others who shared what they knew with us. We intend this book to honor them as well as Virginia's remarkable trees.

Nancy Ross Hugo

Most people, when asked why they admire trees, include "age" in their answer. The fact that trees outlive people by so many decades (and sometimes centuries) inspires awe in us shorter-lived folk. Trees are also older than people evolutionarily. How much older trees are than people depends on how you define a person and how you define a tree, but the first trees recognizable as trees appeared on earth around 400 million years ago and the first men recognizable as men appeared around 3 million years ago—a gap in time wide enough to firmly establish trees' preeminence on the planet.

In the chapters that follow we will describe some tree genera, like *Ginkgo*, that were well established on earth before the dinosaurs (and, of course, before men), but in this one we will be describing individual trees that have the distinction of being among the oldest living trees in Virginia—trees like the baldcypresses on the Blackwater River in Southampton County, which have been scientifically determined to be over 800 years old, sharing historical time with Genghis Khan and King Henry I. We have selected only trees for which there is some scientific or historical basis to believe they are among the oldest living examples of their species in the state and trees that have the genetic potential for long life to begin with.

So how does one determine how old a tree is? Unfortunately, you don't do it by looking at how big the tree is. Most everyone assumes there is a direct correlation between tree size and tree age, but there isn't. "It's no more likely a big tree will be older than a small one than it is that a large person will be older than a small one," explains Dr. Carolyn Copenheaver, forest ecologist at Virginia Tech. After all, the oldest trees on earth, the 4,000-year-old bristlecone pines, are relatively small, and in Virginia, there are some chestnut oaks 17 inches in diameter that are over 250 years old (these grow on rocky mountaintops) and other chestnut oaks the same size but growing in fertile valleys, that are only 50 years old. One can make *some* assumptions about age based on a tree's genetic potential (we know baldcypresses have the genetic potential to live over a thousand years and that boxelders seldom live more than a hundred), but tree spacing and site conditions affect tree size too profoundly for size to be well correlated with age.

Historical documents can help with determining tree ages—Thomas Jefferson's planting records have helped establish tree ages at Monticello, and a Mathew Brady photograph establishes the Civil War presence of the Brompton oak in Fredericksburg—but the only scientific way to date a tree is to count its rings. Because trees put on different kinds of wood in early summer and in late summer, dendrochronologists can count annual rings to figure out how old a tree is. (These rings are visible to the eye because early summer wood is a different color than late summer wood—sometimes lighter, sometimes darker, depending on the tree species.) Unfortunately, to see tree rings, one must cut the tree down, cut a wedge out of it, or use an increment borer to extract a narrow (about 1/4-inch) tube-like sample from the tree. The last option is obviously the least damaging to the tree, but even it wounds the tree. Fortunately, such wounds, similar to those made when tapping a sugar maple, usually heal within two years. Core samples are dried, sanded, examined closely under a microscope, and compared to existing tree ring data to determine the tree's age. As you will see in the following pages, the results can be surprising.

In 2008, this eastern arborvitae (Thuja occidentalis) *along Dunlap Creek in Alleghany County was recognized as the largest in the nation.*

EASTERN ARBORVITAE, ALLEGHANY COUNTY

"It's like Jurassic Park," Anne Lacy Wright says of the unique trees, rocks, and water features behind her home in Alleghany County, and few visitors would disagree. Wright's living room window looks out on a 40-foot-high waterfall that stretches 100 feet horizontally. The waterfall, which probably formed long ago when a cave collapsed, indicates something about the geology of the area, and that geology helps explain the extraordinary nearby trees.

Along the creek into which this waterfall drains grow eastern arborvitae (*Thuja occidentalis*), which are often found on limestone terrain characterized by sinks, ravines, and underground streams. This species loves alkaline (as opposed to acidic) soils and thrives under conditions like those found along Dunlap Creek, where the shoreline is punctuated with huge white (limestone) rocks and honeycombed with caves. These trees also benefit from the turquoise-blue waters of Dunlap Creek.

Like Jurassic Park, this habitat seems to have come to us from another era. The arborvitae there seem "otherworldly" in that their pale trunks rise along the creek like towers of living driftwood. Some of them are unusually large (the largest eastern arborvitae in the state, with a 255-inch girth, grows among them); some are small (one grows like a perfectly formed bonsai specimen on a rock platform in the creek); and some have bald white spires in their crowns, suggesting great age.

No one knows exactly how old the arborvitae along Dunlap Creek are. Jeff Kirwan cored a small specimen along the creek and dated it to 1792, but much larger trees on the site were impossible to age because of their hollow interiors. As a species, eastern arborvitae is one of the most long-lived—some would say *the* longest lived—species in the eastern U.S. (Baldcypress is the other contender.) Eastern arborvitae

specimens over 1,600 years old have been dated in Canada, and while no one claims the arborvitae along Dunlap Creek are that old, Jeff Kirwan believes some may be 500 years old.

An evergreen species with flattened, feathery foliage, eastern arborvitae is variously called American arborvitae, eastern white cedar, northern white cedar, and swamp cedar. In the Cypress family, it is not a true cedar at all, but it does share some *Cedrus* characteristics—such as having durable, aromatic wood. Its common name "arborvitae" means "tree of life" and may refer either to the tree's evergreen foliage or to its medicinal properties. American Indians reportedly served French and British sailors a vitamin C-rich tea made from arborvitae foliage, saving them from scurvy.

"Have you tasted it?" Wright asked as she led the Remarkable Tree team through her trees. We hadn't, but we did, noticing immediately the fruity, almost tropical flavor of the shoot tips. Don't try this at home; even American Indians who still use the plant medicinally say there are "good cedars" and "to avoid cedars" often growing side by side (in high concentrations arborvitae leaf oil can be toxic), but on this day, in this environment, we felt we knew the trees better for having tasted them.

Cold springs (always around 55 degrees F) and "sweet" rock (rich in calcium carbonate) have helped create the habitat in which these old eastern arborvitae grow. This stretch of trees, some of which may be 500 years old, grows along Dunlap Creek, between the villages of Crow and Sweet Chalybeate. Eastern arborvitae (Thuja occidentalis) is native only to the far western part of Virginia, but it grows in gardens throughout the state, where homeowners value it for its evergreen foliage and pyramidal shape.

RED CEDAR, GILES COUNTY

Where the New River cuts a canyon-like swath through Giles County, some of Virginia's most startling old trees grow. These are not giants growing in deep soil, the towering trees one usually associates with old growth and forests primeval. Instead, they are stunted eastern red cedars, more reminiscent of the red cedars one might harvest from an old field at Christmas. In fact, the red cedars growing on Pembroke Cliffs are smaller than most Christmas trees—few are over 6 feet tall, but unlike the typical Christmas tree, some of these red cedars are over 400 years old.

The tendency to associate age with size—assuming the biggest trees to be the oldest—is almost universal. But it is a mistake. In fact, according to forester Tom Dierauf, great size can be a curse to a tree, requiring it to raise water to great heights and to nourish more sapwood. On the East Coast, large trees are also more vulnerable to those two great tree levelers—hurricane-force winds and ice storms. "A situation that prevents the possibility of getting large presents the possibility of getting old," argues Dierauf, and the dry, infertile, Pembroke Cliffs provide just such a situation. There conditions are just right for slow growth, small stature, and long life.

On a good growing site, a red cedar (*Juniperus virginiana*) can grow into a tree 80 feet tall and 3 feet in diameter in 60 years. But on a poor site—like the limestone cliffs overlooking the New River in Giles County, a red cedar only 7 inches in diameter and 6 feet tall may be over 400 years old. In fact, red cedars hanging to the edges of these cliffs are eking out a living under conditions that would make the most optimistic arborist cringe. The cliffs themselves, rising 200 feet above the river valley, were carved out during the Pleistocene Period (a time of repeated glaciations between 1.8 million and 11,000 years ago), and their sheer faces seem more rope-climber- than tree-friendly. Trees, including eastern arborvitae, redbud, sugar maple, and chinquapin oak, as well as red cedar, do grow here, but they cling to the cliff faces and rise from rocky outcrops in ways that seem to defy logic, if not gravity.

There is, in fact, a worldwide association between

cliffs, trees of small stature, and trees of great age. Examples of such an association in this country include the oldest trees in the world—the ancient Bristlecone pines (*Pinus longaeva*), which grow in the White Mountains of California and on other high-altitude, limestone mountainsides of the Great Basin, and ancient eastern arborvitae (*Thuja occidentalis*), which grow on the Niagara Escarpment (part of the cliff formation that forms Niagara Falls) from New York to Ontario. Bristlecone pines, which look not like the towering redwoods and giant sequoias we associate with old growth but rather like enormous pieces of living driftwood, live thousands of years (the oldest known living Bristlecone pine, the Methuselah tree, is about 4,800 years old), and one eastern arborvitae growing on the exposed limestone cliffs of Niagara Escarpment in southern Ontario has been dated at over 1,000 years old.

It was the similarity between the conditions under which eastern arborvitae on the Niagara Escarpment grow, and the conditions under which red cedars (and a few eastern arborvitae) on the Pembroke Cliffs grow, that led biologist Tom Wieboldt to suggest that dendrochronologists meeting at the Mountain Lake Biological Station visit the Pembroke Cliffs. Equipped with harnesses and climbing gear, they took core samples from living trees and cross sections from dead trees, which they later analyzed in the lab, counting what turned out to be some very narrow tree rings. Even in youth, it seemed, the eastern red cedars on these cliffs grew extremely slowly, with saplings only 7 to 11 inches tall proving to be 20 years old. The oldest eastern red cedar the scientists dated turned out to be 475 years old (in 1993), but the researchers concluded that "when one considers that only one cliff was sampled, and that only 101 adult trees were sampled, it is highly probable that much older trees will be found when other cliffs are explored."

Exciting as it is to entertain the idea of even older trees growing on Pembroke Cliffs, most of us are thrilled enough with the knowledge that a small red cedar still growing on Pembroke Cliffs was alive when Martin Luther posted his 95 theses on the door of Wittenburg Castle Church (1517) and over 70 years before Shakespeare wrote his first play.

Red cedars on the Pembroke Cliffs near Blacksburg are small but very old—illustrating the correlation between slow growth, small stature, and great age.

RED SPRUCE, GILES COUNTY

When the National Christmas tree, a 65-foot red spruce, was cut from Highland County in 2004, many Virginians were surprised to learn the species even grew in the state. Much more abundant in northern New England and the maritime provinces of Canada, this striking evergreen, which grows best in cool, moist climates, now grows sparsely in high-elevation Virginia mountains, but it was once much more abundant. "There was quite a bit at the turn of the century," says forester Tom Dierauf. "It was much sought after for lumber, but it was pretty much logged out by the First World War." (Your guitar or piano sounding board may be made of resonant red spruce wood, also known as Adirondack spruce.) According to Dierauf, after logging, areas where red spruce had grown were often burned, destroying the seeds that might have helped the species regenerate, and the remaining red spruce populations in Virginia are now threatened by global warming, which could make even Virginia's mountain habitats too warm for them.

There are no more than about a dozen localities in western Virginia where natural stands of red spruce (*Picea rubens*) grow, and many of them are hard to reach or even see (through binoculars, they show up as dark green patches on some mountaintops), but one area in Giles County is an exception. Not far off the easily accessible War Spur Trail on Salt Pond Mountain, some of the state's oldest—and its largest—red spruce grow. One is Virginia's red spruce champion, a towering tree with a double trunk and narrow crown that looks almost tropical silhouetted against the sky. It is 116 feet tall with a diameter of 4⅓ feet at chest height. Nearby grow other enormous red spruces, several of which were dated by biogeographer David Lawrence and his colleagues in 1992. They found two trees that were at least 260 years old.

At the time, Lawrence and his colleagues were interested in, among other things, the decline of red spruce in this area. But, as it turned out, it was healthy hemlocks in this forest, not red spruce trees, that would be experiencing the greatest mortality. Today, although the woods around them are lush with rhododendrons and thick with species like yellow birch and mountain laurel, skeletal hemlocks remind the visitor how radically altered these woods have been by the woolly adelgid—the insect that has decimated hemlocks in Virginia. Surprisingly encouraging are the young red spruce trees that line the trail. Perfectly shaped and impeccably decked out in dark green needles, they seem poised and ready to keep this area rich in red spruce, as long as the climate, the quality of the air, the weather, insects, and pathogens cooperate.

Red spruce trees along War Spur Trail in the Jefferson National Forest, Giles County, germinated around 1730, more than a century before the Civil War.

WHITE OAK, NELSON COUNTY

If you were to scroll down a list of the life spans of Virginia oak species, you would find lots in the 200- to 400-year range, but, at least when it comes to maximum longevity (as opposed to typical age of mortality), white oak is the Methuselah of the group. Although older white oaks have been recorded, the maximum longevity of the white oak (*Quercus alba*) is usually estimated to be 600 years.

The white oak featured here may not be the oldest in the state, but it probably is the oldest white oak in a setting as extraordinary as this one. Isolated on a hillside on the Oak Ridge Estate in Nelson County, it overlooks mountains on four sides and commands views unobstructed by other trees.

Small wonder it has been the subject of amateur and professional paintings, including one by the American painter and printmaker Rockwell Kent (1882-1971), which is now part of the Lora Robins Collection of Virginia Art at the Virginia Historical Society. Painted in 1956 and entitled "Child Under Tree, Virginia," Kent's oil painting depicts the tree looking almost as large as it does today, with children playing under it and the Blue Ridge Mountains in the background.

Although it is now showing its age—two large branches have broken off, and the tree shows signs of decay—this white oak could dominate its site for many years to come. "Two hundred years growing, 200 years living, and 200 years dying" is one aphorism often applied to white oaks. No one knows exactly how old the Oak Ridge Estate's signature white oak is, but when it was cored in 1986, the tree was found to be "at least 365 years old." "That is as far as their testing equipment went," Preston Tyree, estate manager at the time recalls, so today the tree could be over 387 years old—a venerable tree, to be sure, but no more than middle-aged by white oak standards.

Tree with a view. Believed to be over 387 years old, the Oak Ridge Estate's signature white oak commands stunning views of the Blue Ridge Mountains.

BLACKGUM, GREENE COUNTY

"Tough," "old," and "improbable" were the words that kept popping up when the Remarkable Tree crew visited this tree. "Old" because this blackgum's bark screamed "Age!" in a way that few trees do. The tree's thick bark had flat-topped ridges with crevices so deep you could sink half your hand in them, and it was so hard it felt more like stone than wood. According to forest researcher Tom Dierauf, who alerted us to this tree, blackgums this old are rare in Virginia, but it is not unusual for very old blackgums (which can live 250 to 600 years) to have such startling bark. Unlike most trees, Dierauf explains, the blackgum doesn't slough off bark as it ages; its bark just gets thicker and thicker, providing it nearly impenetrable armor.

The tree also seemed improbable, because nothing in the area around it—save rocks—seemed nearly as old as this tree. Most of this area, near the Pocosin Hollow area of Shenandoah National Park, was logged out in the early part of the nineteenth century, but this and a few other blackgums in the area were spared. Why? For one thing, blackgums, which often have decayed heartwood, are famous for being hollow, making them unattractive to loggers. (Beekeepers have long used hollow sections of blackgum for hives.) Second, even when its heartwood is intact, blackgum is unattractive to those who might use it as firewood because it is nearly impossible to split. And third, because of the way it warps and shrinks (at least without the assistance of a dry kiln), blackgum has been described as "too worthless for a self-respecting lumberman to fight into boards."

So as other trees around it were harvested (and wind and ice storms took their toll on weaker trees),

blackgums in this area, which had been slowly growing in the understory, were released, enabling them to grab a spot in the sun. Today, they tower over nearby trees, but their crowns have a distinctly zig-zag appearance, something that Dierauf explains is characteristic of many blackgums and other shade tolerant trees. According to Dierauf, many shade tolerant trees have deformed crowns because, while they were growing in the understory, wind banged them around against the stouter, lower branches of taller trees, repeatedly destroying their terminal buds (for which side buds took over). Old trees like these can also be "stag-headed," with antler-like dead branches sticking out of their crowns. Such "stag-headed-ness" is usually the result of drought: a tree reaches the maximum height to which it can raise water, then a drought comes along and the tree can't get water to its uppermost branches.

Young, old, with a perfect or irregular crown, blackgum is a beautiful tree in the landscape. Although it is seldom listed as an ornamental, blackgum (also known as black tupelo, bee-gum, sour gum, and Pepperidge) can be as colorful as a maple, as picturesque as a pine. Its summer leaves are so shiny they look as though they have been polished, and the fall foliage of many blackgums is a brilliant red (sometimes mixed with green, orange, and yellow). The tree's fruit, a blue-black drupe, is valuable to wildlife, and despite its drawbacks as a timber tree, its wood is valuable for making things you don't want to split, like tool handles. Add to these attributes the blackgum's potential for long life, and you have a tree worthy of admiration and attention, although the tree near Pocosin Hollow proves neglect has its advantages, too.

Sign of age. Thick, hard bark with flat-topped ridges characterizes this old blackgum (Nyssa sylvatica), which grows near an entrance to the Pocosin Hollow Trail, Shenandoah National Park.

Unlike most blackgums, which grow in the forest understory, this old one towers over surrounding trees. It exhibits the "stag-headed-ness," or jagged crown, characteristic of many old trees.

BALDCYPRESS, SOUTHAMPTON COUNTY

Inaccessibility, good genes, and sensitive stewardship have all contributed to the long life of the baldcypress trees on the Blackwater River near Ivor. Based on corings by Dr. David Stahle, geosciences professor at the University of Arkansas, baldcypress trees on Virginia's Blackwater River are believed to be, if not the oldest trees in the state, the oldest trees for which there is scientific documentation of age. According to Dr. Stahle, who cored about 70 of them in 1985, there are several baldcypress trees in the Blackwater swamp that are over 800 years old. The oldest one he dated, based on tree rings, was 810 years old in 1985, which would mean it was alive when Genghis Khan was a teenager. According to Stahle, he "wouldn't be surprised" if there are baldcypress trees on the Blackwater River that are 1,000 years old, and he thinks it likely that 2,000-year-old baldcypress trees once grew in the swamp.

Interestingly, Dr. Stahle's studies were originally designed not to establish the trees' ages but rather to add to the chronology of weather data provided by tree rings. From Virginia's baldcypress trees, Stahle learned, for example, that there was a strong correlation between periods of extreme drought in Virginia and both the disappearance of the Lost Colony of Roanoke Island and the death rates during the early occupations at Jamestown. The years when the trees put on fat rings (wet years), colonists survived; when the trees put on skinny rings (dry years), they died. Stahle's tree ring data revealed that the Lost Colony disappeared during the most extreme drought in 800 years (1587-1589) and that the alarming mortality and near abandonment of Jamestown occurred during the driest period in 770 years (1606-1612).

Although baldcypress trees on the Blackwater River are the oldest scientifically dated trees in Virginia, they are neither the oldest known baldcypress trees on the East Coast nor are they the largest baldcypress trees in Virginia. The oldest *documented* baldcypresses (*Taxodium distichum*) grow on the Black River in North Carolina, where one living tree has been dated at 1,700 years old. Probably because they grow under more nutrient-rich conditions, however, the baldcypress trees on Virginia's Blackwater and Nottoway Rivers are bigger than those on North Carolina's Black River. The swamps along Virginia's Blackwater River contain many baldcypress trees over 20 feet in circumference and over 120 feet tall, and baldcypresses on the Nottoway, including Virginia's

largest tree (see page 50), are over 35 feet in circumference. Although it hasn't been scientifically dated (and can't be because it is hollow), Virginia's largest baldcypress, "Big Mama," and other nearby baldcypresses on the Nottoway, may be older than these dated trees on the Blackwater.

Famous for their size, longevity, and tolerance of wet growing conditions, baldcypress trees belong to an ancient genus, *Taxodium*, and are among the few conifers that lose their needle-like leaves. (Larch and dawn redwood are two others.) Most conifers are evergreen, but baldcypress trees lose their needle-like leaves in the fall.

The baldcypress tree's durable, insect- and water-resistant wood contributes to the tree's longevity as well as to its timber value. Baldcypress wood has been called "the wood eternal" and has been traditionally used for flooring, ship members, cross ties, coffins, shingles and even water pipes. One story has it that a water main made of cypress logs, bored lengthwise, was laid in New Orleans in 1789, and that when it was dug up in 1914, it showed only a trace of rot around the outer circumference.

A similar story is told in Virginia relative to baldcypress logs found along the edge of the Blackwater baldcypress forest in the early 1980s. Those ax-cut logs, long hidden until extreme drought revealed them, had been submerged for decades until they were discovered, with sapwood rotted but heartwood intact. From those logs, shingles were milled and used to build the roof of St. John's Episcopal Church in Chuckatuck.

The baldcypress trees illustrated here grow in the Pompey Tract—a 76-acre old-growth area now owned by the Nature Conservancy. "George Fenwick was dazzled by it," says naturalist Gary Williamson, who first showed the area to Fenwick, president of the Nature Conservancy's Virginia chapter in the 1990s. Prior to its acquisition by the Nature Conservancy, the area was owned by the Kirk Lumber Company, whose president, J. R. Kirk, was equally enthralled by it. "He tried to preserve the site by donating it to the state in the 1950s," says Williamson, "but the state wouldn't take it." The site was never logged, and Kirk's son Arthur donated the property to the Nature Conservancy in 1994. "It's like walking into a different world," says one Kirk relative, who still marvels at the trees on the site. "It's like going into the Astrodome or Superdome, the canopy is so high."

Dividing Isle of Wight and Southampton Counties, the Blackwater River is home to some of the oldest trees in Virginia—ancient baldcypress trees that have been scientifically dated at over 800 years old.

TULIP-POPLAR, GREENE COUNTY

Unlike most of America's national parks, Shenandoah National Park was established not to preserve wilderness but to create it. By the 1930s, most of the land in the Park had been cleared, and the Pocosin Hollow area, like most of the Park, was home to families that had been living in the area for decades. How a 5-acre part of this area came to be spared the saw and plow, no one knows, but for whatever reason, a small portion of this area remained undisturbed and now houses what naturalist Charles E. ("Mo") Stevens has called "the largest trees in aggregation that he has seen in more than 35 years of exploration of the Park."

Along the trail that descends into the hollow, the trunks of enormous red and black oaks stand out among the other trees, but it is tulip-poplars (*Liriodendron tulipifera*) that dominate the old-growth area. Some of the tulip-poplars there are over 120 feet tall, many have diameters of over 5 feet, and one is nearly 150 feet tall and almost 6 feet in diameter, which is to say that standing among them is like standing in a cathedral with massive columns. The tulip-poplars alone signify that this area is special, but it's not just the standing trees that earn this, or any old-growth area, its "old growth" designation.

There are certain "structural characteristics" that define old-growth forest. Old-growth areas are characterized by lots of coarse, woody debris on the forest floor, by uneven age distribution (a mixture of old, medium, and young trees), by nurse logs (rotting logs on which plant seeds often germinate), and by "pit and mound" topography. The latter, also called "pillow and cradle" topography, is what you see when a big, old tree has been uprooted leaving a deep depression behind the mound of its upturned roots. In parts of Pocosin Hollow, for example, there are almost as many huge tulip-poplars on the ground as there are standing ones, and a hike through the woods requires climbs up and over horizontal trunks as tall as people.

"Some of these mountain laurel are probably as old as any of the trees we're going to see," biologist Nick Fisichelli commented the day he led the Remarkable Tree team into the old-growth area of Pocosin Hollow. And it wasn't just the mountain laurel and the big trees that captured our attention; it was the shelf fungi, the marginal shield fern, the club mosses, the lichen-covered rocks. It was the corky bark of the black locust trees, the aromatic twigs of the yellow birches, and the rotting wood of ancient oak logs spilling their guts onto the forest floor. We reveled in the spicebush, the witch hazel, the serviceberry, the striped maple, and the hophornbeam—a fine challenge trying to tell them all apart in winter. All this, and the fact that the soil under our feet was so soft and humus-rich it gave under our weight like a water bed, reminded us how misguided it can be to focus on individual trees. In the words of one botanist stressing the importance of ecosystems, "You've gotta' hug the entire forest."

Groves of tulip-poplars are now the largest remaining tracts of old growth in the Shenandoah National Park. Fifteen years ago, the most extensive areas of old growth in the Park were stands of eastern hemlock, but those stands have been decimated by a non-native insect pest, the woolly adelgid.

Eastern Hemlock, Giles County

Straddling tool-shed-sized boulders, hemlocks at Mountain Lake seem to marry rock and wood. In some places, the trees and rocks are so connected it is hard to tell where one stops and the other begins. The impression of extreme old age seems to carry over from the rocks to the trees, and, at Mountain Lake, the impression is not misleading. While young in geologic time, many hemlocks at Mountain Lake are old in arboreal time. As a species, hemlocks have long life spans (450 to 800 years, with some 1,000-year-old specimens reported), and living hemlocks at Mountain Lake are no exception. Some living hemlocks there have been determined, through coring, to be at least 427 years old. Nearby dead hemlocks have been dated at 523 years old, but it is the living hemlocks that merit attention here, because healthy old hemlocks (or young ones for that matter) are no longer the given they once were in Virginia.

Hemlocks in almost every Virginia county where these moisture- and cool-temperature-loving evergreens grow have fallen victim to the woolly adelgid, a sucking insect that kills all or most of its host trees, then moves on to other areas where its hemlock host is available. Some of the state's most beloved hemlock habitats, including the Limberlost in Shenandoah National Park and Skidmore Fork in the George Washington National Forest, changed in a matter of years from towering groves of healthy evergreens to graveyards of dead and dying trees. Mountain Lake didn't

Death toll: About 70 percent of the hemlocks at Mountain Lake succumbed to the woolly adelgid in the 1990s, but that was actually a smaller loss than in some other parts of the state. By some estimates, Shenandoah National Park has lost 95 percent of its hemlocks to the insect.

escape the woolly adelgid—brown swaths of dead hemlocks line one side of the lake—but about 30 percent of the hemlocks at the Lake survived the woolly adelgid, a percentage larger than in many other parts of the state.

No one is entirely sure why so many hemlocks at Mountain Lake were spared. Factors cited include the trees' genetic makeup, the drought of 1998-2003, controlled spraying, stem injections, and the introduction of an exotic beetle that eats the woolly adelgid, but for whatever reason (or combination of reasons), woolly adelgid damage was halted at Mountain Lake before it had killed some of Virginia's most picturesque trees.

Naturalists at Mountain Lake tend to take the long view not only of the fate of the eastern hemlock (*Tsuga canadensis*), but of the Lake itself (which shrank dramatically in the 1990s and loses an astounding amount of water per day through natural fissures). Evidence from the wood of submerged white pines (preserved because the temperature of the water is so cold) has proved that parts of Mountain Lake now under 20 to 30 feet of water were dry during the lifetimes of those trees, and additional evidence has shown that the Lake may have been empty as much as it has been full in the course of its 10,000- to 12,000-year history. "People think something unnatural is going on," says naturalist Dave Deshler, referring both to the ups and downs of the Lake and to the ups and downs of the hemlock, "but it's all very natural."

Eastern hemlocks over 400 years old grow near the shores of Mountain Lake, site of an historic mountaintop resort in southwestern Virginia. Where they grow in and among boulders, some of the lake's old hemlocks create rock/tree formations like this one.

LIVE OAK, HAMPTON
The Algernourne Oak

Hurricane Isabel hit Fort Monroe hard, but it didn't take out the Algernourne oak or many of the other massive live oaks on the site. One would like to think the site's stone walls (designed by an aide to Napoleon and constructed under the supervision of Robert E. Lee) and moat (yes, moat, complete with drawbridges) may have helped protect the trees, but the moat actually creates wind zones in which horticulturists try not to plant trees. Lucky for the Algernourne oak, a nearby building helps shield it from the wind, and it has been shaped, not snapped, by weather.

What a tree it is. The third largest live oak in Virginia, it has a crown spread of 97 feet and trunk diameter of over 6.5 feet. Like most live oaks, it is not particularly tall (only 57 feet), but its gigantic, flaring trunk and spreading, sinuous branches give it that expressive, "Gone with the Wind" look so typical of live oaks. (Live oaks grew at Twelve Oaks, the Wilkes' estate in *Gone with the Wind*.) Virginia is at the northern tip of the live oak's range, and you will find them in their natural habitats only in the southeastern part of the state, but at the time this tree germinated, the area that is now Fort Monroe, just across Hampton Roads from Norfolk, was probably maritime live oak forest.

Virginia Tech's R. J. Stipes, professor of plant pathology and physiology, has estimated that the Algernourne oak may have germinated in 1540. How could he know? The date is just an estimate, but it is based on real evidence. In 1997, Stipes and colleagues conducted a study at Fort Monroe during which several live oaks were cored to determine their ages. The Algernourne oak was not cored, but based on data from nearby trees, the researchers came up with an average number of tree rings per inch of trunk diameter. By their estimates, the Algernourne oak was 437 years old in 1977. Readers familiar with the incomparable Angel Oak in South Carolina, which is advertised as 1,400 years old, will see the Algernourne oak as a youngster, but it is important to remember that no one has cored the Angel Oak, a process which, because of the nature of live oak wood, is difficult under the best of circumstances, and that on the East Coast, any tree over 400 years old is a graybeard.

This tree can vie with any in Virginia for "most history witnessed." Because of its strategic significance at the entrance to the James River, the site near which it grows has been home to forts since 1609, when Ft. Algernourne (named for an English lord) was built. That wooden stockade, destroyed by fire, was followed by a series of other fortifications, including two destroyed by hurricanes, that were designed to protect the area first from the Spanish, then the British, then Confederates (the Union held the fort during the Civil War).

Luminaries who may have passed the tree include Edgar Allen Poe, who served as a soldier there; Chief Black Hawk and his warriors, who were "detained" there; President Lincoln, who attended a peace conference there; Robert E. Lee, who served there prior to the Civil War; and Jefferson Davis, who was held prisoner there. And that doesn't include the long, unrecorded native American history on the site or the non-human connections to this tree. Today, the tree grows comfortably along the well-manicured parade ground at Ft. Monroe, where military employees and civilians still stroll past it, but it is also home to colonies of yellow-crowned night herons that nest and roost in the tree. To them the tree is more than an historical or ornamental curiosity; it's a part of the living landscape.

Tree dating of other live oaks in its vicinity indicate the Algernourne oak may have germinated as early as 1540. It is the third-largest member of its species (Quercus virginiana) in Virginia.

chapter two · HISTORIC TREES

The phrase "living witness" has been overused, but when you stand in the presence of a tree that provided solace to a slave girl or had the dismembered limbs of Civil War soldiers piled around its trunk, you do feel a connection to those events more "visceral" than you do in other places. Such combinations not only enhance our experience of the historical event but of the tree as well. It was alive way back then when THAT was happening?

In choosing trees for this chapter, we relied on our list of nominated trees as well as other sources. We found trees nominated to the Remarkable Tree Project particularly interesting because they included many trees that are otherwise overlooked in the usual compendia of historic trees. "This tree is known locally as the moonshine tree," wrote Dennis Anderson in his nomination of a white oak in Floyd County. "Moonshine was left in the hole at the base of the tree for customers to retrieve. Money was left for the moonshiner." Anderson's description provides not just an interesting anecdote about Prohibition but a reflection of the culture of the time—a time when you could leave something in a hole at the base of a tree and come back later to pick up payment, a time when people noticed holes in trees the way they notice holes in cell phone coverage today.

Other lists of historic trees we culled through included the results of a 1930 list of awards in the Virginia Historical Tree Contest as well as trees recognized in a Notable Trees of Virginia Search conducted between 1976 and 1978. Other sources included a wonderful old book of *Historic American Trees* published in 1922, a pamphlet called *Famous Trees*, Miscellaneous Publication No. 295, published by the United States Department of Agriculture in 1938, and the various publications of the American Forestry Association (now American Forests) cataloging *Famous and Historic Trees*. Sometimes, too, we found historic trees in photos intended for other purposes. When Mathew Brady took photographs of Gen. George McClellan's tent under a tulip-poplar at Berkeley Plantation or of soldiers under a white oak at Brompton in Fredericksburg, his interest was in the war, not the tree, but, as it turns out, his photographs prove the longevity of the pictured trees— not to mention the human history they witnessed.

In our travels to visit as many historic trees as we could, it was reassuring—and sometimes surprising—to find trees like the Mount Vernon pecan looking today much the same as it did in 1939, when it appeared on the cover of *Famous Trees*. On the other hand, we discovered many historically significant trees that had died and some that were still around but unrecognized or neglected. Sycamores planted as part of "the first recorded Arbor Day Ceremonies to be held at a Negro school in Virginia" (1908), still grow along Mountain Road in Henrico County in front of Virginia E. Randolph Community High School, but, at best, a handful of the commuters who pass them every day are aware of their significance. Ditto for the southern red oak in the 6600 block of Henrico's Broad Street, which survives next to six lanes of traffic. Thousands of people must pass this tree every day, but no one knows it marks the shady spot where people traveling to Richmond with mules and wagons used to stop for food and water, and that a young slave named Rosa Smith once served Jeb Stuart lemonade under the tree.

Every community should have a Living Landmark program like the one initiated by Piedmont Master Gardeners in 2000 to recognize its historic and significant trees, because there are scores of them in every Virginia county. One could do a book on Virginia trees with connections to the Civil War alone (Gen. Robert E. Lee seems to have tied his horse Traveler to an inordinate number of Virginia trees), but historic trees also include Indian trail trees, pirate lookout trees, survey trees marking property boundaries, memorial trees, hanging trees, and trees with unusual origins—like Hampton's "moon tree," grown from seeds taken to the moon, and Hanover's historic ginkgoes, gifts from the Emperor of Japan.

Here we have tried to mix some famously historic trees (tulip-poplars at Monticello, a white ash at Mount Vernon) with some not-so-famous ones (Sallie's Crying Tree in Marion, the Wilson Tree in Highland County), to illustrate the breadth of the historic tree category, and we have thrown in one "people's choice" tree—a beech associated with stock car racing—just to prove trees are connected to *all* of Virginia history, not just the part that usually makes it into history books.

This live oak (Quercus virginiana) *in Hampton is known as the Emancipation Oak.*

Live Oak, Hampton

The Emancipation Oak

Just off Emancipation Drive on the campus of Hampton University, an enormous live oak spreads across an immaculately kept lawn. Approached from the nearby parking lot, it looks more like a grove of trees than like a single tree, but once you penetrate the wall of green that defines its perimeter, you realize this is one tree with a maze of branches that have dipped to the earth and then headed skyward again. Although it is not tall (only 47 feet), its trunk is almost 17 feet in circumference, and its low-slung branches—which seem too impossibly heavy to spread as wide as they do—cover an area 99 feet in diameter.

To enter the area under this tree's canopy is to leave the world of busy highways and twenty-first century preoccupations (I-64 is within earshot of the tree) and to enter a quieter place where it's easier to imagine the historic events that happened around it. As early as 1861, for example, a freeborn black woman named Mary Smith Peake used the area around this tree as an outdoor classroom, and there, although it was illegal to do so at the time, she taught both free and enslaved African Americans to read and write. Between 1872 and 1875, when he was a student at what is now Hampton University, Booker T. Washington is also said to have read and studied under the tree. But the defining event in this tree's history (at least from a human point of view), was the reading of the Emancipation Proclamation under its branches. By many accounts, it was under this tree in 1863 that a Union soldier read the Emancipation Proclamation to slaves and free blacks gathered beneath it, and many believe this to have been the first reading of Lincoln's Emancipation Proclamation in the South.

Ironically, according to historian Dr. Robert F. Engs, the Emancipation Proclamation didn't actually free the slaves who heard that 1863 reading. Engs has pointed out that a sentence nested in the document exempted slaves in 48 counties, including Elizabeth City (now Hampton) from its provisions and that, technically, Elizabeth City's slaves weren't freed until the Thirteenth Amendment passed in 1865. On the other hand, its unlikely technicalities seemed important that day, and it's easy to believe, as later accounts have suggested, that the sound heard under the Emancipation Oak in 1863 was of African American men and women rejoicing.

Now a symbol of education and freedom, the Emancipation Oak has been beautifully cared for and is protected by a wrought iron fence (as the tree's spread has widened, the fence encircling it has been pulled back, creating the appealing illusion that it has burst its bounds). Nearby concrete slabs, which seem to have once functioned as foundations, also suggest there has been an unusual reversal of fortunes in this tree's lifetime. "For once," one visitor commented, "the buildings got taken down and the tree was left standing."

This massive live oak (Quercus virginiana) grows near Emancipation Drive on the campus of Hampton University. In 1863, the Emancipation Proclamation was read to slaves and free black men and women gathered beneath it.

WHITE OAK, MARION

Sallie's Crying Tree

A thunderstorm, Sallie's Crying Tree, and Evelyn Lawrence—it's hard to know which is the most powerful force in Marion. If you happen to be in the presence of all three at once, expect lightning. On the day the Remarkable Tree team visited this tree, a thunderstorm came up so fast we had to take shelter. Fortunately, the local firehouse stands behind Sallie's Crying Tree on Main Street in this southwestern Virginia town, and we retreated there. Unfortunately, there's no retreating from the message this tree and Mrs. Lawrence have to tell.

Evelyn Lawrence, former elementary and music teacher (44 years), world traveler (over 15 countries), and former grand marshal of the Marion Christmas Parade, is the granddaughter of Sallie Adams (1841-1913), the slave girl whose story Mrs. Lawrence tells. If the story seems impossibly fresh, it's partly because Mrs. Lawrence is a born storyteller with a sharp memory and partly because the story has passed through so few people (Sallie bore Mrs. Lawrence's mother late in life, Mrs. Lawrence's mother bore Evelyn late in life, and Evelyn Lawrence is older than she looks—stretching the number of years between generations but contracting the number of people through whom the tree story passed).

Mrs. Lawrence knows all the details of Marion life as they relate to Sallie's Crying Tree, and she doesn't intend to let her town forget them. A stone marker placed in front of the tree explains: "Sallie, a lonely little slave girl, here in the 1840's, wrapped her arms around this kindly oak tree, and cried daily for her lost family, sold to a Lynchburg, Va. slave master." All this seems like ancient history, reading it on the stone marker beneath the nice white oak wedged between a parking lot, a residence, and the firehouse. But then the wind whips up, the top of the tree, oddly heavy and dense for its trunk, begins to sway, and Mrs. Lawrence begins to talk.

"Sallie was pulled away from her mother's skirts and put on the slave block when she was 5 or 6," Mrs. Lawrence explains. "She was sold to the richest man in Marion, who had a chronically ill wife. She was brought here [site of the home that previously occupied the parking lot] to be a body servant to her. She slept on a pallet next to her mistress's bed. She could never be a child again, because the most urgent time to be alert was at night when her mistress would cry out for help, and if she missed hearing, they would punish her. She was supposed to alert adults if her mistress needed help." According to Mrs. Lawrence, Sallie had no one to talk to so "she told all her sorrows to that tree; it was a live mentor for her."

Sallie's story doesn't end there. She was given away to her former owner's son "like you would give a horse or a dog," according to Mrs. Lawrence, and even after 1865, as a freewoman, Sallie suffered the indignity of being forced to leave the dwelling she occupied on Main Street, not too far from her crying tree, because "Marion authorities said no black person could live on Main Street unless they were in the employ of a white person." Eventually, however, not only did Sallie own her own home, which still stands near the railroad tracks in north Marion, but she grew two maple trees in front of the house, and these, too, still stand (although they have suffered the indignity of having their crowns scalped to accommodate utility wires). "Sallie loved anything that was growing," says Mrs. Lawrence, and she finds it fitting that Sallie died a day after collapsing in her garden in 1913.

It's hard to say which is the stronger force of nature, Mrs. Evelyn Lawrence or the impressive white oak that comforted her grandmother, but together, they represent a significant slice of Marion history. All trees should have such apostles to tell their stories and advocates to guarantee their care.

Standing under the tree after the storm, photographer Robert Llewellyn shielded his camera equipment from water dripping off the tree and noted, "This tree could use some lightning protection." Without hesitation, Mrs. Lawrence responded, "I'll see to it."

The town of Marion, in Smyth County, owns the property on which Sallie's Crying Tree grows, but Mrs. Evelyn Lawrence is the tree's interpreter, and advocate. A white oak (Quercus alba), *the tree provided solace to a slave girl named Sallie Adams.*

SWAMP WHITE OAK, HIGHLAND COUNTY

Oral history figures prominently in many of the stories connected to remarkable trees, but nowhere is oral history more provocative and sometimes harder to authenticate—than in stories of hanging trees. Eight living trees purported to be hanging trees were nominated to the Remarkable Tree Project, and we received reports of several other trees, now dead, that served as hanging trees. (Virginia Beach reportedly had one hanging tree for blacks and another for whites. The hanging tree for blacks, a sycamore, still grows on Cheswick Lane.) Other trees believed to be hanging trees grow in Farmville, Lynchburg, Clifton Forge, Campbell County, and Fairfax County, but it was a tree in Highland County that attracted our attention, because it was said to have "hosted" the last hanging in Highland County and to have "dropped its limbs in shame" because of its notorious past. It was a great story, but when we looked into it, it turned out the tree had witnessed a different kind of historical event.

One of many Virginia trees reputed to be "hanging trees," this swamp white oak near the village of Bolar probably witnessed an Indian attack, but no hangings. Partly because it is so big (the largest swamp white oak in Virginia), and partly because it is so picturesque, it has attracted stories the way some trees do lightning.

Most everyone we ran into at Midway Grocery (the country store nearest the tree, outside Bolar), thought the tree was associated with both an Indian attack and at least one hanging, but stories varied about who had been hung and why. "I think a gal got scalped and then they hung her," one person reported, improbably. "The women was washin' clothes when the Indians came. They [Indians] killed 'em. Then they hung the men," reported another. According to written accounts of the event (both based on oral history), neither story is true, but it does seem true that the historic Highland County swamp white oak witnessed an Indian attack disturbing enough that it has lodged in the community's memory and festered there for over two centuries.

According to local historian Hugh Gwin, the Wilson Tree, as this tree is sometimes called, witnessed an Indian attack on the Wilson family in 1763. Gwin's written account, based on the stories of family and friends, is full of grizzly details, but the gist of the story is this: the Wilson family (mother, father, four daughters and two sons), had a cabin close to the swamp white oak in 1763. While father and sons were away, Indians attacked, wounding the mother, who was at the Jackson River washing. One daughter in the cabin was "knocked down and her skull fractured," and another defended herself with "a hot smoothing iron," until the men returned and drove the Indians away. One son was "carried off to the Indian towns beyond the Ohio."

Chilling as it is, Gwin's account contains no scalping, no hanging, and not even a death, but it does harken to a period when settlers and Indians were fighting for rights to western Virginia, when settlers were suffering, and when stark memories were gathering around what would become a great tree. Although it hasn't kept them consistent, the tree seems to have given the stories of the Indian attack near Bolar something to accumulate around, and today it's easy to imagine the events the stories describe partly because the tree looks old enough to have been around in the eighteenth century and partly because the area is still so sparsely populated one feels a little like a pioneer there even in the twenty-first century.

In terms of helping to keep a story alive, the tree's size must also be a factor. The Bolar swamp white oak is the largest of its kind in the state (70 feet tall and almost 8 feet in diameter), and it towers over the field it occupies the way the Washington Monument does over the National Mall. The only tree in its vicinity, it grows in a swale that captures water flowing off Jack Mountain into the Jackson River, and it shares the ground around its roots with a rich collection of moisture-loving wildflowers. A swamp white oak couldn't have picked a more congenial spot in which to grow. Unlike white oak (*Quercus alba*), which prefers well-drained soil, swamp white oak (*Quercus bicolor*) likes moist sites, including swamps, the borders of streams, poorly drained pastures, and moist meadows like the one in which this tree grows. Although now hollow and in decline, the tree still commands attention and dominates the land around it with the authority of a tree that has owned its spot for centuries and outlived events more numerous and historic than human memory can recount.

SOUTHERN CATALPA, STAFFORD COUNTY

Chatham

Because of the topography around Chatham, so obviously a strategic high ground, it's easy to picture the Civil War scenes played out there, but one spot around this historic home is more evocative than most. It is an area just west of the north wing of the house, below two windows, where two ancient catalpas grow. Through those windows, according to some accounts, the amputated limbs of Civil War soldiers were tossed, and they accumulated at the foot of the trees.

Today the room overlooking the trees is outfitted with air conditioning, folding chairs, and a tourist-friendly video, but during the Battle of Fredericksburg, the room served as an operating room for some of the 10,000 "ghastly wounded soldiers streaming back from the front." It is easy to imagine the horror of that scene, partly because Walt Whitman, who visited the house-turned-hospital, has described the scene for us, and partly because the trees associated with the event are not only still standing but are standing in postures so contorted by age and suggestive of affliction that they seem to epitomize the horror of battle, the texture of healing.

"Began my visits (December 21, 1862) among the camp hospital in the Army of the Potomac, under General Burnside," wrote Whitman in *The Wound Dresser*. "Spent a good part of the day in a large brick mansion [Chatham] on the banks of the Rappahannock, immediately opposite Fredericksburg. It is used as a hospital since the battle, and seems to have received only the worst cases. Outdoors, at the foot of a tree, within ten yards of the front of the house, I noticed a heap of amputated feet, legs, arms, hands, etc—about a load for a one-horse cart. Several dead bodies lie near, each covered with its brown woolen blanket."

An 1863 photograph of Chatham shows two young catalpa trees, each about 25 feet tall, growing outside the north wing of the house, where they still grow, and in 1978 a forester who aged the trees estimated they were between 160 to 170 years old. It is impossible to verify the trees' ages today since they are too hollow to core, but it seems irrefutable that these trees witnessed not only the carnage following the battle of Fredericksburg but also the thriving plantation life that preceded it. (Chatham, now under the jurisdiction of the National Park Service, is one of the few historic properties that can boast visits from Robert E. Lee, George Washington, Thomas Jefferson, *and* Abe Lincoln.)

It is quite likely the southern catalpas (*Catalpa bignonioides*) at Chatham were planted as ornamentals, because this tree's showy blooms and exotic-looking, bright green, heart-shaped leaves recommended it to early landscapers. We also know that northern catalpas (*Catalpa speciosa*) were planted as early as 1737 along the Palace Green in Colonial Williamsburg, where they flourished, according to garden historian Wesley Greene, as one of the first municipal street tree plantings in North America. Interestingly, both species of catalpa are generally thought to be non-native to Virginia, but their original ranges are a matter of dispute.

The two historic southern catalpas at Chatham have the short stature and crooked crowns typical of their species, and their gnarled trunks have more knobs, swirls, holes and tangles of twisted bark than a Hobbit habitat. Joe Ruedi, Chatham gardener, notes that not only have these trees' tops and centers mostly rotted away, but the trees have been bolted, cabled, and had cement blocks (later removed) dropped into them. For all that, they seem surprisingly staunch, and, when we visited in June 2007, they were blooming profusely. Instead of mutilated bodies, a well-kept lawn now surrounds these trees, and their trunks seem to say "everything heals, but sometimes the scars are startling."

Riddled with decay and marred by cankers (abnormal growths sometimes caused by mechanical injury, pruning, or disease), the historic catalpas at Chatham still bloom profusely in late spring. Although often scorned for the debris they shed (spent flowers, cigar-shaped pods), catalpas are beautiful both in leaf and flower.

A war correspondent visiting Chatham a few weeks following the Battle of Fredericksburg wrote that every wall and floor of the house was saturated with blood and that all that had once been elegant at the place was "now wretched." What he might not have noticed, amidst the devastation, were several trees, including these two catalpas, which had survived the carnage.

HACKBERRY, WESTMORELAND COUNTY

George Washington Birthplace National Monument

When you're a tree, it pays to be associated with a famous person, and few trees prove that fact more conclusively than the common hackberry at George Washington's birthplace in Westmoreland County. This property, designated a National Monument in 1930, was home to Washington for only the first three and a half years of his life, but its association with America's first president and his family (which lasted longer than George's residence there) has resulted in tender loving care of this 551-acre property and of its most striking hackberry.

Many native hackberries grow at George Washington Birthplace National Monument, also known as Popes Creek Plantation or Wakefield, but this one has the good fortune to be nestled between the Memorial House, built to honor Washington in 1930-31, and the colonial Kitchen House, also constructed in 1930. The tree probably post-dates Washington (the most generous estimates of its age suggest it may be 200 years old), but, partly because of the care and protection it has received (including extensive cabling and lightning protection), the tree has grown into a tree interesting enough to be a tourist attraction itself.

"Visitors love it," says Rijk Morawe, Chief of Resources Management at Popes Creek. "People want to know what it is and ask 'What are all the bumps? Is that natural?'" The answer to the "bump" question is "Yes, the 'bumps' on a hackberry are natural," because mature hackberry bark is characterized by corky ridges and wart-like projections. This hackberry also exhibits galls (areas of disorganized growth) that contribute to its "knobbiness," and the combination of all these protuberances with the tree's branching pattern—arching gracefully upward but with branches forking, curving, dipping, and ascending in irregular lines—all contribute to the tree's visual interest.

Depending on when you visit, you may also find broad sweeps of snowdrops blooming under the tree or fruit on nearby figs, plantings that contribute to the general feeling of natural abundance on this property.

With elm-like leaves that turn pale yellow in the fall, hackberry makes a good street tree as well as a good choice for dry, windy sites like the one at Popes Creek. Its only serious drawback, from a cultural and aesthetic point of view, is the fact that it often requires pruning to remove "witches' brooms"—thick clusters of twigs that appear near the ends of the branches. A great wildlife tree, hackberry leaves are host to several species of butterfly caterpillars, and its small (¼-inch) fruit is relished by winter birds. People are attracted to hackberry fruit, too, although it's hard to make a snack, much less a meal, from it. "It's a tease," says naturalist and wild food forager Vickie Shufer. "The skin is very sweet—tastes like a date, but there's nothing inside. The thin skin is wrapped around a big, hard seed." This fruit, which gives the tree its name (from the Scottish *hagberry*, a type of cherry) may disappoint, but the tree itself, especially when showcased like the one at Popes Creek, does not.

This hackberry (Celtis occidentalis) *at Popes Creek Plantation in Westmoreland County grows near George Washington's birthplace.*

Tulip-poplar, Albemarle County

Monticello

I never before knew the full value of trees. My house is entirely embossomed in high plane-trees, with good grass below; and under them I breakfast, dine, write, read, and receive my company. What would I not give that the trees planted nearest round the house at Monticello were full grown.

Jefferson to Martha Randolph (from Philadelphia), 1793

On April 16, 1807, Thomas Jefferson noted planting "1. Laurodendron" in an area where one of the most impressive tulip-poplars in Virginia now grows. Would that Jefferson could see this tulip-poplar (*Liriodendron tulipifera*) full grown, because the tree towers over the house in a way that would have made the third President proud. In fact, one wishes the tree had been included in the stark portrayal of Monticello on a nickel, so effectively does this tulip-poplar, and one planted later on the other side of the house, connect Monticello to the sky.

Jefferson's passion for plants is well known, and, as Monticello Director of Gardens and Grounds Peter Hatch points out, Jefferson ranked trees at the top of his hierarchy of garden plants. He planted over 140 species of trees at Monticello and was famous for taking visitors on strolls to visit his "pet trees." Jefferson, who argued forcefully that North American plants were not, as some implied, inferior to European plants, sent tree seeds to friends in Europe, and the lists of what he sent remind us that trees Virginians take for granted were once received like rocks from the moon in Europe. Red maple, black walnut, persimmon, sweet bay magnolia, sassafras, red cedar, red buckeye, pecan, redbud, dogwood, fringe tree, and, of course, tulip-poplar, were among the trees Jefferson shared.

The tulip-poplar believed to have been planted by Jefferson at Monticello models the most impressive features of the species. Its enormous trunk (7 feet in diameter) rises straight and tall (over 120 feet) with high branches reaching dramatically upward like, in the words of Peter Hatch, "a massive hand reaching for the sky." Hatch, who describes this tulip-poplar as among the most studied trees in the world, says it's also "a defiant tree, withstanding years of neglect, mountain-top storms, lashing hurricanes, debilitating ice storms, searing droughts, and both the compaction of trampling feet and the armed embrace of thousands of Monticello visitors over the last 200 years." Some or all of these challenges may finally be taking a toll on the tree, which, in 2006, showed worrisome signs of stress (minor then major limbs loosing leaves prematurely). "We're hopeful it will come back," says Hatch, noting that the only thing worse than losing a tree planted by Thomas Jefferson would be having a tree planted by Thomas Jefferson fall on Thomas Jefferson's house. Undoubtedly, Monticello's tree stewards will be thoughtful in their deliberations regarding the tree, knowing, as they do, that Jefferson was once quoted as saying "the unnecessary felling of a tree, perhaps the growth of centuries, seems to me a crime little short of murder."

Thomas Jefferson, who called the tulip-poplar "the Juno of our Groves," is believed to have planted this one at Monticello in 1807. Another large tulip-poplar, believed to have been planted around 1880, grows on the opposite side of the house, framing Jefferson's home in a way that makes it postcard perfect.

AMERICAN BEECH, PATRICK COUNTY

We expect presidents and their ilk to be associated with famous trees, because some of the dignity of the person gravitates to the tree—and vice versa. But cultural icons can have their tree associates, too, and one of the most appealing is the connection between the legendary Wood brothers (of Wood Brothers Racing) and this beech growing on their family home place in Woolwine.

"We were what you call shade tree mechanics," says Glen Wood, who, with his brother Leonard, founded the racing team that is now one of the most storied in NASCAR history. When Leonard and Glen Wood say they were "shade tree mechanics" in the 1940s, they are not speaking metaphorically. "We had to use something to hoist engines out of our car, and as we didn't have a garage, that tree was the only thing we could do it with," says Glen. According to Leonard, the brothers pulled their race cars (and occasionally a family car) up under the tree, hooked a chain over the limb, then hooked a chain horse to the chain and lifted the engine out so they could work on it.

The American beech had something more than strong limbs and shade to attract the Wood brothers. A spring at its base provided cool, clear drinking water. "In those days we didn't have a refrigerator," says Glen Wood, and in addition to getting drinking water from the spring, the Wood family (five sons, one daughter) kept their milk and butter in a "spring box" there.

Today, the beech that shaded the Wood brothers in the 1940s is a huge, healthy specimen with the smooth bark and sinuous (seemingly muscle-bound) branches characteristic of its species (*Fagus grandifolia*). The spring at its base still provides clear water, and a collection of wild and cultivated flowers—in an arrangement created by the brothers' sister Crystal–grows among the rocky ledges surrounding its roots. "We still gather here in the summer for our reunion," says Crystal, who is understandably proud of her brothers—and also inordinately fond of the tree. "It's a tranquil little place," she explains.

Forget the roar of the speedway; it's the quiet dignity of a massive beech that permeates the setting where Glen and Leonard Wood (along with brothers Clay, Ray, and Delano) worked on their first race cars. The Wood brothers were literally "shade tree mechanics"—using the branches of this beech to help hoist engines out of their cars.

TULIP-POPLAR, WESTMORELAND COUNTY

Nomini Hall

"They're pretty beat up. I'm not sure there's much left of them."

Those words almost persuaded us to cancel a visit to the tulip-poplars at Nomini Hall, Westmoreland County, but two things kept them on our itinerary. First of all, they were dated in a way that none of our other historic trees were: They had been mentioned, several times, in the journal and letters of Philip Vickers Fithian, a tutor at Nomini Hall, who had described them as "tall, flourishing, beautiful Poplars" in March of 1774. If they were only 20 years old at the time he called them "tall and flourishing," that would make them 254 years old in 2008, and trees worth investigating, to be sure.

A second factor in their favor was the fact that they represented something we hadn't yet photographed: the kind of tree allée that was so wildly popular in the eighteenth century and that has been repeated up and down driveways ever since. "All the big mansions had to have their allée," Frank Delano, Northern Neck reporter for *The Free Lance-Star* and local history buff, reminded us the day we visited Nomini Hall, where he was reporting on archaeological investigations at the site. Although the original Nomini Hall mansion burned down in 1850 (to be replaced by the home that occupies the site today), Philip Fithian's description of the impression the trees had made on him on March 18, 1774 could describe their impact today:

"These Rows of Poplars form an extremely pleasant avenue, & at the Road, through them, the House appears most romantic, at the same time that it does truly elegant…" (From *Journal and Letters of Philip Vickers Fithian: A Plantation Tour of the Old Dominion, 1773-1774*, The University Press of Virginia)

Our visit to the trees proved that although the trees are "pretty beat up," they are still impressive—and of even more historical significance than we had realized. Fifteen of the original trees remain, and while some of them have lost important limbs and one is a mere snag, all of them have the sculptural quality only trees that have been worked over by weather for centuries can display, and some look healthy enough to survive for at least another decade.

From Frank Delano we learned they are more than remnants of an ancient allée; they are living witnesses to a significant event in the history of the slaveholding South. According to oral history collected by another reporter, Lawrence Latane, it was under these trees that Robert Carter III announced that he was freeing his slaves. This would have been significant at any time—Carter had over 600 slaves—but it was astounding in 1791, when most of Carter's friends and neighbors were slaveholders (and the Emancipation Proclamation was 72 years away). It seems Carter had undergone a religious conversion leading him to the conclusion that slavery was "contrary to the true principles of Religion and Justice."

"Robert Carter had 'em build this great big pulpit on the lawn right in between them poplar trees and he called everybody out," 84-year-old Eddie Carey, who had heard the story from his grandmother, told Latane in 1991. "It was built way up high so they could see him and he could see them. Some of 'em had never seen him before and he had never seen some of them before. Then he said that he set them free." The catalpa by Robert Carter's grave (he asked to be laid to rest with nothing but a tree to mark his grave) has died and its stump rotted away, but the tulip-poplars under which he freed his slaves still stand. Beat up? Yes, they are beat up, but they're too loaded with import to ignore.

These tulip-poplars (Liriodendron tulipifera) at Nomini Hall were probably planted soon after the original mansion was built around 1730. In his diary of 1773-1774, Philip Vickers Fithian, tutor to Robert Carter's children, described this avenue of tulip-poplars as "tall and flourishing."

WHITE OAK, FREDERICKSBURG

The Brompton Oak

Sometimes it's hard to imagine the horrors a Civil War site has seen—especially when the site is as pastoral as the campus of the University of Mary Washington, but a living oak and an old Mathew Brady photograph bring history to life in Fredericksburg.

The Brompton oak, named for the pre-Civil War home behind it, sits on a ridge called Marye's Heights—a strategic position in 1862. During the First Battle of Fredericksburg, the Confederate Army defended the ridge with cannon and engaged the Union army on the open ground at the bottom of the Heights. Two hundred thousand men fought—the largest number of men ever engaged in a battle on the American continent; 18,000 died. The following year, the second Battle of Fredericksburg also involved a battle for the ridge. Again Confederate artillery defended the ridge around the oak, but this time Union forces overran the Heights and took possession of the home (Brompton) and its nearby oak. Later that year, Confederate soldiers retook the Heights, but the site didn't remain under Confederate control for long. By 1864, during and after the battles of the Wilderness and Spotsylvania Courthouse, Brompton and its grounds served as a hospital for Union soldiers, who were cared for there until they could be sent to larger hospitals in Washington. Mathew Brady took the photo reproduced here, showing Union soldiers recuperating under the tree, on May 19 or 20, 1864.

Chilling in its detail, the photo shows the Brompton oak growing on a small rise, like an overturned bowl, against which a soldier on a stretcher reclines. That rise is still prominent under the tree today. The photo also captures the glassy-eyed gaze of a soldier who has had his left forearm amputated, the stooped posture of men on crutches, the forced camaraderie of wounded men sharing shade. Today a well-manicured lawn has replaced the accoutrements of a field hospital under the tree, and Brompton house, now home to the University's President, receives distinguished visitors rather than artillery fire, but the tree still commands its prominent position overlooking Marye's Heights. Although it is hollow inside and suffers from a root fungus, the Brompton oak appears surprisingly robust (partly due to the expert attention it has received from landscape supervisor Joni Wilson and her staff), and long, low limbs that might have been removed or damaged years ago still dip gracefully to the ground under the tree.

Although we know it was a sizeable tree in 1864, no one knows exactly how old the Brompton oak is. A white oak (*Quercus alba*) can live 600 years or more, but in the case of the Brompton oak, the tree's longevity seems all the more remarkable for the threats the tree has survived. In war, trees often seem expendable—they get in the way of maneuvers, they block strategic views, they are useful for firewood, and they get damaged by gunfire (as Brompton house was), but the Brompton oak somehow managed to survive the Civil War and its aftermath, not to mention all the lightning strikes its high site has invited. Casual observers passing the tree today would never know its history, but this tree has been a living witness to much more tumultuous times.

This Mathew Brady photograph depicts Union soldiers recuperating under Fredericksburg's Brompton oak in 1864. Photo from the Library of Congress.

Immortalized in the Civil War photograph on the left, the Brompton oak still grows on the crest of a hill that overlooked the first and second battles of Fredericksburg.

Osage-orange, Charlotte County

Red Hill

Science sometimes sabotages legends, but science spiced up the history of this Osage-orange at Patrick Henry's last home, Red Hill, in the Charlotte County community of Brookneal.

This tree attracts visitors the way Henry did patriots. Part of its charisma lies in the way it dominates the landscape in front of the residence where Henry died. The tree spreads to cover an area almost as big as a tennis court and its multiple trunks support branches commanding skyline and lawn. But it is the tree's bark, marked with deep, orange-brown ridges and soccer-ball-sized burls, that accounts for its most compelling feature—the aura of age.

Until 2003, two competing legends offered evidence of this tree's age. One held that the tree was grown from plant material brought back from the Lewis and Clark expedition in1806. The second held that the tree was even older—so old, in fact, that Patrick Henry had played his violin under it, and that Henry's physician had wept under the tree when the patriot died at Red Hill in 1799. In 2003, Virginia Tech dendrochronologist Dr. Carolyn Copenheaver proved the tree was too old to have been grown from a seed or cutting sent east by Lewis or Clark and that, in fact, it was old enough to have been spreading considerable shade when Henry died on the Red Hill property in 1799. From a core sample taken, Copenheaver estimated the tree to be at least 300 years old, suggesting it had been growing on the property as early as 1703.

Copenheaver's discovery raised more questions than it answered, because the Osage-orange is native to an area from southwest Arkansas and southeast Oklahoma through east central Texas, an area once occupied by the Osage Indians, for whom it is named. The tree was considered by some to be unknown in the east until Meriwether Lewis sent seeds to Thomas Jefferson (who sent them to others who propagated them) in the early 1800s. Later in the nineteenth century, the tree spread like wildfire because it was used, particularly in the Midwest, but also in the East, as a living fence. (When aggressively pruned, the thorny tree can be trained to form a nearly impenetrable barrier.) Sixty thousand miles of Osage-orange hedges were planted in this country in 1868 alone, and according to Monticello's plant historian Peter Hatch, the Osage-orange was the "most commonly planted plant in America in the mid-nineteenth century." We know what brought an end to "hedgemania"—the invention of barbed wire in 1875—but what accounts for the existence of Osage-orange on the Red Hill property long before the tree was supposedly brought east?

Don't look to birds or other animals for the answer, because botanists suggest one reason for the tree's limited original range is the fact that most animals don't like to eat its bitter fruit. Osage-orange fruits are yellowish green, grapefruit-sized orbs with the convoluted texture of brains, a sticky latex "juice," and hard seeds. In prehistory (more than 10,000 years ago), horses, mammoths, mastodons and camels are said to have eaten, and helped disperse, this ancient tree's seeds, but most modern-day animals (with the exception of squirrels, foxes, and some birds that eat the seeds) avoid Osage-orange fruit, which falls to the ground and decays quickly, with little or no means of long-distance migration.

The wood of the Osage-orange is another story. Highly valued by American Indians, the strong, flexible wood of the Osage-orange was used to make bows (hence its French name "bois d'arc"), and an Osage-orange bow was said to be so valuable to an American Indian that it equaled a horse and a blanket in trade. According to William Clark, "savages" traveled "many hundreds of miles in quest of it."

"Very plausibly, given the nature of trade among Native Americans and the value of this plant, it was growing on the eastern seaboard long before Lewis and Clark introduced it," argues Karen Gorham-Smith, curator at Red Hill National Memorial. Gorham-Smith also points out that not only do artifacts found in the vicinity of the Red Hill property indicate that Indians lived in the area around 1670, but an archaeological study of the site in 1999 found evidence of a "major prehistoric Indian village" on the banks of the Staunton River nearby.

Did American Indians introduce the Osage-orange to the East? No one knows, but the age of the Osage-orange at Red Hill, now scientifically confirmed, suggests sometimes trees are even older—and more interesting in their origins—than we thought.

The Osage-orange (Maclura pomifera) at Red Hill is the largest of its species in the nation. Many fine, old Osage-orange trees grow in Virginia, including extraordinarily large specimens in Henry and Essex counties.

CUCUMBER MAGNOLIA, COLONIAL HEIGHTS

Unlike the historic Osage-orange in Brookneal, the enormous cucumber magnolia in Colonial Heights is probably younger than legend suggests, but even if it wasn't planted in 1718 (as a laminated sign in front of the tree states) or grown from a slip provided by Thomas Jefferson (as a brass plaque in front of the tree suggests), its size, beauty, and historic connections make it one of the most impressive trees in the state. It is also one of the most accessible, as it grows on a park-like piece of property in a modest residential neighborhood within a stone's throw of U.S. Route 1.

It seems improbable, as you drive Route 1 looking for the tree, that such an extraordinary natural phenomenon would be growing in such close proximity to establishments advertising waffles, burgers, and cash loans on car titles, but just around the corner from the highway that cuts its way through Colonial Heights grows a tree that gives the neighborhood a jolt of nobility and dwarfs the tiny Violet Bank museum behind it.

The tree is most remarkable for its spread, girth, and shape. Covering an area almost as large as a baseball diamond, this one tree has the presence of a small grove, so dense is its canopy and so thick are the sinuous branches that reach down from its shed-sized trunk. At several points, horizontal branches thick enough to be trunks themselves reach all the way down to the ground as if to offer pint-sized tree climbers a lift. Never was there a tree that begged harder to be climbed, but, mixed blessing that it is, the tree is protected by law from trespassers, and visitors are asked not to intrude. The tree has obviously been extremely well-cared for, with extensive lightning protection, a wide apron of mulch, and substantial crutches supporting many of the most massive and gravity-defying limbs, but a frequent visitor to the tree might notice that some of the crutches that once supported huge limbs now support nothing.

No one knows exactly how old the tree is, but evidence suggests that although it was neither planted in 1718 nor a gift from Thomas Jefferson, it may have been a substantial tree when Gen. Robert E. Lee and his troops camped on the property (and used Violet Bank as headquarters) in 1864. According to Violet Bank curator Russell Woodburn, the museum has a photo of the tree taken in 1915 that includes a notation on the back saying the tree was planted from a slip brought from White Sulphur Springs in 1833. Certainly, this fast-growing species (*Magnolia acuminata*) was planted (as opposed to germinating on the site naturally), because Colonial Heights is well outside its natural range. The cucumber magnolia is a mountain species, growing wild only in the western part of the state, but it is an adaptable species, often grown outside its range as an ornamental.

The cucumber magnolia takes its name from its pinkish red fruit (shaped like a small cucumber) and is notable for its yellow flowers, its hardiness, and its disease resistance. Few cucumber magnolias reach the size of the one in Colonial Heights, but there is actually one almost as big in Virginia Beach (off Diamond Springs Road at the Virginia Tech Experimental Research Station) and a larger one in Loudoun County (on Main Street in Hamilton). Tree lovers in Hamilton say that, unlike the Violet Bank tree, their cucumber magnolia is associated with peace, not war. Their tree, they point out, symbolizes peace and harmony, because Hamilton, originally named Harmony, is a Quaker-influenced community with the town motto "Living in harmony in Hamilton."

War issues aside, what adds to the "wow factor" of the cucumber magnolia in Colonial Heights is the tree's extraordinary crown spread (110 feet), its proximity to modest homes, and its location on an appealing historic site. At Violet Bank one can peek in the window to see early nineteenth century woodwork, doors, fireplaces, and floors—even General Lee's military coat casually draped over an antique chair, but the most startling "artifact" on the property is this tree growing in the yard.

The cucumber magnolia in Colonial Heights is a deciduous species (one that loses its leaves in the fall). Most cucumber magnolias grow in mixed hardwood forests, but this one grows in a park-like setting, where it has reached the remarkable proportions of over 20 feet in circumference and 110 feet in crown spread.

AMERICAN CHESTNUT, KING GEORGE COUNTY

In Memoriam

You'd think dead trees would be outside the scope of this book, but think again.

No accounting of Virginia's remarkable trees would seem complete without at least homage to the American chestnut, because its demise has been called "one of the greatest natural disasters in the history of forest biology." Until the early 1900s, the American chestnut (*Castanea dentata*) dominated 200 million acres of forest from Maine to Florida and westward from the Piedmont to the Ohio Valley. The tree was central to American culture (remember Longfellow's "Under a spreading chestnut tree"?) and essential to rural people who used its nuts to feed livestock (and themselves), its wood to make everything from cradles to coffins.

It has been estimated that 4 billion American chestnuts were growing in the tree's native range at the end of the nineteenth century and that 25 percent of the standing timber in the East was American chestnut, but by 1950 the tree had been almost completely wiped out. The culprit was a fungus that disrupts the flow of nutrients within the tree and kills its above-ground parts. The fungus probably entered the country on imported Chinese chestnut, which is naturally resistant to the blight.

The American chestnut's demise was swift and startling, but the tree did not disappear entirely. Like a phoenix, the American chestnut keeps trying to come back from roots (and from the few nuts these new shoots produce), but these "comeback" chestnuts usually succumb to the blight before they are 15 feet tall, and only a very few reach 50 feet. The largest living American chestnut in Virginia is a scraggly, but stalwart, specimen growing in an Amherst County pasture. At 53 feet tall and 10 feet in circumference, it doesn't come close to the 100-foot chestnuts of yore, but it does provide cuttings for scientists trying to breed blight-resistant American chestnuts. Skeletons or standing snags of old American chestnuts can also still be found in Virginia forests (one of the largest rises like a monument in the Caledon Natural Area), and handsome, weather-beaten chestnut logs, which refuse to rot, still grace many a forest floor. Travelers enjoying the rail fences along the Blue Ridge Parkway are also seeing remnants of Virginia's great chestnut forests, as the great majority of them were constructed with American chestnut. ("We could build a mile a

day," one retired Park employee told us.)

Virginia is also home to some of the most promising efforts to restore the American chestnut to its former glory. Some of those efforts have involved crossing American chestnuts with Chinese chestnuts in an effort to breed the blight resistance of the Chinese into the American chestnut (and then to breed back out the unwanted characteristics of the Chinese chestnut—characteristics like short, orchard-tree-like stature). Working under the auspices of the American Chestnut Foundation, plant pathologist Dr. Frederick Hebard oversees a 150-acre operation in Meadowview, near Abingdon, where, in June, you can see acres of chestnuts wearing little white bags over their blooms— an effort to protect the "purity" of the crosses. Similar efforts have been going on at the Lesesne State Forest in Nelson County since 1969.

At Lesesne and on hundreds of other plots in Virginia, another approach to restoring the American chestnut is being tested. Since the 1970s, Dr. Gary Griffin and his wife Lucille with the American Chestnut Cooperators' Foundation have been spearheading an effort to breed a blight-resistant American chestnut using only American, no Chinese, chestnuts. Having developed a way to measure blight resistance in existing trees, the Griffins conduct crosses involving American chestnuts with relatively good blight resistance, and then, with the help of hundreds of cooperative growers, monitor the results.

All this is slow, painstaking work, and the growers are, at best, cautiously optimistic about the results. Lucille Griffin, who spends six days a week working with American chestnuts, says she and her husband are getting "about a 10 percent success rate" in terms of producing trees with adequate blight resistance. One especially promising chestnut—the result of an American/American cross, now grows at Lesesne State Forest where it has reached 70 feet and is producing fine crops of nuts. Of the American/Chinese crosses, Dr. Hebard says that "if all goes well," blight-resistant trees (some of which are beginning to be distributed to members of the American Chestnut Foundation) will be available to the public around 2015, and that it may take another 30 to 50 years to find out if the Foundation's chestnuts can compete with other trees in the forest.

American chestnuts of enormous stature dominated forests of the central and southern Appalachian mountains until they were wiped out by chestnut blight in the 1930s and 1940s.

This American chestnut snag in the Caledon Natural Area, King George County, rises like a monument to the past glory of a species that once dominated eastern North American forests. American beech now dominates this forest.

chapter three CHAMPION TREES

What makes a tree a champion? Size and size alone. Those who keep champion tree records define a champion tree as the largest specimen of its species. Ever since the 1940s, when the American Forestry Association (now American Forests) introduced the nationwide champion tree program, trees have been declared "champions" based on a score that combines three measurements: circumference in inches, height in feet, and 25 percent of the tree's average crown spread in feet. The resulting score is quite arbitrary, probably gives "fat" trees an unfair advantage, and results in some oddball winners (no points are awarded for the health or beauty of the tree, for example), but it does provide a method of comparison that has intrigued and delighted tree enthusiasts for decades.

Virginia and 45 other states also have statewide "big tree programs," which identify the largest tree of each species in the state. Some Virginia localities, including Arlington, Blacksburg, Charlottesville, Chesapeake, Fairfax, Falls Church, Roanoke, and Virginia Beach, have also conducted champion tree programs locally. (In Bland and Washington counties, young 4-H members spearheaded such programs.) Champion tree programs are particularly interesting to kids, lovers of record-breaking that they are, and they have been used to teach biology (nominating a potential champion requires accurate tree identification) and math skills (how *does* one measure the height of a tree?). The easiest answer to the last question is "with a clinometer"—a forester's tool, but there is also an old Boy Scout method that involves using geometry, or "twigonometry" as it is sometimes called. You can find instructions for measuring and nominating big trees on the Virginia Big Tree Program website.

Champion tree programs not only uncover some remarkable trees (who knew a sassafras could get as big as the one illustrated on page 64?), but because they involve friendly competition, they also generate interest in trees. The only Virginia tree ever to appear on the front page of the *New York Times* was an American elm in Sebrell that caused a stir when it dethroned a famous elm in Kansas, and champion trees of all stripes seem to make the news more often than their less celebrated brethren. Big tree records are also of interest to botanists, landscapers, and ordinary tree lovers because they remind us how big trees of each species can get, and how much space we should allow them.

More champion trees are dethroned because a larger tree is found than are dethroned because they die or lose limbs (making them smaller), and Virginia's champion tree list changes so fast Jeff Kirwan, who maintains it at Virginia Tech, can hardly keep up with it. Virginia ranks fifth in the U.S. in terms of the number of its state champion trees that are also national champions (56), and that ranking (below only Florida, California, Arizona, and Texas) is maintained partly because Virginia has such fine trees of many species and partly because Virginia has such fine champion tree hunters, like Suffolk's Byron Carmean, who, often with cohort Gary Williamson, has found over 40 percent of Virginia's current champion trees.

Anyone can make a champion tree nomination, however, and we invite you to look at the sample of champion trees featured here and on the big tree website to see if you know of a tree that is bigger. The competition is pretty stiff, but new champions are crowned all the time. Remember that not all champions are behemoths—even the largest trees of some species are relatively small—and your favorite lawn tree could be a champion.

A local celebrity, this state champion cherrybark oak (Quercus pagoda) attracts passersby of all ages to a Colonial Beach (Westmoreland County) front yard.

CHERRYBARK OAK, COLONIAL BEACH

"Can you imagine biking down the road and coming across this tree?"

Luke Sydnor, owner of the home behind the tree pictured here and on the preceding page asked us to imagine coming upon his state champion cherrybark oak by surprise. It's nearly impossible to imagine how startling that would be, because even if you've seen a picture of the tree and know what to look for at 215 Ball Street, the tree hits you like ton of bricks—or, more accurately, like a ton of living wood attached to a leafy canopy that dwarfs the home behind it. This tree is larger and more impressive than any living organism most people will encounter in their lifetimes, yet no one charges admission to see it and it would be easy for a tourist to visit Colonial Beach and never know it's there. To some extent, it has been "discovered" by tree lovers who have seen it pictured or listed in American Forests' big tree publications, but, as Luke Sydnor is fond of pointing out, it still stops unsuspecting passersby in their tracks.

Measurements seldom create an accurate picture of a big tree, and in this case they seem particularly flat and static in comparison to the living, breathing tree. The tree's numbers are these: 105 feet tall, 124-foot crown spread, 26.3-foot circumference at a point 4.5 feet off the ground. But those numbers don't take into account the bulging roots that spread out at the base of the tree like a claw-footed platform (covering an area as big as some dining rooms), nor do they count the height to which your amazement soars when you hide behind this tree (sandwiched between the tree and the house) and *feel* the tree's weight in comparison to the house. Anyone wishing to feel small, vulnerable, and temporary (or uplifted, sheltered, and awestruck) might want to spend a few minutes with the cherrybark oak in Colonial Beach.

Unlike some remarkable trees that are sequestered behind privacy walls, this one is also impressively accessible. "Sometimes I put up a canopy in the front yard, serve coffee, buns, and cut up some melon," says Luke Sydnor, former president of the Colonial Beach Chamber of Commerce, describing his attitude toward visitors. "I share her with everybody. She's God's gift to all of us. I'm just happy to be the one who has her in the yard." Sydnor offers to hold the camera when people stop to take photos with the tree and has hosted bridal groups under the tree. "Some people have pets to get acquainted with people. I have this tree," he says.

According to Sydnor, who grew up near the tree but has lived in the house behind it only since the 1990s, the house behind the tree was built about 60 years ago, and he watched its construction. "They carried out six or eight double-axle dump truck loads of roots," he says. On the other hand, according to Sydnor, some of the workmen digging footings for the house were careful to protect some roots and "turned them to the side" before repositioning them in the ditch line. The tree obviously survived and seems to be in relatively good health.

The state champion black oak grew in a nearby yard (Sydnor's sister's) until it was felled by Hurricane Isabel in 2003. "That was quite a storm," says Sydnor, who weathered it in his home behind the cherrybark oak. "I was here by myself and I could hear it whipping the limbs. I went outside a couple of times and those branches were just dancing and touching the ground and swinging and swirling. It looked like one of those dance shows on TV." Sydnor's cherrybark oak lost only a few small branches, but he was dismayed by the loss of his sister's black oak. "When you've been around a tree like that all your life, that's one of your friends."

Cherrybark oak (Quercus pagoda), which closely resembles southern red oak, gets its name from the fact that, at times, its bark resembles that of black cherry. No one knows how old this state champion tree is, but average and maximum ages for the species have been estimated to be 200 and 275 years, respectively.

WHITE ASH, FAIRFAX COUNTY

Mount Vernon

If you'd like to be reassured that trees still have the power to impress even the most hard-to-impress kids and over-stimulated adults, stand for a few minutes near the Great Ash at Mount Vernon. The tree is situated along the serpentine walkway that leads to the mansion, home of George Washington, where over a million tourists and school kids encounter it each year. Because of the layout of the path, a visitor is almost on top of the tree before it springs into view, but the minute it does, eyes pop, conversations stop, and comments like this erupt:

"That thing is gorgeous."

"Wow!"

"Whoa!"

"Is that a big tree or what?"

"Bet you couldn't get to the top of that!"

"Wonder how old that rascal is?"

"Somebody take a picture of me hugging this tree!"

Even a mother pushing a stroller stops and directs her newborn to "Look at this *big* tree!"

All these visitors know a remarkable tree when they see it. The Great Ash at Mount Vernon, the 2008 state champion white ash, is a 130-foot-tall specimen with a 17.6 foot circumference, which is to say that it is big enough to engage a band of pre-adolescent kids much longer than they would give even the most urgent text message. Its deeply furrowed bark has a braided, textural appearance that invites touch, and its buttressing roots snake, anaconda-like, across the ground. How this tree has survived the millions of footsteps that have trod on its roots and compacted the soil around it is hard to imagine, but survive it has.

For years this white ash was believed to have been planted between 1785 and 1787, when George Washington was planting trees along Mount Vernon's Bowling Green. But, alas, the truth came out in 2006 when dendrochronologists from Oxford, England, cored the tree and found that it probably germinated around 1819. "I think they're still mad they lost the Revolutionary War," says Dean Norton, Director of Horticulture, expressing his disappointment at the dating results. One wonders, however, why a tree needs to have been planted by a famous person to get the praise it deserves; certainly no one who encounters the Great Ash along the serpentine path cares too much who planted it—they're all responding to the tree itself. A tree that germinated in 1819 is no spring chicken, and a fine white ash is a fine white ash whether planted by a president or germinated from a seed dispersed by wind.

Whether on a great estate or in a large back yard, white ash (*Fraxinius americana*) makes a great shade tree. Considered one of the "cleanest" of trees, because it drops so little debris on lawns and sidewalks, it has good fall color (shades of gold to purple), a pleasing, rounded shape, and attractive compound leaves with whitish undersides. White ash is also an important commercial tree, because it grows relatively quickly to a size at which it can be harvested for products that require hard, light, strong but flexible wood. Anyone who swings a baseball bat, wields a hockey stick, or uses a high-quality garden tool with a wooden handle has probably experienced the strength of white ash wood.

In addition to the Great Ash, other visually impressive trees at Mount Vernon include towering tulip-poplars (also growing along the serpentine walk), a picturesque pecan overlooking the Potomac, and a marvelous mulberry anchoring an area west of the upper garden. Of these, only the tulip-poplars are old enough to have been planted by Washington, but the property has other trees old enough to have been planted by the first President and some that predate him. For example, the dendrochronologists who disappointed Dean Norton by revealing the relative youth of the Great Ash also found, at the top of a steep ravine in Mt. Vernon's forested area, a chestnut oak that germinated "no later than 1683"—predating the birth of the first President of the United States by 49 years.

Visitors to Mount Vernon pass this state champion white ash on the way to George Washington's home.

Baldcypress, Southampton County

"Big Mama"

For champion tree hunter Byron Carmean, finding the "Lost Forest" on the Nottoway River was a lifetime achievement. "These trees are going to blow away everything else in the state," he predicted soon after spotting the state's largest baldcypress, a tree he calls "Big Mama," there. Sure enough, soon after discovering "Big Mama" in 2005, Carmean found two state and national champion water tupelos, a state champion swamp cottonwood, and a state and national champion Carolina ash in what would come to be called the "Lost Forest." It wasn't just the size of these trees that astonished Carmean (and later a team from the Virginia Department of Conservation and Recreation's Natural Heritage Program); it was the fact that so many enormous trees were concentrated in a relatively small—37-acre—area and that the trees had gone unnoticed for so long. How was that possible?

Answers lie partly in the topography of the area. Located just south of Courtland, the Nottoway River swamp in which these trees grow is similar to the nearby Blackwater Swamp in that accessibility varies widely with water level, as does the "look" of the trees that grow there. At high water levels, the gigantic buttresses of the water tupelos that dominate this swamp, and the baldcypresses that grow with them, are totally submerged, erasing the most compelling feature of these trees. And even at low water levels, it usually requires a canoe to get from nearby Cypress Bridge to the area in which these champions grow. On the day Carmean and ecologist Gary Fleming spotted these trees, water levels were low, but Carmean still had to go home and grab his canoe before he could reach the trees he suspected would be giants.

This area, it turns out, had been visited in 1937 by Harvard botanist M.L. Fernald, who had reported "enjoying the view, so exotic to northern eyes, the quiet blackish water of the Nottoway [and] giant cypresses with their bulging bases and innumerable tall 'knees'…." But, as Carmean has pointed out to many a person he has led into the swamp, what looks like a big tree from a distance (in this case, the easy-to-reach shore) can be a world-class tree up close (in the harder-to-reach swamp). What the discovery of the Lost Forest really needed was 1) an eye as practiced as that of Carmean, a retired horticulture teacher who hunts champion trees as a hobby, and 2) a person tenacious enough to go home (to Suffolk), get his boots and his canoe, and come back to investigate.

It's also worth noting why these trees had escaped logging. According to Gary Williamson, another naturalist who explores big tree sites with Carmean, these trees were probably already hollow, and therefore of little interest to loggers, when the great clearing of baldcypress swamps took place in the late nineteenth and early twentieth centuries. No one knows exactly how old the trees are, but based on core samples taken from nearby baldcypress logs, giant baldcypress trees in the area have been estimated to be over 1,000 years old.

Because of their great size and age, Williamson calls the baldcypress trees on the Blackwater and Nottoway rivers "the redwoods of the East," and the most impressive tree among them is Big Mama. The largest tree in the state, it grows in a slough on the north side of the Nottoway River. Because of the way other trees obscure its silhouette, it is hard to appreciate from afar, but up close it miniaturizes any person in its presence. Its mammoth, bulging base is over 12 feet in diameter—larger than the floor space in some kitchens—and its trunk doesn't constrict until well above human heads. It is 123 feet tall and has lost many of its limbs (a fact that Carmean believes may have helped it weather Hurricane Isabel), and its high, remnant branches with feathery foliage give it an "old man with thinning hair" sort of appearance.

According to geoscientist Dr. David Stahle, trees like Big Mama represent remnants of baldcypress-water tupelo forest that once covered more than 40 million acres in the southeastern U.S., and of which only about 12,000 uncut acres remained at the time Virginia's "Lost Forest" was discovered. At the time of this writing, International Paper owned "Planet Nottoway," and the Virginia Department of Conservation and Recreation's Natural Heritage Program was negotiating for the purchase of a 374-acre portion of the tract that includes Big Mama and the "Lost Forest." "It will protect a rare and enchanting remnant of undisturbed swamp, essentially unchanged in character since before European settlement," wrote Natural Heritage ecologist Gary Fleming, describing the importance of the purchase.

For Byron Carmean, the protection of the land is more important than his personal achievement in identifying the significant trees, but it's worth noting that, with the discovery of the "Lost Forest" champions, Carmean had become the nominator or co-nominator of 21 of Virginia's 56 national champion trees. The statistics may seem irrelevant to most of us, but calling our attention to rare botanical treasures is not.

The largest concentration of champion trees in the state grows in the "Lost Forest" near Cypress Bridge in Southampton County. Dubbed "Big Mama," this baldcypress (Taxodium distichum) is the largest tree in Virginia.

OVERCUP OAK, ISLE OF WIGHT COUNTY

You're walking through cut-over woods, trying to keep from getting tripped up by grapevine or ripped by greenbrier, when you enter the floodplain of the Blackwater River, where the going gets a little easier (albeit wetter) and the tripping hazards change to cypress knees and downed wood. The green hawthorn, deciduous holly, and river birch are of interest, but nothing is notable for its size until suddenly, through a screen of other trunks, you see a trunk that is totally out of scale with everything around it. As you approach, it gets bigger, and bigger, and bigger.....

"We all just gasped when we saw it," says Byron Carmean, who, with Mike Rasnake and Gary Williamson, discovered this overcup oak in November, 2007. The date in itself is amazing, given how unlikely it is that such a big tree could go undiscovered so long. How this one was overlooked becomes clearer when you visit it, however. The tree is about 100 yards from the banks of the Blackwater River, but you can't see it from the river (this stretch has been pretty much impassable since Hurricane Isabel), and the sandy road that leads into these woods (so soft it feels like driving on a pillow) seems to promise nothing but cut-over pine forest. Carmean speculates this overcup oak was probably passed over when the area was logged "because it was so limby."

The trunk of this tree, even high into its crown, is massive (26 feet in circumference), and it is 109 feet tall with a 102-foot crown spread. Gently curving low branches give it a graceful silhouette, and a "fur" of resurrection fern softens the contours of its upper branches. There is an unmistakable twist in the tree's trunk—a feature that Carmean thinks may have contributed to the tree's strength over the years. How many years? Overcup oak (*Quercus lyrata*) is a slow-growing species usually estimated to have a maximum life span of around 400 years, but Carmean thinks this tree could easily be 450 years old. The tree seems all the more stalwart for having survived what many of its neighboring trees did not. "Nature threw something at these trees that even native trees couldn't handle," says Carmean, pointing out dead river birches and other trees that didn't survive the floods accompanying hurricanes Floyd, Isabel, and Ernesto, when the waters of the Blackwater rose 15 feet up some trunks, and stayed there for weeks.

Overcup oak is native only to the eastern half of the state, but it can be planted all over Virginia. It's a good choice for lowlands and poorly drained sites. It belongs to the white oak group, so it produces a new crop of acorns every year, which is a boon to wildlife, and its acorns are particularly interesting to naturalists. The cap of the overcup oak acorn covers the nut underneath almost entirely (explaining the tree's name), and these big, round acorns have a property that sets them apart from other healthy acorns: they float. Most acorns float only when they have been hollowed out by acorn weevil larvae (a bad sign if you want them to germinate), but overcup oak acorns are "designed" to float. One of the overcup oak's major methods of dispersal is through acorns traveling on water.

While the overcup oak pictured here, a state and national champion, grows on private property, hundreds of acres of publicly owned natural lands nearby provide habitat for this and other interesting tree species (including the longleaf pine). The Antioch Pines Natural Area Preserve, owned by the Commonwealth of Virginia, and the Blackwater Ecological Preserve, owned by Old Dominion University, together make up the 1,200-acre Zuni Pine Barrens Preserves, which in addition to providing other ecological services, could be the place where the next millennium's champion overcup oak might grow.

Hurry, the water is rising! With that warning, champion tree hunter Byron Carmean led photographer Robert Llewellyn and other members of the Remarkable Tree crew to this state and national champion overcup oak (Quercus lyrata) in Isle of Wight County.

SILVER MAPLE, BLAND COUNTY

I t's easy to see why Virginia's largest silver maple has thrived: it grows in a shallow bowl between two gentle hills, with Brushy Mountain rising up behind it. And, as if the topography weren't enough to channel adequate water to it, an active spring bubbles up near its base. Silver maples (also known as soft, white, water, creek, and river maples) will grow most anywhere, but as their common names suggest, they prosper, and achieve their greatest size, in areas where they receive lots of moisture. This site, near an abandoned farmhouse in Bland County, certainly fits the bill.

This tree, like silver maples in general, probably grew fast, and even though it looks old (flaky bark, enormous trunk, some rotten wood and a large missing limb), it is unlikely to be over 125 years old, the average maximum age for silver maples. Like many other fast-growing trees, silver maples pay for their fast growth with weak wood and are notorious for breaking up in wind and ice storms. For this and for the fact that their greedy roots can buckle sidewalks and clog drain fields, landscapers don't much like them, but many property owners do, and with equally good reason.

Not only are silver maples the fastest-growing American maple species—able to turn a new home site into one with some "big tree gravitas" in a hurry—they have the enormously appealing habit of kicking up the silvery undersides of their leaves whenever the wind blows. Watching wind move through a silver maple is like witnessing the passing of a ghost, so responsive are these leaves to something you can't otherwise see, and many would argue that although a silver maple exhibits less fall color than a sugar maple or a red maple (its fall leaves are a pale yellow often tinged with brown or green), it makes up for its relatively nondescript fall show with bravura performances in summer thunderstorms.

A spring, marked by a spring house near the base of the state champion silver maple, helps explain why it has prospered.

YELLOW BUCKEYE, ALLEGHANY COUNTY

an Miles, facilities manager at Claytor Nature Study Center in Bedford, was fossil-hunting when he encountered this yellow buckeye (*Aesculus flava*) on the Cowpasture River in Alleghany County. From the road, he thought the tree might be 4 feet in diameter, but as he approached the tree, he realized the best thing he'd find that day—or year—wouldn't be fossils. "I was awestruck by its enormous bole," says Miles. "It was a mass of sculpted bulges embraced by sinuous vines, and with an entry door to a spacious room inside it, complete with window!"

Miles contacted local foresters and asked them to measure the tree, which turned out to be 7.9 feet in diameter, 94 feet tall, and 69 feet in crown spread—a new state champion. Later, when compared with the nation's largest yellow buckeyes, it was dubbed a national champion. What's fun about this discovery is not just that it thrilled Dan Miles, but that it took place in 2007, proving

Crevices, cracks, and shelf-like burls provide landing pads for seeds of other species that sprout in the bark and soft wood of this yellow buckeye (Aesculus flava).

trees larger than reigning champions can still be found.

The tree Miles found isn't hidden. Although it is partially obscured by smaller trees growing beside it, it grows in an open field where boaters and fishermen must pass it often. The land on which the tree grows is currently part of Walter L. Robinson River Access Park, which is in turn a part of the George Washington National Forest. According to local foresters, when the land on which the tree grows was acquired in 1970, it was being farmed and the hollow tree was being used as a hog house—with hogs penned in near the tree, which they used for shelter.

It's quite a shelter. The interior of the trunk—big enough to accommodate several people if they could squeeze through the "door"—is white with age and lit from above by light streaming through holes in the upper trunk. The exterior of the trunk looks like something boiling and melting—with some of its bark coming off in flat, smooth plates, other parts of its trunk covered with large, swirly burls and other craggy outgrowths.

Although it is sometimes planted as an ornamental and is native to western Virginia, yellow buckeye is much less common in Virginia than it is in other parts of its range. (According to *Silvics of North America*, it is most abundant in the Great Smokey Mountains of the southeastern U.S.) It is a fast-growing species, which usually correlates with short life, but experts disagree on yellow buckeye's longevity; some list the tree as short-lived (to 80 years), others as long-lived (to 300 years). A lover of moist, deep soils with good drainage, yellow buckeye grows particularly well in cool coves, on north-facing slopes, and in river bottoms like the one on the Cowpasture River. Because its young shoots and seeds contain poisonous compounds, it is sometimes removed from pastures. The name of the tree reportedly comes from its large, dark brown nuts, which look almost polished and carry a pale scar that reminded those who named the tree of a deer's eye.

Yellow buckeye wood is soft and makes poor lumber, but the tree is handsome in the landscape and makes a fine shade tree. "[It's] the most beautiful of the large-growing *Aesculus*" says plantsman Michael Dirr. Other assets of the yellow buckeye include its showy, upright clusters of yellowish, late spring flowers and its dark green, palmate leaves, but a large yellow buckeye can impress even without them. When the Remarkable Tree team visited the champion yellow buckeye in Alleghany County, it was neither in leaf nor flower, but its bark, size, and shape rendered it by far the most distinguished denizen of the riverbank.

This yellow buckeye on the banks of the Cowpasture River (south of Clifton Forge near the village of Long Furnace) had never been nominated to Virginia's Big Tree Program when Dan Miles brought it to the attention of foresters in 2007. One of the largest trees in Virginia, it now reigns as the national champion yellow buckeye.

SERVICEBERRY, TAZEWELL COUNTY

Burke's Garden

This champion tree is small, but it's enormous for a serviceberry. The way the champion tree program works, even trees that are typically small of stature get to compete, because they are compared to others of their kind (white oak to white oak, serviceberry to serviceberry) rather than to every other tree in the woods. Serviceberries, for example, seldom get over 40 feet tall (and many are multi-stemmed shrubs in the 10- to 15-foot range), but this one is not only 44 feet tall, it has a single trunk 100 inches in girth, making it the largest known serviceberry in the country.

It seems fitting that this tree, as beautiful as it is big, grows on the farm of Louise Hoge, who, in the 1970s and 1980s, was among the most prolific "big tree nominators" in the state. Newcomers to the "big tree list" wondered why so many trees had Louise Hoge's name by them. Part of the reason was that Louise Hoge had a great eye for trees, and part of the reason was that Hoge lived in Burke's Garden, where the trees seem as superlative as their setting. (Sometimes referred to as "God's Thumbprint," Burke's Garden is a topographically rare basin, rimmed on all sides by Garden Mountain.)

"It's like Shangri-la," Robert Llewellyn kept saying as he wandered through the pasture surrounding this serviceberry in Burke's Garden. The day was harsh, the wind sharp, but the tree seemed gentle and forgiving as it released its tiny white petals—and even some flower clusters—to the wind. The woods of nearby Jefferson National Forest were also dappled with serviceberry—these less far along in their April blooming, with their buds still hanging in graceful clusters from delicate twigs. Peeking out from under forest trees, serviceberry blooms before the trees around it have started to leaf out, but it is far less conspicuous than better known pear, dogwood, or wild plum, for which it is frequently mistaken.

Shadbush, shadblow, sarvis-tree and Juneberry are other names for this refined but staunch native tree. It's called shadbush and shadblow because it blooms when the shad are running; it's called Juneberry because its small, berry-like fruits, beloved by birds, mature in June. Serviceberry fruit is also relished by people, some of whom consider it superior to highbush blueberries, and American Indians relied on it as an ingredient in pemmican—a ceremonial food consisting of dried bison meat, juneberries, and spices.

Some say this tree's common names that include the words "sarvis" and "service" derive from the word "sorbus," a common name (and genus name) for trees with similar fruit, but the most appealing explanation of the serviceberry name derives from the tree's blooming time. Legend has it that ministers traveling mountain roads on horseback couldn't reach their parishioners in the mountains until early spring when the roads became passable, so settlers postponed their weddings and baptisms until then. Because the ground was too frozen for digging graves, funerals, too, were postponed until graves could be dug, and services held—a time coinciding with the blooming of the tree that came to be known as "serviceberry."

Not a dogwood, not a pear: Serviceberry is often mistaken for other early, white-flowering trees, especially now that the non-native Bradford pear has escaped into the wild. Serviceberry has smaller flowers, and usually blooms earlier, than dogwood, and it is usually more understated in appearance than the more floriferous pear. This downy serviceberry (Amelanchier arborea) in Burke's Garden, Tazewell County, is a state and national champion.

LAUREL OAK, CHESAPEAKE

If you were trying to hide a champion tree, you couldn't find a much better spot than behind a home on Currituck Drive in eastern Chesapeake. This suburban neighborhood, with its modest ranch houses, doesn't draw attention to itself and neither does the tree. Someone looking hard might notice that the canopy of leaves showing above the roof of one home is unusually broad, but because it's not startlingly high, few passersby would give it a second look. In fact, it seems quite possible there are homeowners in this neighborhood who have no idea there's a behemoth in their midst.

To see the tree you need an invitation from the owner to step into his small backyard where the trunk dominates the yard the way an elephant might a closet. Everything around it—plastic lawn chairs, children's play equipment, a grill—seems dwarfed and temporary in comparison to this massive living thing. The largest laurel oak in Virginia and the second largest in the nation, the tree has an enormous trunk (almost 7.5 feet in diameter) that rises close to the house and says, emphatically but not accusingly, "I was here first." The tree seems happily domesticated, sporting a chain once used to hoist engines when the area around it was a farm, and now supporting a baby swing. Roughly level with the roof of the house, there is a depression in the trunk that gathers water (probably promoting some rot), but that platform-like area has also served as an invitation to tree climbers, some of whom have carved their initials, but no dates, in the tree. Although fast-growing laurel oaks are not

typically long-lived, the tree's owner believes the tree to be over 300 years old, and even if it's not that old, it looks it.

According to local lore, the farmer who owned the property where the tree grows stipulated that this laurel oak must never be cut down. (As with many champion trees, the tree's size is also a disincentive to cutting it down.) This tree has also been favored by at least one owner—its current one—who treated the tree with care by pruning judiciously, not vengefully, after it dropped a limb on part of his house.

Like many of Virginia's champion trees, this one was "discovered" by big tree hunter Byron Carmean. About twenty-five years ago, Carmean was teaching horticulture and forestry at the Chesapeake Center for Science and Technology when one of his students, Ricky Lehman, told him, "I know where a big tree is." Together, Lehman (who lived on a nearby farm) and Carmean visited the tree and nominated it to Virginia's Big Tree Program, where it has been a "star" ever since.

Although most laurel oaks grow only about 60 feet tall with a 40- to 60-foot spread, this one is 82 feet tall with a crown spread of 87 feet. The tree is semi-evergreen, keeping some of its narrow, lance-shaped leaves all year and dropping others, in the words of its owner, "all year." Native only to the southeastern U.S.—from the Gulf Coast, east to Florida and north to southeastern Virginia—laurel oaks are said to reach their greatest size and beauty in northern Florida and in Georgia, but this laurel oak hidden in a Virginia subdivision proves the locations of fine trees will sometimes surprise you.

This laurel oak (Quercus laurifolia) in Chesapeake is the largest of its species in the state and the second largest in the nation.

WEEPING WILLOW, TAZEWELL COUNTY

Burke's Garden

There may be no more expressive tree in the landscape than the weeping willow (*Salix babylonica*), and the bigger it is, the more eloquent it is.

This weeping willow in Tazewell, the biggest one in the nation, creates an umbrella of shade 102 feet wide, and when even the gentlest breeze stirs it, every pendulous branch seems to tremble. In a stiff breeze, the branches all move in unison—a ballet of branches—and a strong wind whips the tree into a maelstrom of movement.

No wonder there is so much romance associated with weeping willows. This one, which grows in the type of moist, low place weeping willows love, has a wide, double trunk, basket-weave bark, and a crown laden with twisted, dead branches that threaten to fall every time the tree dances. An old outhouse stands within feet of the tree, and a carefully hand-lettered wooden sign, partly decomposed, rests in the crotch of a branch. Although it may not have been read by more than a handful of people in a decade, the sign still announces proudly "Champion weeping willow."

Weeping willows are famous for growing fast (as much as 6 to 8 feet a year) and large, but this tree far exceeds averages. Weeping willows usually get about 30 to 60 feet tall and 1 to 3 feet in diameter; this one is 102 feet tall and 7 feet in diameter. Because it sits in a somewhat protected hollow, it has been sheltered from some of the fiercest winds that sweep through Burke's Garden, the Tazewell community in which it grows, but it also seems to have been toughened by the years. Like all weeping willows, it leafs out very early in the spring (looking much more yellow than green), and the contrast of its delicate early foliage and drooping catkins against its deeply fissured and time-scarred bark is striking.

No one seems to know who, if anyone, planted the Tazewell weeping willow champ, or when. Chances are it either grew from a cutting that was rooted deliberately (cuttings root easily in water), or it grew from a branch or twig that washed or blew into this auspicious spot. Many are the stories of weeping willows in Virginia and elsewhere that rooted from a willow crop or switch accidentally dropped into receptive soil or from a cutting brought back from an exotic place, like Napoleon's tomb at St. Helena. All the weeping willows in England are said to be descended from one twig, rooted by the poet Alexander Pope, who took it from a package (tied with willow twigs) that Lady Norfolk had received from Spain. It's unlikely that story is true, but it, and others like it, crop up like cresses around weeping willows.

This picturesque weeping willow, ranked the largest in the nation in 2008, enjoys a low spot next to Route 727 in Burke's Garden.

BLACK WALNUT
WILLIAMSBURG, ORANGE COUNTY, AND WESTMORELAND COUNTY

As if to prove champion trees can be dethroned overnight, the black walnut champion we had selected and photographed for this chapter—a walnut growing in Colonial Williamsburg—was dethroned in 2007. So we photographed the new champion growing at Montpelier in Orange County. Then *it* was dethroned by a black walnut growing at Spring Grove Farm in Westmoreland County. It's not easy keeping track of champion trees, much less planning chapters around them!

What our tree chase proved, however, is just how fickle the champion tree selection process can be. For example, the Williamsburg walnut lost its title to the Orange County tree not because it had gotten smaller or the Orange County tree had gotten bigger, but because the rules for measuring big trees had changed. When measured according to new rules put forth by American Forests, the point value of the Orange County tree went up, because its girth was measured differently. When it had been measured in 2004 (in accordance with the old rules), it had been measured at 4½ feet on the uphill side of the slope at its base; in 2007, in accordance with the new rules, it was measured at a median slope position, which placed the tape lower, around a broader portion of the trunk, and the tree gained girth points. The walnut in Westmoreland, which had always been a contender for champion status, wrested the title from the Orange County walnut when it was remeasured by a county forester and found to be both taller and larger in girth than when previously measured.

Because we had become attached to them and thought others would enjoy seeing them, we've included the two dethroned champs here along with the new Westmoreland champ. The Westmoreland champ grows along the edge of a woodland in Mt. Holly, where its owner can enjoy it from her den window. At over 20

feet in circumference, it is by far the most massive of these three walnuts, but because it is less isolated in the landscape (it grows among a clutch of other trees), the tree doesn't call attention to itself. The Williamsburg walnut grows near the corner of Francis Street and Nassau Avenue in Colonial Williamsburg. Its setting—an open field in which oxen graze—contributes to its impact, but it would be impressive anywhere. At 108 feet, it is the tallest of the three trees, and has the open, rounded crown of a field-grown walnut. It has dominated its site for as long as anyone associated with Colonial Williamsburg can remember and helps shelter the nearby Custis yew, which is believed to be the oldest living plant in Colonial Williamsburg.

The Orange County walnut, which grows at James Madison's home, Montpelier, has a different kind of beauty. It stands at the top of a hill overlooking a grove of smaller walnuts, and the repetition of their shapes creates a visual echo. The tree is also notable for the way it leans and for the

This former state champion black walnut grows in Colonial Williamsburg.

orientation of its branches, which define an area once occupied by a partner tree. Right next to this tree, until the mid 1990s, grew another walnut, almost as big as the near-champion, and regular visitors to Montpelier remember well when the impact of the existing tree was doubled by its partner.

While it's unlikely a walnut as big as any of these grows in your yard or your neighbor's (each of these trees is over 100 feet tall and the smallest is almost 19 feet in circumference), walnut trees of substantial size *are* often found in ordinary backyards (they like open, sunny spots), where they are alternately loved and loathed. Walnuts are infamous for the debris they drop—lots of twigs and golf-ball-sized fruit—but that same fruit is the source of the delicious black walnuts used in cooking. Walnuts also have a chemical in their roots, bark, leaves, and fruit that can inhibit the growth of neighboring plants, making them tricky to deal with around a garden, but there is a certain stalwart quality to a walnut that adds "gravitas" to the landscape.

Walnuts are also impressive in winter silhouette—dark bark, abruptly angled branches—and one sure sign of the end of summer is a shower of pale yellow walnut leaves falling on the lawn. Black walnut (*Juglans nigra*) is also highly valued for its wood (especially for furniture and cabinetry), but don't get too excited about making a windfall if a walnut topples over in your yard. According to Charlie Becker, manager of utilization and marketing for the Virginia Department of Forestry, a walnut in a Virginia churchyard did once sell for over $10,000, but it's highly unlikely the average backyard walnut would fetch such a price. For one thing, most backyard walnuts aren't 100 to 150 feet tall, 2 to 3 feet in diameter, or possessed of a trunk that grows 40 to 50 feet straight up before branching—the kind of walnuts lumbermen really want. For another, most backyard walnuts are too difficult to remove (think utility lines, nearby buildings) and too filled with perilous objects (nails, old hammock hooks, etc.) for lumbermen to be interested in them. According to Becker, having a backyard walnut a lumberman would want is about as likely as winning the lottery.

Once a state champion, the black walnut in the snowy scene grows at Montpelier in Orange County. It was dethroned by the larger black walnut (left) in Westmoreland County.

SASSAFRAS, LEE COUNTY

Every school child in Virginia has probably plucked leaves from a sassafras—or should have. It's the tree that makes such a good addition to leaf collections because its leaves come in three shapes—mitten-shaped, three-lobed, and elliptical. But it's unlikely many school kids (or even adults) have plucked leaves from a sassafras as big as this one. Most of us know the sassafras as a small tree or multi-stemmed shrub that grows in hedgerows, in abandoned fields, and along the edges of woods, where it can be notable for its spring flowers (chartreuse green), its fall color (ranging from pale yellow to dramatic apricot and red), or its fragrance (pleasantly pungent), but seldom for its size. It is one of the virtues of champion tree programs, however, that they alert us to trees like this one, a gorgeous old specimen almost 6 feet in diameter.

This sassafras, which occupies a Lee County pasture, is the largest of its species in the state, but there are a surprising number of oversized sassafras trees in Virginia. Sassafras trees of near-champion size grow in Shenandoah, King and Queen, and Rockingham counties, and historically, large sassafras trees were common in the mid-Atlantic. In addition to noting its use for bowls, timber posts, and medicines, John Brickell, in his 1737 *The Natural History of North Carolina*, noted that sassafras is "very common" and "grows large, its Wood being sometimes above two Feet over." Because it is a pioneer species and regenerates from roots after fire, thickets of small sassafras trees would have also been abundant in colonial (and pre-colonial) America, where it appeared in old Indian fields.

Small wonder sassafras was so important to colonial economies. The search for it inspired many a New World exploration, and it was reportedly being loaded onto French ships off the coast of South Carolina as early as 1588. In his *Joyfull Newes Out of the Newe Founde World* (1574), the Spanish botanist Nicholás Monardes devoted over 20 pages

to the virtues of sassafras, and in the Virginia Charter of 1610, sassafras led the list of natural products the British Crown demanded of the Virginia colony as a price for its charter. This "tree of high price and profit" was known to have essential oils in its roots, leaves, and twigs, which were believed to cure everything from lameness to liver aches. American Indians, who had been using the plant medicinally for hundreds if not thousands of years, taught colonists how to make teas and poultices from sassafras, and by the 1600s patrons of London coffee houses were as devoted to their saloop (a drink made of sassafras tea and hot milk) as contemporary coffee drinkers are to their lattes. According to some reports, the sassafras market in England bottomed out only after it became commonly known that sassafras tea was a good remedy for syphilis—and then no one wanted to be seen drinking it.

Wild foods enthusiasts still make sassafras tea from sassafras roots, but sassafras tea that includes "real" safrole—the oil in sassafras—is no longer available commercially. Like root beer, which was originally flavored with sassafras, sassafras tea is now flavored artificially. Sassafras tea was banned from interstate commerce in 1960, when the Food and Drug Administration found it to be carcinogenic. The sale of sassafras oil is also closely monitored by the Drug Enforcement Administration, because it is used in the clandestine manufacture of the drug MDMA (ecstasy).

Gone, too, are the days when sassafras supported small industries in Virginia. According to forest historian Henry Clepper, sassafras roots were once harvested by the ton in Virginia, and those roots were then distilled and their oils used in the manufacture of medicines, perfumes, scented soaps, and candies. Still with us, however, is the distinctive fragrance of sassafras, which can be had by anyone willing to snap a twig, abrade its bark, and inhale. Fortunately, this kind of ecstasy is still legal.

Virginia Tech Extension Agent Harold Jerrell uses his walking stick, which happens to be made of sassafras, to estimate the girth of the champion sassafras in Lee County. The tree is over 18 feet in circumference.

This state champion sassafras (Sassafras albidum) has probably benefited from growing in a shallow sinkhole where water flows toward its roots.

TULIP-POPLAR, BEDFORD

It has not been easy seeing the Bedford tulip-poplar decline. This is a tree that reigned as Virginia's largest tree and the largest tulip-poplar in the nation for over 30 years. As one of the first really impressive trees nominated to Virginia's Big Tree Program, it drew publicity to the program and inspired many a tree lover (including an author of this book) to develop a strong interest in remarkable trees. But that was the 1970s, when the tree grew in a woodland and the closest habitation was a pen for hunting dogs, not a subdivision.

First the property around the Bedford tulip-poplar was developed, and the tree was protected in a small park. Then the tree began to decline, and it was surrounded with a chain-link fence—to protect neighborhood children from the tree or the town from liability, or maybe both. In the summer of 2007, after the tree lost part of its trunk and a limb estimated to weigh 6 tons, concerns about the tree falling onto a nearby duplex escalated, and the tree was radically pruned. (It was not removed, because, among other things, the price tag was too high: $40,000.)

"I lost sleep over that tree," says Randal Nixon, Director of Parks and Recreation for the city of Bedford. According to Nixon, a local school is propagating seeds from the Bedford tulip-poplar and plans are afoot to make memorabilia from some of the wood it has shed. Nixon also thinks the tree may continue to bloom and grow a while longer.

Now diminished to the point that only its old friends would want to visit it, the Bedford tulip-poplar is still the third largest tulip-poplar in Virginia, but it has a very bad haircut. Unflattering photos of the tree circulate on the Internet like knives to the heart of those who knew the tree in its prime. We feature the tree here because, having reigned so long, it seems to deserve recognition in this chapter, and because we love it. Trees enter your life the way people do, and sometimes one person or one tree has more influence than another. This tree, to some of us, has been an avatar.

The shrinking of the Bedford tulip-poplar is partly conveyed by these figures: when it reigned as champion, the tree was 138 feet tall and had a crown spread of 135 feet. It is now 52 feet tall and has a crown spread of 67 feet. And its girth has shrunk from 34 feet (almost 11 feet in diameter) to 30.5 feet (about 9.7 feet in diameter).

No one knows, and no one will probably ever know, how old the Bedford tulip-poplar is. Because the tree is hollow, it's impossible to count its rings. It grows in an extremely favorable environment—in a hollow, near

a seasonal stream and possibly a spring, and, like all tulip-poplars, it has the genes for long life. By some estimates, the typical age of mortality for a tulip-poplar is about 200 years, but tulip-poplars 450 years old have been reported. In contrast to long-lived trees that grow slowly partly because they are putting energy into things like producing strong wood and insect defenses, tulip-poplars support their long life with rapid growth. According to ecologist Craig Loehle, a tulip-poplar is able to keep ahead of decay only so long as it can maintain a rapid growth rate, and on poor sites, the tulip-poplar is not nearly so long-lived as it is on favorable ones.

The Bedford tulip-poplar never had the "look" of a typical tulip-poplar. The tallest hardwoods in North America, tulip-poplars usually have straight, tall trunks that are frequently clear of branches 80 to 100 feet off the ground. The Bedford tulip-poplar was—and is—shaped more like a laughing Buddha, with a fat "belly" and massive branches close to ground. It does, however, have an excess of the quintessential characteristic for which this species is famous—volume. Ranked by volume, tulip-poplar (*Liriodendron tulipifera*) is the species with the greatest volume (sheer mass of wood) in Virginia's forests, and the Bedford tulip-poplar is "voluminous" in the extreme.

Relatives of magnolias, tulip-poplars are ancient trees with beautiful cup-shaped flowers. It is the resemblance of these flowers (green with yellow and orange markings) to tulips that results in part of the tree's common name. Why the tree is referred to as a "poplar" is less well understood, but it may have something to do with Europeans seeing a resemblance between this North American tree and European poplars (it is unrelated to the poplar). Other common names for the tulip-poplar include tulip-tree, yellow-poplar (a reference to the color of the tree's wood), and canoewood, a reference to the fact that early Americans fashioned dugout canoes from tulip-poplar logs. (The tree's wood is light and floats easily.)

In the woods, tulip-poplars are easily identifiable even in winter when they hold their flower-like seed pods aloft. When the sun strikes these pale woody structures, it seems to light them, and the sides of mountains sometimes glow with tulip-poplar "candles."

When we photographed the Bedford tulip-poplar in the spring of 2007, the tree was blooming and many of its cup-shaped flowers were on the ground. "I think it may flower again this spring," said Randal Nixon optimistically in early 2008. "It just doesn't want to go."

This 1986 photo depicts the Bedford tulip-poplar in its prime. Photo by Nancy R. Hugo

Once Virginia's largest tree, this tulip-poplar grows in Bedford's Poplar Park, which was created to protect it. The tree is in decline and lost its title to a tulip-poplar in Chesapeake in 2008.

chapter four COMMUNITY TREES

You're on the trail of a mulberry in White Post, but you happen through Upperville, and something there startles you. New trees are being planted in median strips and the town seems to have given up a lane of traffic on an already narrow road to accommodate them. It seems Upperville is involved in a major "traffic calming" effort and the trees in the medians are part of that effort. Traffic may be calmed, but the heart of a tree lover races: another example of trees contributing to the community.

Too often trees are part of the "taken-for-granted" background of our communities; they are appreciated only when they are threatened—or mourned when they are lost. But if the number of communities lobbying to have their trees featured in this book is any indication, community tree hugging is on the rise. Not only are communities realizing the economic value of trees (see Urban Forests, page 184), they also recognize the fact that trees can be community symbols and that of all the "green amenities" a community might boast, trees are often the most beloved and apparent. Trees, which are usually a community's oldest living residents, also provide a consistent bridge between human generations, something we share not only with our neighbors but with the parents and grandparents of our neighbors.

There are all sorts of ways to define a community tree, and in this chapter we've included trees that meet more than one of those definitions. Some define a community tree as a "familiar feature of the community," and by that definition, a community tree can be not only the sugar maple that everyone in town loves and talks about as it comes into color; it can be the white oak along the Appalachian trail that is known to hikers up and down the East Coast, or a sycamore that is known and appreciated by the community of commuters who pass it on the way to work every day.

One could also define a community tree as a tree a community has taken active steps to protect or celebrate, and within that category alone there are hundreds of trees—far more than we could feature—that deserve recognition. Notable among them are a white oak grove at Boyce Crossing in Clarke County protected by conservation easement (and a cooperative developer); a black walnut in Montgomery County with "two miles of cousins" trying to save it from road-widening; and a white oak in Oakton, one of the last surviving oaks for which that community is named, growing on a curve that would now be a lane of traffic had Hunter Mill Road not been realigned to go around the tree.

A tree lover could also take inspiration from the ways Virginia communities have found to celebrate their trees. For example, every ten years Chesterfield County has an official "Measuring Ceremony," complete with invitations and media coverage, to re-measure the Nunnally oak planted at its courthouse in 1814. Old Town Warrenton has a tree walking tour (complete with map and useful information about each species), Vienna once held an "oldest tree" contest, and Lynchburg recognizes a Heritage Tree with a plaque (and publicity) each year.

Community trees are celebrated on county auto decals (not a bad way to educate the public about heritage trees), and seedlings from treasured trees have been propagated and distributed as part of "community-building" activities in Bridgewater and Elkton. Virginians celebrate trees through full-fledged festivals, including Charlottesville's Dogwood Festival, the Shenandoah Apple Blossom Festival, and Highland County's Sugar Maple Festival, and through small town Arbor Day festivities as well. All these activities not only bring background trees into the foreground, they help turn collections of people into communities.

This "centerpiece of Sperryville" is a sugar maple (Acer saccharum) believed to have been growing on this site since the 1890s. Most of the year it draws little attention to itself, but in the fall it looks like a fire raging in the middle of town.

RED MULBERRY, HENRICO COUNTY
Lewis Ginter Botanical Garden

"It's absolutely irresistible to kids," says John Bouton, a long-time buildings and grounds superintendent at the Lewis Ginter Botanical Garden, describing the reclining red mulberry in the Children's Garden there. There does seem to be a magnetic pull to the tree—something easily witnessed when school groups, so dutifully lined up as they enter the Garden, are allowed to scatter and find their own places of interest. Straightaway, they make for the tree.

Even before the creation of the Children's Garden, which surrounds the tree, this old specimen, noted for its gnarled bark and reclining habit, was in decline. The decision of whether or not to protect the tree from kids or to allow them to enjoy it (its branches and split trunk seem to reach down and invite climbing) was a hard one, but advocates for tree climbing prevailed, and today almost 17,000 students and who-knows-how-many-other children have access to the tree each year. The wear and tear on the tree is unmistakable, but so is the positive impact the tree has on kids who have been allowed to ride its limbs, scale its trunk, and experience its bark, leaves, and fruit up close.

The tree was probably planted on the property for the same reason many landscapers today avoid it—for its fruit. Prior to its incarnation as a botanical garden, the Lewis Ginter property was owned by Miss Grace Arents, a noted gardener and horticulturist, who, in addition to her philanthropic activities, used the property as a showplace for the most progressive horticultural and agricultural practices of the time. (She occupied a home on the property from 1917 to 1926.) In addition to planting ornamentals and food crops, Arents planted fruit trees, and according to John Bouton, who interviewed many people who knew her, Miss Arents "actually planted that tree for the mulberries."

Although the tree is more often maligned than praised for its fruit (birds love it, but it is unwelcome on sidewalks, cars, and laundry drying on a clothesline), red mulberry fruit was a valuable food source in pre-colonial America. In *Jamestown Narratives*, a collection of eyewitness accounts of the early years of the Virginia Colony, account after account refers to instances in which American Indians fed red mulberries to settlers. "This people gave us mulberries, sod wheat and beans…" wrote Gabriel Archer, who also reported that the Powhatan king Arahatec "caused his women to bring us victuals, mulberries, strawberries…." According to Archer, "the Great King Powatah" (son of Powhatan), also served Captain Christopher Newport a meal that included strawberries and mulberries "new shaken off the tree, dropping on our heads as we sat."

Native to Virginia, red mulberry (*Morus rubra*) is considered a more valuable tree than common or white mulberry (*Morus alba*), which was imported to this country from China for the silkworm industry, but both trees grow fast, and because they are usually stout and spreading (and sometimes falling over), they provide climbable branches and what has been called "a ruined antique look" in a hurry. Among Virginia's most picturesque mulberries are Virginia's former state champion red mulberry at Wingfield House in Bedford, a nearly prostrate white mulberry outside Jefferson Hall at the College of William and Mary, a gnarled old paper mulberry (*Broussonetia papyrifera*) behind the Orlando Jones House in Colonial Williamsburg, and, of course, the much-loved red mulberry at the Lewis Ginter Botanical Garden in Henrico County.

Kid magnet: Thousands of school children in the Richmond area, as well as young tourists, have climbed the reclining red mulberry at the Lewis Ginter Botanical Garden in Henrico County.

SUGAR MAPLE, ROCKBRIDGE COUNTY

Follow Swope Lane toward Brownsburg Turnpike. Where the road ends in a T, turn right. There you will enter an area known locally as "Avenue of Trees" or "Maple Lane," where sugar maples form a natural tunnel that turns brilliant reds, yellows, and oranges in the fall. It is a landscape created by Rockbridge County residents who had the foresight to plant sugar maples there perhaps over a century ago.

"My great, great grandfather was involved," one Rockbridge resident suggested proudly. "The people of New Providence Church planted them," suggested another. Still another account, in a local newspaper, attributes the planting to Brownsburg residents William Frank Patterson and Walter Reese. Patterson's daughter-in-law, now in her 80s, confirms that Patterson was involved "over 100 years ago." Although nearly everyone we talked to thinks it happened in the late nineteenth century, pinning down the exact date of the planting proved impossible. What proved easy was pinning down exactly when some of the trees in the treasured tunnel were cut down by VDOT. "Six in 1999, 28 in 2004," Rockbridge conservationist Catharine Gilliam informed us, and her 2004 numbers were confirmed by VDOT.

There is disagreement in the Brownsburg community about whether or not it was necessary for VDOT to cut down any of the approximately 150 sugar maples that originally formed the tunnel over Brownsburg Turnpike. According to VDOT roadside manager Scott Nye, the 2004 removal was necessary because the trees had structural defects, rot, and decay that made them a threat to motorists. Not all Brownsburg residents agreed, but there is agreement that even though the integrity of the original tree line has been compromised, it is still a natural wonder. And every tree that was removed has been replaced by a healthy new one.

It is not just the size of the trees and their fall color that make this tree tunnel a remarkable one; it is the old trees' roots. Many of them cling to the roadside embankment like wooden buttresses, and their shapes, which are displayed like sculptures along the line of sight out a car window, are as impressive as many a museum piece.

The trees also provide shade and respite from heat coming off the asphalt road, which may be one reason, in addition to enjoying their beauty, that motorists find tree tunnels so appealing. Unfortunately, in the winter, such shade can be a liability, preventing roadway ice from melting, among other things. Although this was not the reason for the Brownsburg trees' removal, this is the reason many tree canopies that might form tunnels are cut back, but there are ways to deal with such a situation other than cutting trees down. Selective pruning can let in more sunlight, regular maintenance can reduce the possibility that old branches will break under the weight of ice and snow, and barrels of sand or salt can be put out near trouble spots and applied as needed. "That's the way they do it in the northeast," says arborist Joel Koci, who notes that "a little bit of planning goes a long way" toward preserving tree tunnels like the one in Rockbridge.

In autumn visitors come from miles away to experience the technicolor tunnel of sugar maples (Acer saccharum) along Brownsburg Turnpike, a planting prized by Rockbridge County residents.

CHINQUAPIN OAK, LURAY

Look for this chinquapin oak, and you will find Luray—not just the historic buildings and picturesque landscapes but the people. The tree grows in the middle of town, across from the Page County court complex and next to the county administration building. Townspeople believe it germinated in the 1750s, which would mean it occupied its site more than 20 years before the signing of the Declaration of Independence and about 60 years before the founding of Luray (1812), which helps explain why, when new construction threatened it, concerned citizens sprang into action.

"Office Versus Oak," read the headline in *The Daily-News Record.* "County Officials Revamp Plans Because of Tree." The county had purchased the property on which the tree grows in 2003 with the intention of building new county offices on the site, but, in addition to citizen concerns that the construction might damage the tree, there was another issue. In her last will and testament, a previous owner of the property had stipulated that "…the old oak tree in my backyard…be untouched except for safe upkeep, forever, no matter who may own the property."

Working with architects who had already designed plans for the building, county officials first hoped to modify the plans in a way that would allow the construction to take place without damaging the tree, but when an arborist pointed out how large the root protection zone of the tree needed to be—74 feet in all directions from the trunk—plans began to shift. The county realized that with the tree on one side and an historic old school on the other, there just wasn't enough room for the building and its associated parking. In 2007, plans for Page County's new office complex moved to a new site.

"The tree's going to stay, that's for sure," says Charles Newton, president of the Page County Tree Board, which supports efforts by the Luray Town Council, the Luray Tree and Beautification Committee, and the Luray Parks and Recreation Department to keep Luray a "Tree City." To earn "Tree City U.S.A." status (awarded by the National Arbor Day Foundation), a community must have a Tree Board or Forestry Department and a local tree ordinance, it must spend at least $2 per capita on trees, and it must promote Arbor Day. At this writing, 28 Virginia communities had Tree City designation for time periods ranging from one to 27 years.

That's the fact of the matter. The spirit of the matter is that in a Tree City like Luray you find more than the requisite tree projects; you find people organized to champion and celebrate trees. Imagine, for example, stopping to have lunch in Luray, picking up a "mural tour" brochure, and discovering there's a mural painted as a tribute to an enormous white oak cut down years earlier but still mourned by many in the community. When you finally find the mural, you feel as if you've been on a treasure hunt that has brought you into contact with Luray, its trees, its people, and finally with this quote from the Nature Conservancy's John Sawhill (the caption local artist Chris Anderson chose for her mural): "In the end our society will be defined not only by what we create but by what we refuse to destroy."

This chinquapin oak (Quercus muehlenbergii) grows on Court Street in Luray, where it has been protected from development that might have damaged its roots. "They finally recognized roots really are a part of the tree," says Charles Newton, president of the Page County Tree Board, who, with Luray's Tree and Beautification Committee and others, helped present the tree's case to county officials. The second largest chinquapin oak in the state, the tree clings to a hillside overlooking Hawksbill Creek, where its canopy spreads to cover an area 132 feet in diameter.

LIVE OAK, VIRGINIA BEACH

Let this tree stand for all the trees neighbors love without owning. Granted, not every neighborhood has a tree this extraordinary (it's almost 6 feet in diameter), but there is nothing unusual about neighbors feeling connected to trees in others' yards. After all, in many cases, depending on how long they've lived in the neighborhood, neighbors may have longer connections to nearby trees than the trees' owners do.

Located in the Fairfield neighborhood of Virginia Beach on a welcoming cul-de-sac, this live oak was nominated to the Remarkable Tree Project by a neighbor who lives about 1,000 feet away. "I can see the top of its canopy out my back window," says Kristina Villaire, who jogs by the tree regularly and considers it an important influence in her life. "That tree is what made me want to be an arborist," she says. "I'm from New England, and we just don't have trees like that up north." Villaire, who decided she wanted to "be someone who could take care of trees like that" and who "wanted to be around people who like to be around trees" is now an arborist with the City of Chesapeake.

This tree's owner, Charlene Hood, is equally attached to the tree. "Once I stepped out in that back yard and saw that tree it was all over," says Hood, who says she'd never have bought the home she's now lived in for twelve years if it weren't for the tree. "We were looking for something to rent, not to buy, and the house was too small for our family and dogs." Now the tree, which Hood has dubbed "Mini" is a member of the family.

"Everybody comes by and checks on her and says 'hello,'" says Hood.

"Busloads of strangers drive by to get a glimpse of her. When my garden club holds its plant sale, we advertise it as 'under the old oak tree.' People probably come as much for the tree as the plants." Hood even has a section under "T" for "tree" in her Rolodex, where she keeps the numbers of people interested in Mini's health and history.

No one knows exactly how old the Fairfield live oak is (ages of 300 to 500 years have been suggested), but it was almost certainly on the site when the property was part of Fairfield Plantation. The site of the Fairfield Plantation house, about two blocks from the tree, is now occupied by the Fairfield shopping center, but the bodies of many members of the Walke family, who owned the plantation, still lie buried within 20 feet of the Fairfield live oak. The tree harkens to a time when busy Kempsville and Witch Duck roads were dirt roads connecting Ferry and Fairfield plantations, and when, instead of commuters and soccer moms, those roads carried horses and buggies transporting goods to and from nearby Kemps Landing on the Elizabeth River.

Except for some hollow areas, which make the tree resonate like an organ when an owl hoots inside, the Fairfield live oak seems healthy. It did, however, lose two limbs to Hurricane Isabel. "I ran out of the house jumping over trees and power lines in my yard to see if that tree was OK," recalls Villaire. Luckily, the falling limbs resulted in "only a small hole" in Charlene Hood's garage roof, and Hood, who feels the tree has protected her more often than it has harmed her, was less concerned about the damage to her garage than she was impressed by the size of limbs that came down. "Those limbs were bigger than most trees," she marveled.

The owner of this live oak, beloved in its Fairfield neighborhood in Virginia Beach, calls it "Mini," a tongue-in-cheek tribute to its extraordinary size. The live oak (Quercus virginiana) is a semi-evergreen southern tree whose natural range extends only into southeastern Virginia in a narrow belt along the Coastal Plain.

Sweetgum, Chesapeake

This sweetgum has seen the neighborhood around it rise, decline, and rise again. It has known the sounds of children attending Bible school (under the tree in the 1950s), teenagers dancing (in the nearby community center), and of jackhammers ripping up nearby streets and bulldozers razing nearby buildings. With the help of a legendary city arborist (Chesapeake's Miklos Lestyan), an appreciative Parks and Recreation Department (led by Bobby Clifton, who stole his first kiss under the tree in 1957), and an active citizenry (a public library and five churches are within walking distance of the tree), the tree has held its ground in Johnson Park, South Norfolk. In fact, it has more than held its ground; it has thrived.

"I don't know what the red fence means," librarian Jean Cooper commented apprehensively, when a member of the Remarkable Tree team stopped in to talk to her. We were happy to report the red fence was a good thing—it was protecting the root zone of the tree while nearby construction was taking place. And, not only that, in a reversal of fortunes that few trees experience, the tree was about to see its habitat enhanced. As part of a neighborhood revitalization effort that would include trading boarded up buildings for offices, condos, and shops (as well as a hip new name, SoNo, for South Norfolk), this tree was about to have the incredible good fortune of having the street beside it and the overhead utility wires near it removed.

It couldn't have happened to a nicer sweetgum. Much maligned because of

their spiny seed capsules—the woody gumballs that annoy many a homeowner but entertain many a child—the sweetgum (*Liquidambar styraciflua*) actually makes a fine lawn and park tree. With few disease or insect problems, the tree is relatively fast-growing and has good fall color. Often, on a single tree, star-shaped sweetgum leaves exhibit fall colors ranging from yellow-green to orange, scarlet, and a maroon so deep it's almost black. As a lawn tree, its only needs are generous space for its root system (this is not a tree to shoehorn into a hole in the sidewalk) as well as tolerance for its gumballs (again, not a good fit with urban sidewalks, although there are sweetgum cultivars that don't bear gumballs). The tree even has an important place in the pantheon of wildlife foods, serving not only as a seed source for small mammals and birds (goldfinches hang on gumballs like Scrooge to money) but also as host plant to the luna moth.

As few people seem to realize but the Johnson Park sweetgum illustrates, a native sweetgum in the right place can also be as ornamental as many a more vaunted tree. This one, which Mik Lestyan estimates to be around 200 years old, has the spreading, rounded crown characteristic of old sweetgums (younger trees are usually straight-trunked and pyramidal), fine fall color, and commanding presence. As one of the largest and most well-proportioned sweetgums in Virginia, it combines size, beauty, and community connection in a way that does the sweetgum, and South Norfolk, proud.

This sweetgum in the South Norfolk borough of Chesapeake proves a sweetgum in the right spot can be a community treasure. Located in the northwest corner of Johnson Park, this tree has the requisite requirements for sweetgums in urban areas: plenty of room for its roots and somewhere for its gumballs to gather without penalty.

WHITE OAK, CRAIG COUNTY
The Keffer Oak

When most of us think of community trees, we think of trees beloved by towns or cities whose residents value and protect them, but there are trees valued by communities defined more by shared experience than by home address. Consider, for example, the community of hikers who share the Appalachian Trail (AT) and know its features the way some city dwellers do their parks and pubs. These hikers, or at least those who have traveled the trail between Craig Creek Valley and Sinking Creek Valley in southwest Virginia, value a white oak known as the Keffer oak as landmark, rendezvous point, and natural treasure. It is mentioned in trail guides, backpacking journals, and hiker's blogs, and pictures of it pop up on the Internet with a frequency that would put many a beloved urban tree to shame.

How you first experience the Keffer oak has a lot to do with the direction from which you approach it. Northbound on the AT, you approach the tree passing through a wooded area that has been bordered by predictably vertical tree trunks, when suddenly the vertical pattern is broken by a huge horizontal branch visible in the distance. It is larger in diameter than the trunks you have been passing, and, as the trail opens onto the tree and the pasture it borders, you soon discover it is attached to a tree with dozens of such branches and a trunk over 18 feet in circumference.

Approached from the other direction (southbound on the AT), the entire tree is visible immediately from a distance of almost a quarter mile, because there is nothing but pasture (punctuated with stiles to help you cross fences) between you and the tree. The tree's silhouette (broad, rounded crown with wide-spreading branches) rises above the woodland behind it like a monarch among minions, and the path hikers have trodden through the pasture targets the tree like an arrow.

Everyone stops to admire the Keffer oak, named for the family that once owned the property on which it grows. There is a semi-permanent fire pit behind it (camping is allowed in the Jefferson National Forest), and a stile to help you cross the barbed wire fencing behind it. "Kids love the stiles," says Vicky Herrala, an AT hiker who visits the tree often. There's a family-friendly .6-mile hike to the tree from Rt. 630 near Newport, Virginia, and more serious hikers will encounter it on the 11.7-mile stretch of the AT between Sinking Creek Valley and Craig Creek Valley in Craig County. Hikers traversing the entire 2,174-mile length of the AT will want to take a particularly long look at the Keffer oak, because the next comparably large tree on the trail—the tree reputed to be the largest tree on the AT—is the Dover oak, near Pawling, New York.

*One of the largest blazed trees on the Appalachian Trail, the Keffer oak, northwest of Blacksburg near Newport, Virginia, serves as a landmark and rendezvous point for hikers. A white oak (*Quercus alba*), the tree is over 18 feet in circumference.*

AMERICAN SYCAMORE, HANOVER COUNTY

Sycamore Tavern

Trees often seem married to their surroundings, and, in fact, they are, drawing sustenance from the soil, air, and weather conditions around them. But the American sycamore (*Platanus occidentalis*) at Sycamore Tavern seems more married to its site than most. There is something about the way the structure of this tree responds to the architecture of the building behind it, with its branches highlighted against the tavern's steep, shingled roof, its white bark echoing the white clapboard behind it, and its trunk melting into the lawn, that hints of a long history of shared circumstances.

The children of the Sycamore Tavern/Page Library History Camp, who nominated this tree, cited a long list of community connections between the tree and the village of Montpelier in Hanover County. "It has provided shade for history camp, children's story time, special events, weddings, and receptions," they wrote. They also noted that "the roots are an interesting shape and have hollow places which house baby rabbits from time to time." Some residents remember when a taller protuberance from the tree's roots served as a "love seat" for courting couples, and when, during the Great Depression, schoolchildren used a sister sycamore out back as a jungle gym. "They'd slide down through the trunk from top to bottom—and exit out a hole in the trunk!" says Judy Lowry, librarian at the Page Library of History and Genealogy, which now occupies the tavern. But the connections between the Montpelier community, this place, and this tree go back even further.

No one knows when the tree germinated, but the tavern it now shades was built around 1732. According to Lowry, the tavern (known first as Higgason's, then as Shelburne's Tavern) served as a stop on the stagecoach line between Richmond and Charlottesville, and anyone riding that route probably visited there, since the road beside the tree (now Rt. 33 or Old Mountain Road) was a major thoroughfare, and the tavern was a stop where the stagecoach changed horses. Although there is no tangible evidence of it, local residents believe Thomas Jefferson, James Madison, and other notables visited there. Did they pass beneath the sycamore? It's unlikely the sycamore was big enough to "pass under" during the tavern's early history, but many tavern-goers probably passed by, if not "under," the tree. In the course of its subsequent history, the tavern served as a residence, a rectory, a shoe shop, an apothecary shop, a grog shop, a cafeteria (for the school behind it), a home economics classroom, a lending library, and now a research library. And all the while, the tree out front continued to grow.

Re-named Sycamore Tavern in the early twentieth century for its by-then-massive sycamores, the tavern underwent additions and restorations, then more additions, and more restorations, and all the while, the tree continued to grow. When it was named to the state and national registers of historic places in 1974, Sycamore Tavern was famous for, among other things, its massive mantle (5 feet wide, 7 feet tall), its impressive chimney (5 feet wide, 2.5 feet thick), and for the fact that so many of its construction materials were original. Today, the tavern's status as an historic place helps protect its sycamore trees from road widening among other insults, and the namesake sycamore out front, made entirely of original materials, is 4 feet thick, 71 feet tall, and still growing.

Close to Rt. 33 in Hanover County, this American sycamore at Sycamore Tavern has witnessed countless comings and goings in the village of Montpelier.

SOUTHERN RED OAK, LYNCHBURG

This is a tree that no one—and everyone—sees. Near the busy intersection of Lakeside and Memorial Streets in Lynchburg, it is the kind of tree passersby take for granted as they catch their rides in the E. C. Glass High School parking lot, ride by on school or city buses, or walk home from school on nearby sidewalks. From a distance, it seems to be just one of many nice oaks on the school grounds, but the Lynchburg Tree Stewards knew this tree was extraordinary when they dubbed it a Heritage Tree in 1998 and when they nominated it to the Remarkable Trees of Virginia Project in 2007.

They knew, for example, that the closer you get to the tree, the bigger you realize it is. At almost 19 feet in girth and over 100 feet tall, it is about three times as large as other nearby southern red oaks, and it has such a beautiful, well-branched shape that it is often used as a symbol on Lynchburg literature. It also grows in a spot where it has been experienced by generations of students and visitors at E. C. Glass. "I remember it from when I used to go over there and watch my son play baseball," one parent recalls. "Oh, yeah, I played co-ed softball near that tree in the 1980s," remembers another. "The band would sit under the tree when it got hot," says a recent student. And, as if to prove the tree's enduring connection to the community, the girl's soccer team spilled out of school and onto the lawn around the tree on the May day the Remarkable Tree crew visited it. "We run around the tree as part of our warmup," one team member explained.

There must be thousands of current and former students who know this tree without knowing they know it, which is why it was such a fine gesture for the Lynchburg Tree Stewards to select it for special recognition in 1998. Each year, Lynchburg Tree Stewards select a Heritage Tree, donate a plaque for it, and honor its owner with a certificate. They also conduct an Arbor Day tree-planting ceremony at an elementary school, and, throughout the year, they prune and plant trees on public property in the city. "We work closely with the city arborist," says Marge Denham, a founding member of the Lynchburg Tree Steward program, who is particularly enamored of the E. C. Glass southern red oak. "It's so fortunate to have such a good open space to grow in," she says. "If only all our trees had that."

Soccer players, band members, and baseball fans—generations of them—have practiced and sought shelter under this southern red oak (Quercus falcata) *at E. C. Glass High School in Lynchburg.*

BUR OAK, ELKTON

lkton may have other celebrities, but it would be hard to imagine one more appreciated than the bur oak that stands outside the town's municipal building. Calls to Elkton about this tree are not only answered, they are answered by friends, relatives, and colleagues of the person you originally called. It seems everyone in town has some connection to the tree. Some are growing new trees from its acorns (the Downtown Revitalization Committee once sold saplings from the tree's acorns as a fundraiser), some attended summer concerts on the lawn of the municipal building and remember sitting in the bur oak's shade, and others just commune with the tree when they pay their taxes at the treasurer's office. Elkton residents are also proud of the fact that "a gentleman from Richmond" visits the tree every year to collect its acorns, which he grows into seedlings and sells all over the country. "He brings a bucket of water, and takes the ones that don't float," says Charlie Dean, revealing, correctly, that acorns that float have been hollowed out by acorn weevil larvae and are won't germinate.

This bur oak's mystique comes partly from its size, partly from its age, and partly from the fact that bur oak (*Quercus macrocarpa*) is uncommon in Virginia. The Elkton bur oak, the largest of its species in Virginia, is almost 20 feet in circumference and spreads to cover an area almost 100 feet in diameter. No one knows how old it is (the bur oak's average and maximum ages are 200 and 400 years, respectively), but many believe it to be older than the municipal building, which was built as a home in 1840 and served as a hospital during the Civil War. According to local historian K. C. Billhimer, a photograph taken in 1905 shows the tree "was huge then."

The native range of the bur oak barely makes it into Virginia (it extends only into several northern counties, including Rockingham), and it is more common in the Midwest than in the East, but this is a fine, prized oak where it grows. It grows tall (to 100 feet), has a massive trunk, and is distinguished by large, bass fiddle-shaped leaves and unusually large acorns (up to 1½ inches long) that have distinctively fringed caps. (Don't confuse them with sawtooth oak acorns, which also have fringed caps.)

Unfortunately, the Elkton bur oak is also distinguished by a disturbingly healthy crop of English ivy growing up its trunk and well into its crown. At the time of this writing, town officials planned to remove the ivy gradually and in a way that would do no harm to the tree's bark, but they had struggled to decide the best way to do that. To keep from changing the tree's environment too quickly, most experts suggested cutting the ivy vines near the ground and allowing them to die on the tree gradually, but town officials were wary. At the height of Elkton's ivy controversy, mayor Wayne Printz was quoted in the *Daily News-Record* as saying, "We had better not touch anything [on that tree] until we know what's going on. That's an old tree. If the good Lord takes it out of here, that's one thing. But if Wayne Printz takes that tree out of here, I'll be moving back to God knows where."

"It's the hub of the town," says Dorenda Flick, clerk in the treasurer's office, describing Elkton's municipal building and the state champion bur oak that shades it.

SUGAR MAPLE, HIGHLAND COUNTY

As you round Maple Sugar Road off Mountain Turnpike in Highland County, trees that seem more like monuments than living things appear. Many of them have lost major branches as well as their tops, and their spacing seems unnatural, as if they had been arranged like statues.

If the spacing of these trees seems too regular, maybe it is because decades of traffic between them—both by people and grazing animals—has kept the land between them open. And, if they seem particularly beleaguered, maybe it's because the wind and the lightning here are fierce. If the trees seem old, trust that impression, too, because although these trees aren't as old as sugar maples can get (around 400 years), they are old by maple standards (perhaps 250 years), and they are downright ancient for trees that have been working as hard as these have.

Four generations of the Rexrode family, the family that owns this sugar maple grove and others like it on their 345-acre farm, have been tapping these trees for maple syrup. They've done it the old way (using buckets to catch the sap), and they've done it the new way (using plastic tubing), but every year, with few exceptions, they have tapped over 500 trees on the property. Maple sugaring has never been as important in Virginia as it is in New England and Canada, but in Highland County, where there is a long legacy of maple sugaring, the tradition survives.

At one time, almost all the farms in Highland County produced their own maple syrup; today only about a dozen farms produce maple syrup in any quantity, but the county is still filled with "sugar shacks" in which the water was boiled from sap and with groves of hard-working sugar maples, still scarred by tap holes.

Farmers fear a lack of young people interested in the process will further erode the maple sugaring tradition in Highland County, but weather may be a handicap as well. The sugar maple's preference for cool climes makes it vulnerable to global warming, at least in its southerly habitats. If conditions in Virginia become warmer, the sugar maple will find it harder to reproduce and survive here, and just as maple sugaring has given way to the supermarket, the sugar maple may give way to other species.

The sugar maple (*Acer saccharum*) is happy in Highland County, and in other areas west of the Blue Ridge, in a way it isn't in other parts of the state. "It's almost like there's a sign on top of the Blue Ridge Mountains saying 'No sugar maples beyond this point,'" one forester has observed. Natural stands of sugar maple are scattered east of the Blue Ridge, and people plant them outside their natural range, but, in general, the sugar maple is a northern species that suffers from extended heat—hence its western and northern range in Virginia.

Sugar maples on the Rexrode farm have been beaten up by the weather, but they, and others like them, have supplied sugar to this Highland County community for generations. Sap flows best on warm days following cool nights (usually between December and March); a 50 degree day following a 20 degree night is ideal. The Highland Maple Sugar Festival that takes place in March may be the longest-running festival of trees in Virginia.

chapter five UNIQUE TREES

One wag has described a tree as a "leafy green ball with a stick up the middle," but you won't find trees fitting that description here. In this chapter, you'll find unusual trees, including trees with unusual shapes and growth habits, trees with unusual origins, trees growing in unusual locations, and trees with unusual connections—to each other and to inanimate objects.

"Enclosed are 8 photos of unusual trees we found in our wanderings," two tree enthusiasts wrote in the letter accompanying the trees they nominated to the Remarkable Tree Project, and with those photos (which included a photo of a tree you could paddle a canoe through and a tree shaped like the letter "H") and with the help of other nominators and the benefits of our own travels, we began a list of unique trees that was as eclectic as it was long. In terms of shape, we marveled most at the other-worldly trees on the Nottoway River (trees like the water tupelo pictured here and on page 89), but we also found backyard mulberries in gnarled and grotesque shapes.

Trees growing in unique-to-outlandish locations also seemed to fit the "unique tree" bill. Among the trees of that description nominated to the project were a red maple growing out of a boat at False Cape State Park, trees growing out of trucks in Madison and Rockingham counties, and a tulip-poplar growing through the roof of a country store in Bedford. Also nominated was a red maple growing out of a rock that looks as if it has been cracked, egg-like, to release the tree, and an indomitable eastern red cedar growing on a high concrete bridge abutment.

Trees with unusual origins seemed to fit this category, too. In this chapter we have featured a towering coast redwood that was originally purchased as a souvenir seedling in California, as well as a "moon tree" grown from seed that traveled on the Apollo 14 mission to the moon, but many others deserved recognition. For example, there are sycamores in Patrick and Campbell counties that would make any list of trees with interesting origins. According to the tree's nominator, the Campbell County sycamore began life when, in 1826, someone stuck a sycamore switch into the grave of Joseph Poindexter, a Captain in the Bedford militia during the American Revolution. It took root, grew, and "pushed the gravestone aside, breaking it in half." That tree, now 110 feet tall, currently dwarfs all the surrounding trees and shades the entire graveyard.

A somewhat similar "rooting" story took place in Patrick County, when, in 1944, Leonard and Delano Wood, then ages 8 and 10, cut a small sycamore sapling and used it as a haystack pole. By summer's end, the pole had sprouted leaves above the hay line. The tree, pictured on the Remarkable Tree website with the Wood brothers, now in their 70s, standing beside it, is currently 112 feet tall and has a 70-foot crown spread.

And then there are the trees unique because of the objects they have grown into or around. As any homeowner who has watched a hammock hook disappear into a tree knows, trees *do* grow, and there are Virginia trees that have engulfed everything from pump handles to the family silver (the latter reportedly hidden from the Yankees in a Hanover elm). The most interesting object we found a tree embracing, though, was a tricycle that has been almost completely engulfed by an enormous willow oak in Ashland. And the trike isn't on the ground; it's 20 feet up in the tree, the spot to which it was hoisted 100 years ago.

With this and other trees featured in this chapter, we hope to illustrate not just the range of possible unique forms, locations, and origins of trees but also how tenacious and opportunistic they are. And to anyone who says a tree is just a green ball with a stick up the middle, we say "Look again!"

Water tupelo (Nyssa aquatica), Southampton County

WATER TUPELO, SOUTHAMPTON COUNTY

Cypress Bridge

So other-worldly is the Cypress Bridge area of the Nottoway River that photographer Robert Llewellyn has called it "Planet Nottoway." Others, like naturalist Gary Williamson, have called it "a Disneyland of trees." Oddly enough, both descriptions seem apt given the phantasmagorical nature of the trees, tree buttresses, tree knees, tree snags, and other woody formations in the area, but, of course, you're not usually up to your shins in mud or smelling cottonmouth musk at Disneyland.

On the day the Remarkable Tree team visited this site, no cottonmouths (nor snakes of any kind) were spotted, but the air of the place was ripe with the fragrance of camphor weed, a native plant Williamson describes as smelling like "cottonmouth musk." The mud around the site's unusual trees and tree formations was also like a catalog of critter travels—with deer, raccoon, wild turkey, and turtle tracks making deep impressions in the muck. "My toe's stuck," lamented Davis Luck, the stalwart three-year-old we had invited to join us for the tour. Davis had just discovered the boot-grabbing quality of the mud, but he was also describing why the area may be more like another planet than a theme park—nothing is simulated or sanitized there.

This is the "Lost Forest" area (described in Chapter Three) that big-tree hunter Byron Carmean discovered in 2005—a remnant old-growth area filled with champion

trees and tree formations unlike those anywhere else in the state. The water tupelo arch pictured here has been described as "the weirdest tree on earth," which may be an overstatement, but not by much. The gnarled architecture of the arch tree would be remarkable even if the tree were dead, but the tree is very much alive, as is the water tupelo pictured on the preceding page.

On this site, there are hollow trees shaped like teepees—some big enough to accommodate a human family of six (not to mention hosts of bats and possibly even bears), there are trees with see-through crevices resembling keyholes, and there are trees with shapes that inspire names like "teapot tree" and "lobster tree." There are also trees that Carmean calls "menagerie trees"—trees that have grown up on top of one another, or on the stumps of rotting trees, creating what looks like one entity. One such "menagerie tree" includes an overcup oak, a winged elm, and a black oak—all growing from the ancient

The interior of the "teepee tree" (the same water tupelo pictured on page 86) is as unusual as its exterior. No one is entirely sure what has caused the "disorderly growth" on the interior of this tree, but some have suggested that the tree's cambium has grown inward, through fissures, because there is no interior pressure to prevent its doing so.

stump of a water tupelo. Some of the trees in this swamp are also "perch trees"—trees whose roots seem to perch high above some invisible object, which, in a way, they do, because the stumps on which their seeds germinated have long since rotted away.

In this area along the Nottoway River there are more water tupelos than baldcypress trees. This is, however, the site that houses "Big Mama," the state champion baldcypress (*Taxodium distichum*) and largest tree in Virginia, as well as two former national champion water tupelos (*Nyssa aquatica*). Both the baldcypress trees and the water tupelos form bulging bases called buttresses that are often completely hidden when the water level of the swamp is high. When the water level is low, as it usually is in late summer, the buttresses loom large and reveal, in the twists and turnings of their wood, adaptations to eons of swamp living.

Equally impressive are the cypress knees, cone-shaped protuberances that rise up from the swamp like gnome homes. Cypress knees on the Nottoway reach almost 10 feet in height (their height being related to the high water level of the swamp), and they are so thick one naturalist has suggested they should be called not cypress knees but "cypress thighs." Some of these knees (or thighs) are like ancient pieces of driftwood, but others are actively growing and have pinkish tips. According to Williamson, early Virginia colonists used hollow cypress knees as buckets and beehives. Many if not most of the ancient tree trunks in this area are hollow as well, and when Williamson knocks on one, the noise resonates through the woods like the sound of an enormous drum.

The dead wood in the center of this water tupelo arch has rotted away, but a strip of living tissue keeps leaves and new growth at the top of the arch alive. This and other unusual formations grow in what has been called the "Lost Forest" near Courtland in Southampton County.

BALDCYPRESS, CHESAPEAKE

Lake Drummond

The Great Dismal Swamp, all 111,000 acres of it, has been logged at least once, and most of it has also been subjected to periodic fires, but not only does the swamp, now a national wildlife refuge, shelter some large, old trees, it shelters some remarkably picturesque ones. "We don't know why they were left," says visitor service specialist Deloras Freeman. "Maybe they were too difficult to log or impressed the logger too much."

Certainly no logger would have been much interested in harvesting the misshapen baldcypresses that hug hummocks along the eastern shore of Lake Drummond, nor the hollow trees that grow 150 feet out into the lake, but what treasures they are to anyone interested in unique trees. These baldcypresses seem like relics of a remote and distant past, and their mystique is enhanced by the difficulty of getting to them.

Think of the eastern edge of Lake Drummond, the 3,100-acre lake in the middle of the Great Dismal Swamp, as a gallery of wild and wonderful baldcypress trees, sculpted by water and wind into some of the most outlandish shapes imaginable, but don't expect to visit it on foot. None of the refuge's trails leads to the lake's eastern shore, and access to the trees even by boat isn't all that easy. Visiting the trees in a boat is worth the effort, however, if only to see the way the dark waters of the lake mirror their shapes.

Like baldcypress trees (*Taxodium distichum*) pictured elsewhere in this book, these exhibit the wide, sometimes flaring, sometimes dome-shaped, buttresses characteristic of

Unflatteringly called "the Feeder Ditch," the 3.5-mile stretch of flat water that leads from the Dismal Swamp Canal into the Dismal Swamp can be as impressive as the swamp itself.

Check out your Virginia road map, and you'll find an almost perfectly round, blue circle southeast of Suffolk. That's Lake Drummond, in which this "horseshoe tree," a baldcypress, grows.

the species—buttresses designed to help anchor them to soft, wet soils on which they usually grow. They also have the cone-shaped protuberances called "knees" that are believed to help the trees obtain air for the submerged portions of the tree ("woody snorkels," some have called them), and their limbs are furry with resurrection fern, which seems to die, then springs back to life, when rain "resurrects" it. Each tree has its own personality—there's the ghost tree, the giant bonsai tree, the horseshoe tree—but what really sets these trees apart from other interesting baldcypress trees in Virginia is the backdrop of Lake Drummond.

One of only two natural freshwater lakes in Virginia (the other is Mountain Lake in Giles County), Lake Drummond is a shallow (usually only about 6 feet deep) lake that covers over 5 square miles. Looking from one side of the lake to the other, you see a lot of sky, an enormous expanse of flat water (on a still day, that is; wind can whip Lake Drummond into a frenzy), and a whiskery horizon line (that's the trees on the other side of the Lake). Shaped like a dinner plate and 20 feet above sea level with three rivers running out of it, there's nothing quite like Lake Drummond anywhere else in Virginia—and nothing quite like a baldcypress silhouetted against it.

Dubbed "the ghost tree" because of the spectral shapes in some of its wood, this baldcypress grows near the eastern shore of the Great Dismal Swamp.

Until recently, part of the lake's mystique derived from a theory of its origin—that the impact of a meteorite ignited a fire that burned into the peat that formed the lake's basin. According to Freeman, researchers at Old Dominion University have squelched that theory, seeing no evidence of an impact crater at Lake Drummond but much evidence that a large fire alone probably burned through the peat layer that once covered the sand under the lake (creating the depression in which the water has gathered). For those who cling to the meteorite theory, there is still the fact that "magnetic anomalies" consistent with large iron ore deposits exist on the eastern side of the lake, but whatever its origin, the lake and surrounding swamp now provide habitat for a wide range of important plant and animal species, including some of Virginia's most striking baldcypress trees.

*This picturesque baldcypress (*Taxodium distichum*) grows along the eastern shore of Lake Drummond in the Great Dismal Swamp National Wildlife Refuge. The refuge stretches from southeastern Virginia into northeastern North Carolina.*

AMERICAN SYCAMORE, AUGUSTA COUNTY

Leaning sycamores aren't all that unusual—sycamores and black willows, among other trees, lean out over rivers all the time. But this sycamore on the North River in Augusta County takes leaning to a new level. "Zacchaeus could almost have walked up this tree!" says Gary Huffman, an Augusta resident, referring to the Biblical tax collector who climbed a tree to see Jesus.

In addition to leaning at a more acute angle than most trees of the non-vertical sort, this one is much larger and therefore more startling in its extreme posture. How can it possibly be holding all that volume up, and for so long? "It's been that way ever since I was a kid—about 50 years ago," says Huffman, who notes that not only does the tree seem perfectly healthy and unlikely to topple, but it has endured at least two floods of the North River, when water was 12 to 15 feet up its trunk.

Oddly enough, what one looks for at the base of this tree—an upturned root that might explain its angle—isn't there. Instead, a stump rises directly beside the tree, suggesting the leaning sycamore was once double-trunked and twice as big as it is now.

Even without its missing half, Augusta's leaning sycamore is massive (over 5.5 feet in diameter), and it is as thick 20 feet from its base as it is at ground level. It is also surprisingly graceful, with branches reaching away from its leaning trunk like the arms of a wide receiver stretching out for a pass. It's not unusual for a sycamore to seem humanoid (skin-like bark, curves suggestive of musculature), but this sycamore seems more humanoid than most, and one feels nothing but admiration, if not empathy, for the way it has turned what might have been a life-threatening tilt into something more like a Yoga pose.

This massive sycamore (Platanus occidentalis) leans at almost a 45-degree angle but shows no signs of falling.

SILVER MAPLE, ROCKINGHAM COUNTY

This tree is actually the second silver maple that has occupied this old delivery truck. The first, an even bigger tree, grew through the truck's windshield, and presumably germinated there with no outside help. That tree, according to Bob and Susan Threewitts, who own the cattle farm on which the tree-truck resides, was killed by groundhogs 15 or 20 years ago, and one of the Threewitts' hired hands replaced it with this silver maple (*Acer saccharinum*). Where the truck came from and who abandoned it in the field, no one seems to know. "It's been there as long as I can remember," says Susan, "and that's at least 50 years."

Red Cedar and Black Cherry, Suffolk

rees growing in or on other trees are not uncommon; most everyone has seen a small tree growing in a crotch or crevice of a larger one, but the eastern red cedar/ black cherry combination tree in Cedar Hill Cemetery, Suffolk is a tree marriage of a higher order. The red cedar alone would be worthy of attention. A massive old specimen 14 feet in circumference, its peeling gray bark and knobby trunk speak "age" as eloquently as many of the tombstones in this cemetery, but a closer look reveals this particular red cedar to have an even more extraordinary attribute. It is not a solitary tree; it is a tree in which a black cherry has germinated and grown so large its bark can be seen through a vertical crack in the trunk of the red cedar.

On the other side of the red cedar, 10 feet off the ground, a branch of the cherry, over 2 feet in diameter, emerges from another opening in the cedar trunk, then it forks and wraps its way up and around the cedar to form a combination of two trees so closely entwined they look like one. It's quite likely the black cherry germinated when a bird dropped a seed on rotting wood inside the red cedar. This happens all the time, but what is not common is for the secondary tree to grow so large its trunk seems to expand the trunk of its host tree and for the secondary tree to find a higher opening in its host from which it can extend a limb this large.

Another astonishing fact about this tree is that it seems to have escaped the notice of even the best "remarkable tree hunters" until 2007. Byron Carmean, the retired horticulture teacher famous for finding so many champion trees in Virginia, had an hour to kill (his wife was visiting a nearby gym), when he took a stroll in Cedar Hill Cemetery and happened by this tree. "What is this?" he thought when he spied the cherry's bark through the crack on the west side of the cedar, then felt his jaw drop even further when he found the huge cherry branch growing out of the cedar's east side. That such trees are hiding in plain sight proves just how many unusual trees remain to be discovered, and celebrated, in Virginia.

Byron Carmean found this impressive tree combination in Cedar Hill Cemetery, Suffolk. Inside an old eastern red cedar (Juniperus virginiana) grows a black cherry (Prunus serotina) that has exploited the rotten wood inside the cedar and grown into a large tree itself.

TULIP-POPLAR, GLOUCESTER COUNTY

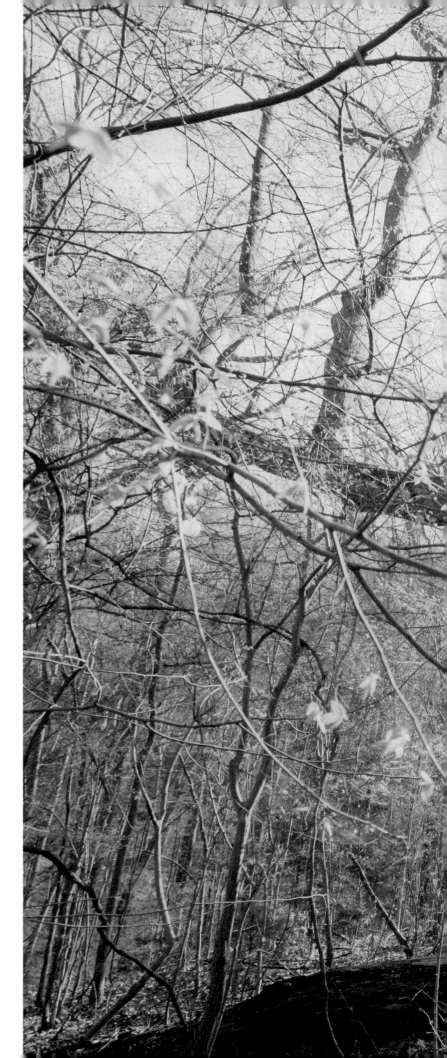

Many churches can trace their histories to "brush arbors," temporary structures fashioned of poles and leafy tree boughs under which worshippers met, but at Zion Poplars Baptist Church, real trees, in an extraordinary configuration, served as the nexus of the church's first congregation. Near the site of what is now Zion Poplars Baptist Church in southeastern Gloucester County grow the remnants of what was, in 1866, a grove of seven tulip-poplars (*Liriodendron tulipifera*) united at the base. This peculiar clustering of trunks was viewed by local African Americans as a natural wonder and "an awesome act of God." According to church historians, the seven united poplar trees represented a "kind of Zion, or sacred place" where God met with his people. The founding members of Zion Poplars Baptist Church first met under the trees in 1866 and continued to meet there until 1894, when a nearby church building was erected.

This kind of gathering was significant for many reasons, not the least of which is the fact that, until the Civil Rights Act of 1964, in many parts of the South blacks were prohibited by law from gathering in large numbers in order to "give or receive, educational or religious instruction." An 1804 Virginia statute, for example, prohibited slaves from assembling "for religious purposes, unless they were attending church with their white masters or with a white family." The gatherings under these Gloucester tulip-poplars were also significant because they harken to earlier West African traditions in which natural phenomena were revered and trees served as "sanctuaries for praying, healing, religious sacrifice and purification."

Today, although only four of the seven original trunks remain, it is easy to see why these trees engendered reverence. In this massive tree assemblage, one huge, hollow, log-like structure connects the bases of four trunks, one of which is almost 6 feet in diameter and two of which are over 3 feet in diameter. The log-like base connecting the trunks is about 24 feet long, and the end nearest the current church is open to a height of 3 feet, inviting the visitors to look into the tunnel of wood under the existing trunks. "That is one *old* piece of wood," photographer Robert Llewellyn commented as he peered into the cavity.

How and why seven large tree trunks grew in such a straight row has been the subject of much speculation. One possibility is that seven trees germinated from seeds that sprouted on a "nurse log"—an old, rotten log that provided a propitious place for their germination, but the more widely held view is that one large tulip-poplar, now the base of the remaining "trees," blew down in a storm, and the seven startling trunks that grew up from it were all suckers or re-oriented branches from the original tree. Genetic testing could resolve the issue of whether the seven Zion tulip-poplars were really one tree or seven, but the issue is irrelevant to anyone who experiences this spectacular tree structure in its historic setting. Although the grove that inspired the first members of Zion Poplars Baptist Church is clearly in decline, it still exudes the aura of a sacred place.

In 1866, the founding members of Zion Poplars Baptist Church first met under this unusual tulip-poplar grove in Gloucester. The church (built in 1894) and its trees are now on the Virginia Landmarks Register and the National Register of Historic Places.

Coast Redwood, Suffolk

Behind the R.W. Baker Funeral Home in Suffolk is a tidy little cottage garden complete with clematis-clad arbor, dogwood, camellia, azaleas, and old farm bell. It could be a cottage garden anywhere in Virginia, except for one thing: a towering coast redwood.

In the center of this cottage garden rises a massive coast redwood (*Sequoia sempervirens*) that has grown so fast and so furiously its roots have lifted the ground around it, creating a 3-foot mound from which the tree's huge, reddish-brown trunk rises. By West Coast standards, this redwood is a baby (the tallest living things in the world, coast redwoods grow over 360 feet tall and live more than 2,000 years), but Suffolk is not the West Coast (which provides perfect growing conditions for these trees), and this tree is only 54 years old.

Virginia is actually home to many impressive coast redwoods. Two beautiful specimens grow on the southwest side of James Blair dormitory on the William and Mary campus, and the state champion coast redwood grows near the butterfly garden at the Norfolk Botanical Garden. Although it is unlikely the tree will ever grow in the East as well as it does on the Pacific Coast, where even temperatures and high levels of year-round moisture favor the trees, the species does grow in Virginia, and at surprisingly fast rates.

The Suffolk sequoia is a case in point. It is growing fast—90 feet in 50 years—compared to 100 to 150 feet on good sites in the West, and it grew from a sapling with an interesting history. In 1954, Robert and Allie Baker, owners of the R.W. Baker Funeral Home, were in California attending a funeral directors' meeting when Hurricane Hazel struck Virginia. "They tried for days to get in touch with us but couldn't," recalls the Baker's son Robert, who now lives above the funeral home with his wife, Marie. According to Blake Baker (grandson of the elder Robert Baker), when his grandparents heard the news of the hurricane (a Category 4 storm and the strongest ever recorded to strike so far north on the East Coast), they thought all was lost. "This made my grandmother stop and dig up this tree and nurse it cross country to Virginia," wrote Blake, in his remarkable tree nomination. Returning to Virginia, Allie Baker dug up a flowering quince and planted the sequoia where the quince had been. Fifty-four years later the tree is almost 90 feet tall and 184 inches in circumference, actually taller than the state champion in Norfolk but smaller in circumference.

Having been moved to Virginia because of a hurricane, the Suffolk sequoia was almost felled by another hurricane. Marie Baker, who watched the tree from an upstairs window during Hurricane Isabel, says the wind was blowing so hard the tree would disappear and then come back into view. "Come on girl, ride it," she thought, as she coached the tree through the storm. "I talked to her for about two hours. It sounded like popcorn popping when her branches snapped off. They went 'Pow! Pow! Pow!'" The next day, says Marie, "We found pieces of her three blocks away. She'd lost half her weight."

Today the Suffolk sequoia looks fit and full, with only the back quarter of the tree showing evidence of its pruning from Hurricane Isabel.

Hurricane Hazel brought this coast redwood (Sequoia sempervirens) to Suffolk; Hurricane Isabel almost wiped it out.

AMERICAN SYCAMORE, HAMPTON

The Moon Tree

Virginia has trees that have been shipped here from all over the world, but when it comes to miles traveled, a sycamore in Hampton puts Virginia's other well-traveled trees to shame. It has been nearly to the moon and back.

The seed of this American sycamore (*Platanus occidentalis*) was transported by Apollo 14 astronaut Stuart Roosa, who orbited the moon while his fellow astronauts made the historic lunar touchdown in 1971. "The seeds didn't go down to the surface," a NASA representative explained at a rededication of the Hampton moon tree in 2006, "but they did get within a couple hundred miles of the surface, which is closer than you or I have ever gotten."

When Roosa decided to take tree seeds with him on his mission, scientists were curious about the effects zero gravity, radiation, and other factors might have on the seeds' viability. And, of course, some ordinary people had visions of bizarre mutations dancing in their heads. There was, in fact, one scene that would have worked well in a horror movie. When the mission returned to earth, the canister that held the moon tree seeds burst open, shooting the seeds out into the decontamination chamber. Evidently, no damage was done (to the seeds or to earthlings), and the 500 or so seeds taken on the mission—of loblolly pine, sycamore, sweetgum, redwood, and Douglas-fir—were germinated by the Forest Service and distributed across the U.S. and to some foreign countries. Oddly enough, though, no one kept track of exactly where the moon trees had been sent, and it wasn't until Dr. Dave Williams, planetary scientist at NASA's Goddard Space Flight Center, began trying to track the trees down 30 years later that a master list of moon tree locations was generated.

Of the hundreds of moon tree seedlings that were distributed in 1976 (many of them as part of bicentennial celebrations), Williams was able to locate only about 60, and some of those were dead. Missing was the tree given

to the Emperor of Japan and dead was the tree planted at the White House, but alive and well were two of the moon trees planted in Virginia. One, a relatively unheralded sweetgum, grows near Hamilton in Loudoun County, where it occupies farmland slated to become athletic fields (it has been promised protection by the current property owner).

Virginia's second moon tree, our sycamore in Hampton, has had star status ever since it was planted at Booker Elementary School in 1976. Booker Elementary was awarded the tree when a Booker sixth-grader won a city-wide poetry contest with her poem "A Tree Lives." The sapling, described as having five leaves and looking "travel weary" when it arrived, was first planted in front of the school, then moved to the courtyard, where it now towers over the flat roof of the school building.

It was Debbie Blanton, a coordinator for the Hampton Clean City Commission, who alerted NASA's Dr. Williams to the existence of the moon tree growing at Booker. And it was she, with the help of the school's Earth Patrol Environmental Club, who used the opportunity of the tree's "rediscovery" to interest a new cohort of schoolchildren in the tree.

The 2006 rededication ceremony included everything the ceremony 30 years earlier might have included, with some updates. There were well-scrubbed children making heartwarming speeches, local dignitaries vying for attention, an inspiring principal, flags, a sheet cake with green icing, and table decorations (trees) made with paper towel tubes. But at this ceremony, Miss Selden, the principal, read not Joyce Kilmer's "Trees," but "Tree Magic," a poem she'd found on the Internet. There was even a rumor circulating that one student was thinking about selling seeds from the Booker moon tree on e-Bay. The times had changed but the sentiments hadn't, and fifth grader Chantal Lewis summed up the feelings of all assembled when she proclaimed, "I'd like to tell the space people who took it to the moon 'thank you' because some people don't care about trees."

This American sycamore at Booker Elementary School, on Apollo Street in Hampton, was grown from a seed that orbited the moon.

WILLOW OAK, ASHLAND

The Tricycle Tree

Let the tricycle tree in Ashland stand for all the trees in Virginia that hold vestiges of human activity in their wood. A lumberman can ruin a good saw hitting the nail that held a birdhouse or the hook that held a hammock in a tree whose wood has long since grown over it, but in Ashland, a willow oak at 505 South Center Street holds fast to something more visible, and more interesting.

Imbedded in a limb (or what's left of a limb) of this oak is an antique tricycle. So encircled is it now by wood that it looks as if the tree has grown a rusty wheel. The tricycle wheel is the last vestige of ground-to-limb dumbwaiter service initiated by brothers William and Reed Blincoe (who lived in the house behind the tree) and their friends in 1908. The boys wired the tricycle's handlebars firmly to a limb, put a long rope around the rim of the front wheel, and used the wheel as a pulley to hoist toys and treasures up to their tree house. One hundred years later, the tree still clings to their invention and shows no signs of letting go.

A misconception about the Ashland tricycle tree is that the tricycle wheel has gotten higher as the tree has grown larger. But tree limbs do not get higher as trees grow; they maintain their positions relative to the ground. (Low limbs may die and fall off, and higher limbs grow larger, creating the impression that a large limb has "climbed," but it hasn't.) The tricycle in the Ashland willow oak is no higher now than it was in 1908 when the Blincoe boys positioned it there, making their accomplishment seem all the more impressive, since the tricycle is 20 feet off the ground.

On December 9, 2005, an ice storm tore a limb—the limb above the rim of this tricycle—from Ashland's tricycle tree, but the tree, with the tricycle still embedded in its wood, stands firm.

This willow oak (Quercus phellos) in Ashland is notable for both its size (6.5-foot diameter, 116-foot crown spread) and for its booty. The tree clings to the wheel of an antique tricycle, positioned there 100 years ago to help pull treasures up to a tree house. Can you find it?

chapter six FINE SPECIMENS

One of the criteria we used to choose the trees for this book was the "wow" factor. If a tree elicited a "wow" from any one of us, it got special consideration, and a tree that elicited a chorus of "wows" was considered a likely candidate for inclusion.

The trees in this chapter are all "triple-wow" trees. Although they may not be the largest of their species in the state (those are featured in our Champion Tree chapter), they are trees that we considered remarkable for their form, beauty, or overall presence. They are trees that seemed like particularly good representatives of their species or that had some charismatic quality we considered remarkable.

Of course, not everyone is impressed by the same trees, and in some cases, one needs to be familiar with the species in order to appreciate a good representative of it. There is at least one tree we've included in this chapter that is probably overlooked by three-quarters of the people who walk by it every day, but the shortleaf pine-lovers among us thought it was fabulous. On the other hand, some trees elicit wows from their entire communities. "People are always sending the owner pictures of this tree in her yard," the nominator of a sugar maple in Floyd County wrote. "The owner once received a Christmas card from a doctor she knew that had her tree on the card. He wrote in it, 'Merry Christmas, this is a picture of your tree in your yard.'"

Many "wow" trees also have peak seasons, and while they may be appreciated all year, they are lionized when they bloom or reach peak color. "It's nicely put together," "It puts its branches in all the right places," and "It's enormous without looking heavy" were some of the appreciative comments we heard made about the Yorktown cherry illustrated here, and those comments would apply to the tree year-round, but it's when the tree is in bloom—a diaphanous mass of pale pink petals—that it generates gasps. The same seasonal splendor applies to a number of tree nominees we received, including a red buckeye on Virginia Avenue in Richmond, a crape myrtle on Rugby Road in Richmond, and a pink dogwood in front of the former South Hill Elementary school in South Hill. In some communities, in fact, there is a "communal wow" when certain trees reach peak bloom or color. "We start passing the word when it begins turning," says Chester's Margie Fox of a particularly colorful sugar maple on Old Hundred Road there.

In addition to paying homage to bloom and color, however, we have tried to include other show-stopping qualities in this chapter—the bark of a particularly shaggy shagbark hickory, the horizontal branching pattern of a statuesque beech, the graceful vase-shape of American elm—because these are tree qualities that can be appreciated all year and because we wanted to highlight as many species-specific "wow" qualities as we could. We have tried to present a representative sample of fine specimens, but, as always, the universe of trees from which we had to choose was too large to do it justice, and even as we photographed the trees we had selected, we kept running into additional trees we wished we could feature (check out the Japanese maple, the Osage-orange, and the river birch pictured in the Index). In the end, we realized the best we could do would be to draw attention to a very few of Virginia's finest trees in the hope that we might be training the eyes of readers to see the outstanding trees in their own communities and to appreciate more "wow" qualities in the trees they already know.

Higan cherry (Prunus subhirtella), *Yorktown*

HIGAN CHERRY, YORKTOWN

The see-through quality of this Higan cherry near the historic Moore House in Yorktown makes it possible to appreciate the tree's structure and flowers at the same time. And somehow the contrast between the delicate flowers and the sturdy branches adds emphasis to both. Not only is the tree a fine specimen, perfectly proportioned and graceful from every angle, but it seems to be in near-perfect health. So many bees were visiting its flowers on the April day the Remarkable Tree team visited it that the entire tree seemed to buzz, and what looked like a quiet tree from a distance had the kinetic energy of a Saturday night disco up close. The slightest breeze further animated the tree by sending a shower of pale pink petals to the ground.

Like many trees that grow into remarkable specimens on land that has had a series of owners, this one's beginnings proved hard to track down. According to Dorothy Geyer, landscape architect for the Colonial National Historical Park, the tree must have been planted after 1929, since it doesn't show up in a 1929 aerial photo of the area. Geyer suspects it was planted by the Park Service, which now owns the property, but no one knows for sure. Certainly the tree postdates historic events that took place on the York Plantation (terms of the British army's Revolutionary War surrender were negotiated there), but even though the tree may be young by "old tree" standards, it proves that even trees planted in the twentieth century have the potential to "wow" us in the twenty-first.

This fine Higan cherry (Prunus subhirtella) near historic Moore House in Yorktown was probably planted in the 1930s. Specimens like this one remind us that a tree "only" 60 to 75 years old is nothing to sneer at, especially if it belongs to a relatively short-lived species.

SHORTLEAF PINE, PRINCE EDWARD COUNTY

"And then there's Cinderella in the basement, but you probably wouldn't be interested in *her*."

That's not exactly the way this shortleaf pine was introduced to the Remarkable Tree team, but it's close. We were touring the Hampden-Sydney campus—being shown fine southern red oaks, an impressive southern magnolia, a noteworthy Osage-orange, among other trees—when one of the Hampden-Sydney representatives mentioned, almost as an aside, "Tom's tree." Evidently Tom Gregory, director of Hampden-Sydney's physical plant, had a long history of championing this tree, and others had a long history of teasing him about it. Who could possibly care about a shortleaf pine? Well, as it turned out, we did, because we had been searching for just such a fine example of one.

Shortleaf pine (*Pinus echinata*) seldom gets the respect it deserves. For one thing, many people confuse it with Virginia pine (*Pinus virginiana*), which is scrubbier and less disciplined in growth habit. For another, although this is a common Virginia tree, it is less often seen in an open situation, where it can show off its graceful silhouette, than it is in a forest of other pines or mixed hardwoods. It also sometimes suffers from pine bark beetle damage and from littleleaf disease, both problems that can be fatal to shortleaf pines and that have greatly reduced their numbers.

In 1940, according to Department of Forestry statistics, there were nearly 1.4 million acres of shortleaf pine in Virginia; in 2003 there were around 72,000 acres, a statistic that reflects not only the tree's pest and disease problems, but the fact that it doesn't compete well with faster-growing loblolly pine. Not only does loblolly outrace shortleaf in pine plantations (where a faster-growing pine means faster profits), but if both pines are seeding into an abandoned field, loblolly will overtop shortleaf before the shade-intolerant shortleaf can establish itself.

Many foresters and tree farmers are experimenting with ways to help the shortleaf make a comeback, because not only is this a valuable forest and timber tree (with wood harder, stronger, and of higher quality than loblolly pine), but it makes a beautiful landscape tree. Naturalist Donald Culross Peattie may have captured the shortleaf pine's appeal best when he described its "boughs that sweep grandly to the ground," its pyramidal outline against a southern sky, and the "thin high whisper" of its needles on a hot day. Peattie even described the "warm resinous aroma" that the sun bakes out of its needles and the way the tree "tinctures" the rainwater dripping from its needles.

Such a tree deserves to be brought up from the cellar and, if not married to a prince, at least planted and admired more widely.

Graceful in silhouette, shortleaf pines like this one at Hampden-Sydney College in Prince Edward County are often underappreciated in the landscape. Shortleaf pine (Pinus echinata) is a relatively long-lived species, with some trees achieving ages of over 300 years.

American Elm, Roanoke

Virginia elms have experienced their fair share of Dutch elm disease, a fungal disease estimated to have killed 100 million American elms nationwide, but many fine American elms survive in the state. Some are being managed for the disease (with preventive or therapeutic fungicide injections), some are resistant to it (one in 100,000, by some estimates), and some have not yet been infected. As a result, fine American elms still grace many a Virginia lawn, school ground, park, and golf course—not to mention the many fine American elms surviving in the wild. New disease-resistant American elms, like 'Princeton' and 'American Liberty,' are also being planted across the state.

Choosing which elm to feature here was a challenge. It seemed important to mention old elms like those at Waynesboro High School, Clark Elementary School (Charlottesville), and Nokesville Elementary School (Prince William), which have become icons at those schools and call attention to the generations of kids who have sheltered under the high canopies of elms during fire drills, band practices, and bus-loading. The former state champion American elm growing at the new state fairgrounds in Caroline County deserved a mention (dethroned by a larger elm in Chesapeake), as did the Sebrell elm, a legendary American elm that once grew in Southampton County. Before succumbing to Dutch elm disease in 1988, that tree had earned the distinction of being the only Virginia tree ever featured on the front page of the *New York Times*, where it was described as having wrested the title of largest American elm in the country from a famous elm in Kansas.

In the end, we decided to feature a fine American elm in Roanoke, not only because it was a gorgeous specimen— large, healthy, and beautifully shaped—but because it allowed us to call attention to an underappreciated tree habitat: the golf course.

Golf courses are more often notable for the trees they displace than for the trees they protect, but a properly managed golf course can be a tree haven.

"Personally, I'd rather play an older course with nice mature trees [than a new one]," says assistant golf course superintendent Bill Keen. "It's more aesthetically pleasing." Keen is prejudiced, of course. He works at the Roanoke Country Club, constructed in the 1920s by a world-renowned golf course architect who often used trees as focal points. But Keen is qualified to speak about golf course trees in general because not only is he responsible for the good health of the trees under his care, he knows the challenges they face.

"Trees and grass don't get along. That's the main problem," says Keen. "Trees will trump the grass every time, as far as sunlight, water, and nutrients, go." Insensitive golf course maintenance can also be a nightmare for trees. Large mowers injure trees, herbicides designed to kill broad-leaved weeds can weaken and kill trees, and irrigation, over- or under-used, can do the same. For golf courses and trees to co-exist, there must be a healthy balance between conditions conducive to growing grass and conditions conducive to growing trees.

At the Roanoke Country Club, the three nine-hole courses are named for trees (Crabapple, Redwood, Dogwood), greens committees have a long history of championing trees, and trees are planted to honor young winners of a junior tournament. Each winner—about 40 of them so far—has had a tree planted in his or her honor, and these trees, complete with plaques indicating when the tree was planted, seem to give the place the air of an arboretum.

Tree-sensitive maintenance has helped protect this old American elm (the same tree pictured on the right) at the Roanoke Country Club. So far it has shown no signs of succumbing to Dutch elm disease, the nemesis of thousands of American elms. The French botanist and explorer André Michaux referred to the American elm (Ulmus americana) as "nature's noblest vegetable," and this fine specimen at the Roanoke Country Club proves his point. The tree was used to frame "hole #1 on the Crabapple nine" when the golf course was constructed in the 1920s.

American Beech, Falls Church

Proving his genius as a tree observer as well as a composer, Beethoven once said, "Every tree seems to say 'Holy, holy.'" He's right, but some trees say "holy, holy" more eloquently than others, and the American beech in front of Sleepy Hollow United Methodist Church in Falls Church not only says "holy, holy," it sings it.

Church members have created a short gravel path to this massive beech, and a wooden cross has been positioned beneath it, so it must have many visitors, but there are multitudes that pass this tree every day in their cars and never notice it, even though it is clearly visible from busy Sleepy Hollow Road.

From a distance (and in this photograph), it's hard to tell how big—and eloquent—the tree is, but walk under this American beech and you will feel its enormity. "It gets bigger as it goes up!" one observer commented, noting, correctly, that while most trees are biggest at the base of the trunk, this one is biggest at its "heart"—where its branches diverge. It's not the biggest American beech in Virginia (that honor belongs to an American beech at the Upper Brandon Plantation in Prince George County), but this beech is tied with one at Westover plantation in Charles City County for second, and neither of its competitors, although stunning, can touch this one for beauty.

There is something decidedly feminine about all beeches, with their smooth, skin-like bark and graceful, dipping branches. British writer Will Cohu, author of *Out of the Woods: The Armchair Guide to Trees*, has gone so far as to describe the European beech, a close relative of the American beech, as "slinky" and to note that a mature beech "looks as if it has just emerged from a wax and a massage." "Even when a couple of hundred years old," he observes, "she looks like a million dollars." Like sycamores, beeches don't have shapes, they have figures, and this one's figure is near perfect. It is well-proportioned all the way around, and its trunk and branches melt and merge, sometimes appearing to fuse, like something molten. As is the case with many beeches, this tree's thin, gray bark has proved irresistible to carvers, and the names of lovers, and other scribblers, rise high into its crown.

Slow-growing but long-lived (to 400 years), the American beech (*Fagus grandifolia*) is a native tree with a long and storied history. Because it has always been associated with good land, many beech woodlands were cleared by early settlers to create farmland. Settlers fattened their hogs and turkeys on beechnuts, and beechnuts were an important food for the now-extinct passenger pigeon. Although good mast years—years of heavy crops—come along only every two or three years, beechnuts, rich in fat and protein, are still an important wildlife food. Beech wood has never been particularly important commercially (it warps badly, making it unsuitable for most construction), but because it is odorless and tasteless it has been used to make items like churns, barrels, and cutting boards, as well as items that need to wear well, like tool handles and thresholds.

Some deciduous trees attract our attention only part of the year, but American beech is a stunner year-round. Its light-colored bark and unusual branching pattern (parallel planes of nearly horizontal branches) are unmistakable, and its leaves—silver tipped in early spring, deep green in summer, yellow-green to bronze in fall, and tan to almost white in winter—are downright artful. Almost all lovers of beeches are drawn to their winter leaves, which have become almost translucent by the end of winter and hang on to their branches like hankies to a clothesline. *Marcescent*, which means withering but not falling off, is a word descriptive of such leaves.

You'd think a tree with so much going for it would be all the rage in the nursery trade, but it isn't. American beeches are too slow-growing and cast too deep a shade (little grows under them) to interest most suburbanites. And the trees are too intolerant of compacted soils and too big at maturity for most urban situations. (Most cultivated beech varieties, some of which are smaller, are forms of the European beech.) American beech has, in fact, been called "the Indian of trees," because it takes so much better to woodlands than it does to city conditions.

More often than not, the few grand American beeches found in urban or suburban situations grew up long before those areas were developed (examples include a fine American beech near the corner of Lawson Hall Road and Diamond Springs Road in Virginia Beach and beeches for which the Round Tree subdivision in Fairfax may have been named), but it's not impossible to find an appropriate place close to people to plant a beech. Parks, golf courses, or expansive lawns can be good sites for the American beech. Do consider planting one (or even better, nurturing one where it already grows), because in addition to being a beautiful tree to look at, the American beech offers the world's best rendition of "holy, holy."

Ninety-five feet tall and 14 feet in circumference, this American beech in Falls Church is one of the largest beech trees in the state. In the fall, its luminous yellow leaves create what naturalist Donald Culross Peattie once called "a golden light that hallows all around it."

YELLOWWOOD, ARLINGTON COUNTY AND FREDERICKSBURG

"Rare and refined" are the two words that describe yellowwood best. This tree is native to small areas of the eastern U.S., but nowhere is it common even within its range. Although it grows wild in nearby states, no botanist has ever found it growing wild in Virginia. There are, however, fine yellowwoods in the state, because the tree is a valuable ornamental and has been planted in parks, gardens, and arboreta, where its rounded form, clean foliage, and May-blooming flowers lend elegance to the landscape.

At Arlington Cemetery a beautiful yellowwood grows in Section 23 just north of the Spanish American War memorial, and in Fredericksburg the state champion yellowwood grows behind the colonial kitchen at Kenmore, George Washington's sister's home. Other places to find yellowwoods include The Virginia State Arboretum in Boyce; Old City Cemetery, Lynchburg; and the Norfolk Botanical Garden's Flowering Arboretum.

This is a tree that should be planted more. An excellent small shade tree, the yellow-wood (*Cladrastis kentukea*) has no serious pest or disease problems, tolerates drought, and shares space agreeably in a garden (because it has a deep taproot that steals less from the upper soil than other trees might). Its bright green foliage and fragrant white flowers

(terminal clusters of pea-like blooms resembling wisteria) drip from the tree's branches like white rain, and few trees, other than willows, are more responsive to wind. A flowering yellowwood touched by wind is like a harp played by a sensitive hand.

The reason the yellowwood isn't planted more frequently probably has to do with two things. First, the tree isn't well-known, and second, it is both slow-growing and slow to bloom. A typical yellowwood doesn't bloom until it is about 10 years old (or about 15 feet tall), and nurserymen prefer fast-growing and fast-flowering trees to the slow-growing, slow-to-bloom ones. The yellowwood also has a habit of blooming in profusion only in 2-to 4-year intervals, making a peak year more exciting (but less predictable) than it is with many other ornamentals. On the other hand, these drawbacks to mass-marketing make the yellowwood an even choicer selection for those who appreciate its rarity and uncommon beauty.

The yellowwood takes its name from the color of its freshly cut heartwood. This light, strong wood, which takes a high polish, was once used by Cherokee Indians for carving and by others for gunstocks. The yellowwood is also the source of a yellow dye, which, according to naturalist Donald Culross Peattie, was probably the source of "many a yellow stripe in a piece of old-time homespun" before synthetic dyes became widely available.

According to urban forester Stephen Van Hoven, this yellowwood at Arlington National Cemetery was probably planted around 1890.

The state champion yellowwood grows at historic Kenmore in Fredericksburg. Grandly positioned on the upper garden terrace, this tree, with the species' characteristic smooth, gray bark, is 68 feet tall and 4.4 feet in diameter.

BLACK LOCUST, WYTHEVILLE

One of the great pleasures of producing this book has been the privilege of calling attention to trees like this state champion black locust in Wytheville. Located on a quiet street in this small, southwest Virginia town, this tree has long been appreciated in its neighborhood ("It's more valuable than the house," one previous owner contended), but few Virginians are aware that *any* black locust could be as big and beautiful as this one.

Black locusts often have a ragtag look, with lots of dead wood in their crowns, and even this one has large fungi protruding from its trunk, a sign of decay. In summer, you can recognize black locusts along Virginia interstates because of their brown, skeletal leaves—the result of leaf miner damage from which the trees usually recover, but only after they've put on a rather unsightly show. On the other hand, in May, a black locust is a sight to behold. Cloaked in fresh green leaves and creamy-white, wisteria-like flowers, a black locust often looks like two trees combined into one: a young tree dripping with delicate flowers, and an old one hanging onto old wood. Many a homeowner has removed such a "half-dead" black locust from the lawn, forgetting the tree is also "half-alive" and probably also forgetting the honey-scented fragrance these trees' flowers add to the landscape.

No one is threatening to cut down the Wytheville black locust, because not only is it the biggest black locust in the state (95 feet tall and over 14 feet in circumference), it seems to be in reasonably good health. Sheila Wyatt, whose family admired the tree long before they bought it and the home behind it twelve years ago, says its foliage has never been disfigured by leaf miners (well-fertilized lawn trees are less vulnerable than forest trees) and that, most springs, its branches drip with pendulous flowers. Unfortunately, a late frost robbed it of most of its flowers in 2007, the year Robert Llewellyn took its glamour

portrait, but the tree was no less impressive for that. So lush was its frond-like foliage, it looked like a tropical tree, and its massive trunk and deeply furrowed bark were so breathtaking, and so unexpected, that the experience of encountering the tree was like finding a priceless antique in a yard sale.

Wytheville is obviously comfortable habitat for the black locust, a tree that originally grew no farther east than the Appalachians but that has naturalized all over Virginia (and the rest of the country). Partly because it is a nitrogen-fixing tree that improves the soil wherever it goes, black locust can grow most anywhere, and does. Virginia Indians were the first to move black locust east of its original Virginia range; they planted it near their settlements to provide valuable wood for bows (and possibly longhouses and palisades). Strong, dense, and rot-resistant, black locust wood was also used as corner posts in some of the first Jamestown homes, and a hundred years after the founding of Jamestown the British naturalist Mark Catesby reported these durable posts were "yet standing" and "still perfectly sound."

Other noteworthy attributes of black locust include its heat value (as high as that of anthracite coal) and its root system (wide-spreading and particularly useful for erosion control). Black locusts have also been credited with drawing lightning to themselves, thus protecting a house from harm, and many an old homesite is still surrounded by black locust trees planted for this purpose. Some tree species *are* more lightning prone than others, and black locust is among them, but no one is entirely sure why.

Luckily, the state champion black locust in Wytheville isn't the tallest tree in the neighborhood, and it is certainly not being used as a lightning rod. Instead, under the care and protection of the Wyatt family, it seems likely to live at least as long as the oldest black locusts—about 100 years—and to enjoy that life in the company of appreciative neighbors.

The frond-like leaves of the black locust have a bluish-green cast and a feathery appearance.

The lush foliage and rounded crown of this state champion black locust (Robinia pseudoacacia) in Wytheville give it a silhouette quite different from many of Virginia's black locusts, which have uneven crowns and foliage damaged by leaf miners.

SWEET BIRCH, FLOYD COUNTY

"There's a line to this tree on weekends." It wasn't entirely surprising to hear photographer Jason Gabris describe how popular this sweet birch is to families. After all, the tree is enormously photogenic—with lichen-covered bark and wide-spreading branches that swoop down like arms to pick up waiting children. But it was surprising to learn how many people have long-term connections to the tree and who know it in all seasons and all weathers.

Gabris, who was photographing the tree in a driving rain when we encountered him, has been photographing the tree for 12 years—ever since he proposed to his wife under it. And Betty Gordon, volunteer in the Rocky Knob Information Center office directly across the road, says she has taken hundreds of photos of the tree. "People from all over the world see it," says Gordon, "but I watch it all year. In spring, it's a beautiful green, but it has multiple colors all year. I've adopted that tree. It's mine."

How nice for any tree, much less a sweet birch, to be getting all this attention. Sweet birch is sort of a connoisseur's tree. Hikers in the Appalachians know its smooth bark marked with lenticels (breathing pores), and naturalists like to call attention to its cone-like fruits and its catkins, but the tree is nowhere near as well-known as the maples, oaks, and tulip-poplars that dominate children's leaf collections. For children in western Virginia (including the western Piedmont), where this tree grows, sweet birch should be moved up into the "must know" category, because it can be known in one of the ways that is most memorable: through the nose. Scratch the bark of a sweet birch and you will immediately encounter the pungent fragrance of wintergreen.

The essential oils in sweet birch (*Betula lenta*) are reportedly identical to the essential oils in the woodland groundcover called wintergreen (*Gaultheria procumbens*). The latter was the original source of the wintergreen flavoring used in medicines and candy, but because sweet birch provided the oil in greater quantity and with more ease for collectors, the tree, according to biologist Rebecca Rupp, was almost wiped out in the nineteenth century. (Appalachian mountaineers reportedly collected the trees by the thousands, because it took 100 sweet birch saplings to produce a quart of wintergreen oil.) Luckily for the sweet birch, chemists learned to make wintergreen oil synthetically, and it is now synthetic wintergreen oil—not the natural oil of creeping wintergreen or of sweet birch—that is used in wintergreen flavorings. Sweet birch is also the source of the sap used to make birch beer, a drink Euell Gibbons described as having "the kick of a mule" and "definitely not suitable for children."

Also known as black birch and cherry birch, sweet birch grows best in moist, fertile soils and is often found growing near mountain streams, but it will also straddle rocks and grow on dry, steep mountainsides where it can eke out a living in the narrow vein of humus between boulders. This one occupies a site less challenging than a steep mountainside, less benign than a streamside, and it seems to be wildly happy there. Its wind-sculpted form and lichen-covered branches reflect in their colors and forms the geology and weather patterns of their upbringing. Although shorter than the tallest sweet birches (which can exceed 80 feet), this one is, overall, the largest of its species in the state. It's only 42 feet tall, but it has a circumference of almost 11 feet and a whopping crown spread of 68 feet. Unlike some champion trees, which are bigger than they are beautiful, this one is as beautiful as it is big, and it has the admirers to prove it.

South of Roanoke near milepost 169 on the Blue Ridge Parkway, this state champion sweet birch attracts photographers the way some trees do bees.

Branches that tangle near the heart of this sweet birch resolve themselves into gracious dips and curves near their tips. The branches are as lichen-covered as nearby rocks.

EASTERN COTTONWOOD, WINCHESTER

This eastern cottonwood (*Populus deltoides*) is big, beautiful, and probably about as old as a cottonwood gets—60 to 100 (occasionally 150) years. Growing in a riparian buffer zone across from Winchester's Whittier Park, it occupies a rise—obviously left to protect the tree—in an area recently planted and spruced up as part of a project to improve the Opequon Watershed. Kids (and adults) rollerblading by seem to take the tree for granted, but to anyone arriving from out of town, the tree is a "gotta-pull-over-and-take-a-closer-look" tree. It's not the largest eastern cottonwood in Virginia—that honor belongs to a fatter cottonwood in Fauquier—but this one is the prettier one, with a full, symmetrical crown, deeply fissured bark, and branches that rise vertically, then gracefully dip to the ground again, on all sides.

Incredibly fast-growing (up to 4 to 5 feet a year in youth), cottonwoods are equally fast-dying and quick to decay, and for that reason, among others, they never got much respect in the East, where long-lived trees with more valuable wood were available. But in plains and prairie states, where a fast-growing tree—or any tree for that matter—is a godsend, cottonwoods found growing along stream banks and rivers provided pioneers the wood they used for everything from cabins to coffins.

Cottonwoods get their name from the cottony fluff on their tiny seeds, which are released after the fruits of female trees mature in summer. If you've ever stood in a grove of cottonwoods (or in the vicinity of a large cottonwood tree) at seed-dispersal time, you'd think you were in the midst of a snowstorm. According to Winchester city arborist Tim Stern, the Winchester cottonwood has never produced "snow," so it must be a male.

Another interesting feature of these trees is their long, pointed leaf buds, which are so sturdy and sharp they could be featured on *CSI* as a crime weapon, and the tree's broad, triangular leaves, which respond to the slightest breeze. "All summer long," the naturalist Donald Culross Peattie once wrote, "there is the constant motion of the leaves, heavier and coarser than the music of Aspen foliage, a sound like a sudden gush of water that as quickly stops, like the rustle of heavy shirts, like distant pattering applause."

Native to about two-thirds of Virginia's counties, the water-loving cottonwood can tolerate dry soils and city conditions, so you'd think it would be a favorite of nurserymen, but no; even though it is fast-growing, the cottonwood is too weak-wooded and drops too much debris (branches, leaves, twigs, catkins) to make it a favorite of nurserymen or homeowners. Plantsman Michael Dirr has written that the cottonwood is "impressive in river bottoms and should remain there," but anyone who has seen the cottonwood across from Whittier Park, or the equally impressive specimens in Colonial Williamsburg (near the corner of Francis Street and Nassau Avenue), in Arlington (along the George Washington Memorial Parkway near the LBJ Grove), or elsewhere, knows this tree has more going for it than it is sometimes given credit for.

This beautifully proportioned Eastern cottonwood grows across from Whittier Park in the city of Winchester. The second largest cottonwood in Virginia, its trunk is 6.5 feet in diameter.

PECAN, SUSSEX COUNTY

When Oscar and Glenice Parker moved to their home, Bollingham, in Sussex County in the late 1940s, they measured the huge pecan in their backyard. It was "16 feet and some inches" in circumference. In 2006, Byron Carmean and Gary Williamson re-measured the tree and found that it had grown an additional 2 feet in girth, making it, with its 18.25-foot circumference and 142-foot height, the second largest pecan in Virginia. The Parkers say that although they treasure the tree and have ignored all suggestions they cut it down to protect their historic home, the tree's growth has been imperceptible to them. "We've grown along with it, I guess," says Mrs. Parker.

Choosing from among the several extraordinary pecan specimens nominated to the Remarkable Trees of Virginia Project was hard. A stunning pecan towers over the southeast wing of the mansion at Mount Vernon in Fairfax County, a handsome pecan graces the gardens at Westover in Charles City County, and the state champion pecan dominates a farm yard in Isle of Wight. Westmoreland, New Kent, and Goochland counties have notable pecans, as does the city of Lynchburg, but we chose the Parker's fine specimen in Sussex because it impressed us with its health, its size, and its form.

Unlike the state champion pecan, it has a single trunk, and unlike some of the other fine, old pecans in Virginia, this one is remarkable for its lack of disease, its vigor, and the apparent solidity of its trunk. Although it has lost at least two large branches ("You should have seen it before; it had a limb 2 feet in diameter that reached way over to the gate," says Mr. Parker), its looming trunk seems to rise forever to a thick canopy that has, incredibly, survived both lightning and wind. This is no small accomplishment given the beating other trees on the Parker's property took from Hurricane Isabel. Based on other damage to the property, it seems, in fact, that, in a reversal of the usual pattern, the house served as a windbreak to the tree.

No one knows the age of the Sussex pecan or where it came from, but the possibilities are intriguing. Although the pecan is not native to Virginia, it was being planted in Virginia as early as the late eighteenth century—if not earlier. Between 1790 and 1807 Thomas Jefferson reported several sowings of pecans at Monticello (records suggest some came from seed sources in

Philadelphia, others directly from the Mississippi Valley), and Jefferson shared pecan seeds with friends like George Washington, who planted them at Mount Vernon. The intriguing possibility, though, is that American Indians had brought the pecan to Virginia earlier. Certainly the value of this tree was well-known to American Indians, who not only traded its nutritious nuts—a staple of their diet—but reportedly planted them along trading routes to ensure a steady supply. The word "pecan" comes, in fact, from an Algonquin Indian word meaning "all nuts requiring a stone to crack" and probably referred to all hickory nuts, including the relatively thin-shelled pecan.

How appealing it is to imagine an Indian connection for the Sussex pecan! If not planted by Virginia Indians, perhaps it is the progeny of a tree planted by Virginia Indians. The tree looks old enough to entertain such a possibility, and the longevity of pecans (average maximum life spans of about 300 years, with 350-year-old-specimens reported) does nothing to quash such a thought. As if to feed the fantasy, Oscar Parker explains that "this was all Seacock Indian territory" in 1701 when his family acquired the property that now includes Bollingham. On the other hand, a farm hand who died in the 1990s once mentioned that he was living when the tree germinated in the corner of a fence line, but Mr. Parker doubts this. "I don't think anyone who looks at that tree could believe it's just a hundred years old."

Only when the Sussex pecan falls and its rings are counted (assuming its heartwood is intact), will anyone know for sure how hold it is, and often such revelations are disappointing. In 2004, for example, one of the pecans near Mount Vernon was removed after being damaged by Hurricane Isabel, and a ring count revealed it couldn't have been one of the pecans planted by George Washington between 1785 and 1787; instead, it probably germinated between 1850 and 1860. Since photos taken in the late 1800s indicate the iconic pecan still growing at Mount Vernon was about the same size as the pecan lost to Isabel, Mount Vernon's Director of Horticulture, Dean Norton, believes, it, too, probably germinated between 1850 and 1860, making it old enough to be worthy of veneration but not old enough to be connected to George Washington.

The Parkers are grateful for their pecan no matter who planted it or when it germinated. Even as she explains how much debris it drops and how much time she spends cleaning it up (pecans are notorious droppers of leaves, nuts, and catkins), Mrs. Parker emphasizes, "We just love it so much; we don't want anything to happen to it."

The second largest pecan in the state, this pecan (Carya illinoensis) in Sussex County grows at Bollingham in Wakefield.

Shagbark Hickory, Lee County

"It's a woolly mammoth of a tree," said Harold Jerrell, friend of the owner of this shagbark hickory, as we stood in Charles Turner's pasture on Tall Hickory Farm. His description seemed apt, because this tree seems like a relic of another age, and it is not only enormous—the largest of its species in the state—it is the shaggiest shagbark hickory most people will ever see. The bark creating the "shag" on this 129-foot hickory pops loose from the trunk in plates, some of which are 6 inches wide, and they curl up at the tip more like a hairdo than trunk-covering.

No wonder Charles Turner named his farm for this tree. The tree is a remarkable specimen, but this species is remarkable, too, for its importance in American history. Nuts from shagbark hickories were a staple in the diets of American Indians and early colonists, and, because shagbark hickory nuts are particularly sweet, they are still the hickory nut of choice for wild food enthusiasts. "I just finished making shagbark hickory milk, and am eating it two times a day—as stock for oatmeal (with maple syrup) and soup," one such enthusiast wrote us, noting that he was "trying to get out of the industrial food chain, and into God's." According to the early American naturalist William Bartram, who described the process of making hickory milk in detail (pounding the nut pieces, steeping them in boiling water, then straining off the oily "milk"), American Indians stored shagbark hickory nuts in their towns, and Bartram observed "a hundred bushels of these nuts belonging to one family." The word hickory, in fact, comes from an Algonquin word, "pawcohiccora," meaning hickory milk.

The shagbark hickory (*Carya ovata*) is native to North America and grows wild in about two-thirds of Virginia's counties, but nowhere is it common, and you shouldn't expect to see trees as shaggy as this one very often. Only mature shagbark hickories exhibit the shaggy bark for which they are famous, and you'd never know from the smooth bark of a young shagbark hickory that it would grow up to look like a "woolly mammoth." (Other old shagbark hickories with really impressive bark grow at Oatlands in Loudoun County and in Washington County.) No one knows how old the shagbark hickory at Tall Hickory Farm is—Charles Turner says it looked as big as it is now 31 years ago when he bought the farm—but it could well be over 200 years old, since this species has a recorded longevity of 300 years.

Another mystery surrounding this tree is the reason for its shaggy bark. Of what advantage would such bark be to the tree? No one was able to answer this question definitively for us, although forester Tom Dierauf suggested the shaggy bark might serve as a squirrel-guard—discouraging squirrels from harvesting the hickory nuts, which they relish and often harvest when they are tender, before they are fully mature. Such extravagantly peeling bark would also shelter bats, butterflies, and other insects, an advantage to those sheltered, but of no obvious advantage to the tree. Whatever its function, such bark is a show-stopper and one of the great wonders of the Virginia woods.

This champion shagbark hickory near Jonesville in far southwestern Virginia is 3.6 feet in diameter and almost 130 feet tall. Only mature shagbark hickories exhibit the shaggy bark for which this species is famous.

chapter seven NOTEWORTHY SPECIES

Early on in the planning for this book we considered organizing our chapters strictly by tree species. "Too much like a text book" was the response of our focus group (friends and family), so we decided on the more "reader-friendly" approach of organizing our trees under categories such as old, historic, unique, etc.

There were some trees, however, that seemed to fit none of the "remarkable tree" categories we had selected—or fit so many of them that they could have been included anywhere. In many of these cases, we realized it was less the attributes of one particular tree in a species that we wanted to highlight but rather the attributes of the group. There are, for example, many fine dogwood and redbud specimens in Virginia, but it is the impact of dogwood and redbud on Virginia *collectively* that makes them so remarkable. And while we found several noteworthy hickories in our travels, it was hickory in general—the value of the species to wildlife, the impact of hickory color in November—that we found ourselves wanting to emphasize. In some ways, this chapter became a catch-all for every tree that seemed more significant as a species than as a specimen (loblolly pine, for example, can grow into a remarkable specimen, but it is as a commercial species that it makes its biggest impact on Virginia).

Our sample of noteworthy species is way too small to represent the innumerable ways a species can be remarkable, but we try, here and elsewhere, to highlight some of the qualities that make the tree universe so interesting. Some species are remarkable for their ability to grow in seemingly inhospitable environments (baldcypress growing in a swamp, for example, or sweet birch growing on rock), others for their adaptability (blackgum can grow everywhere from a swamp to a mountaintop), others for their tenacity (picture a live oak, pruned and shaped by the wind). Still other species are noteworthy for their abundance (almost a billion and a half red maples grow in Virginia) or for their rarity (the roundleaf birch, which had dwindled to a few dozen trees in 2003, is now making a comeback in southwest Virginia). For the properties of their wood, species like paulownia, black walnut, and hickory are remarkable, and for their ancient lineage we value the ginkgo and the magnolia.

In terms of species richness overall, Virginia, with about 200 native tree species, is impoverished if you compare it to the tropics and sub-tropics (Cuba alone has thousands of species of native trees), but rich if you compare it to Europe (all of Britain has only about 40 native tree species). Virginia's species richness (as compared to Europe's) derives partly from its geography and partly from its history. For example, many European tree species were wiped out during the ice ages when they could not migrate far enough from the glaciers (the east-west orientation of Europe's mountains forms a barrier to southern migration), but in eastern North America, where glaciers stopped short of Virginia and the orientation of our mountains allowed southern migration, temperate species survived.

We may not be Costa Rica, but if you add to Virginia's native species the many non-native trees and naturalized species in the state, you have enough tree species to keep the most devoted tree enthusiast busy learning about them for years.

Red maple (Acer rubrum), Barboursville

RED MAPLE, GREENE AND GLOUCESTER COUNTIES

If you were to count the number of trees of each species in Virginia, you'd find more red maples than any other tree. This comes as a surprise to people who might have guessed oak, but there is a reason for red maple's abundance. For one thing, red maple can grow almost anywhere—in wet or dry soils, in low-lying areas and on mountaintops. Red maple is also an opportunistic species that increases significantly when other trees in its vicinity decline (or have been harvested or lost to fire). Although it is itself highly susceptible to fire, red maple will come back from the roots after a fire. It will also move into habitats where other trees have succumbed to Dutch elm disease, gypsy moth infestations, chestnut blight, and other problems, and, for that reason, there is probably more red maple in some Virginia localities today than there was in pre-settlement Virginia. Fire suppression has also benefited existing red maples in Virginia forests.

Another misconception about red maples is that they all have red leaves. Not so. Even in the fall, red maple, which has green leaves in spring and summer, may or may not have red leaves. As the photo on the preceding pages illustrates, red maple *can* have brilliant red fall foliage (and almost all the cultivated varieties in subdivisions do), but "wild" red maples have fall foliage that varies from dull yellows and maroons to bright yellows, oranges, and reds. It was probably the red maple's early spring flowers—small, usually red, and appearing in dense clusters before the leaves—that led to the tree's name, and not its leaves at all.

The largest red maples in Virginia grow in swamp-like situations along the Nottoway and Blackwater rivers in Southampton County, but one of the most impressive red maples in Virginia grows in a Gloucester County front yard. Its fall foliage is relatively lackluster, but its shape is startling. From the road it looks like just a big red maple, but up close you experience how extraordinarily well-branched and "thick in the middle" it is. As a result of removing some of the trees and shrubs that used to surround it, Brownie Bartley, who has lived behind this tree her entire life, has provided motorists an improved view of her tree, and she says it is often pictured on Christmas cards and visited by passersby.

Red maple is a relatively short-lived species (few red maples live longer than 130 years), but the Bartley's red maple may have already surpassed that. Lore in the Bartley family has it that Brownie Bartley's great, great grandfather planted the tree. "My grandfather was born in a small, square house that stood close to where our house stands now," says Bartley. "And we believe that house was built in the 1860s." It's also possible the tree germinated from a seed and has always grown on the spot it now occupies, but whatever its provenance, it certainly owns its site now. "When we took the old house down and built our new house in 2007, we protected the tree with caution tape and the contractor watched every truck that came in to make sure it didn't damage the tree," says Bartley. "We've lost a lot of trees to hurricanes, and I didn't want to lose this one to construction."

Although it is a favorite of many landscapers and beloved by the general public, many foresters are not fans of the red maple. They consider it "inferior and undesirable," because it is "often poorly formed and defective, especially when grown on poor sites." This may be true, but it is also true (as other foresters have observed) that red maple can probably thrive on a wider range of soil types, textures, moisture, pH, and elevation than any other forest species in North America. Then, too, red maple—spring *and* fall—is one of the best sources of color in the state, and there are many specimens, like this fine one in Gloucester, that may not be "disciplined" but they are dramatic.

As this stretch of red maples along a stream in Greene County illustrates, red maples aren't always red.
The fall leaf color of a red maple can vary from yellow to orange to red, with combinations in between.

At 92 feet, this red maple in Gloucester County is not remarkably tall, but it is so thick in the middle it looks like the "plus-size" version of Acer rubrum.

Redbud, Botetourt and Albemarle Counties

It was impossible to choose only one tree to feature as Virginia's most remarkable redbud, because it is in groups growing along roadsides, streams, forest edges, and rocky slopes that redbud makes its most impressive show. Occasionally you'll find a beautiful specimen growing alone (like the one pictured below), but more often it is the raspberry glow created by a thousand redbuds that makes you want to shout "Why is this tree not more appreciated in Virginia?!"

Let the lobbying begin: Be it resolved that peak redbud season (usually between late March and early April) should receive as much press as peak fall color and peak dogwood season. Be it resolved further that every Virginia schoolchild be taught to identify this tree, because, truth be told, it has more dazzle (at least from a child's perspective) than a dogwood. With its electric pink flowers, heart-shaped leaves, and bean-like pods, the redbud is almost impossible to confuse with anything else, and even though its name is somewhat confusing (the tree's pea-like flowers are pink-to-raspberry and occasionally white, not red), the name is easy to remember. "Judas tree" is another common name that has the potential to help lodge this tree in people's memories, because it involves the legendary story of Judas Iscariot, who is said to have hanged himself on *Cercis siliquastrum*, a Eurasian relative of the eastern redbud (*Cercis canadensis*). Prior to Judas's betrayal of Christ, all redbud flowers are said to have been white; after the betrayal, Judas's shame or blood is said to have turned the tree's flowers red.

In addition to its ornamental value, redbud is an important native tree for its value to wildlife. Along with the flowers of red maples and willows, redbud flowers provide one of the earliest sources of nectar for bees. The 3-inch pods that follow the flowers (pods that often remain hanging on the tree into early winter) enclose flat seeds often eaten by birds. Not only does the tree bloom early in the season, it blooms early in its lifespan (often flowering as few as five years after germinating from seed), and it grows so fast a seedling seems to turn into a small tree overnight. The trees are relatively short-lived and irregular in growth habit, and redbuds often exhibit as much dead as healthy wood, but there is beauty even in the most bedraggled redbud, especially in spring, when its pink lights are turned on.

This eastern redbud above blooms along the edge of a field in Botetourt County, but the tree is equally at home in suburbs and cities. Because of its relatively small size, physical beauty, and wildlife value, redbud is among the native ornamentals often recommended for small yards.

More riveting than dogwoods, redbuds, like these along Route 626 in Albemarle County, light up Virginia roadsides in early spring.

American Sycamore, Rockbridge County and Accomac

Skin-like bark, graceful limbs, and torso-like trunks give the American sycamore an almost feminine appearance, but if the American sycamore is a woman, she's an Amazon. As a species, American sycamore (*Platanus occidentalis*) is one of the largest native trees in the eastern United States, and individual trees have dimensions that, if the trees really were women, would send them to the nearest spa immediately. The largest sycamore in the United States (a tree in Ohio) has a girth of over 35 feet, and Virginia's current champ has a 27.5-foot waistline. (Sycamores can also grow to heights of 150 feet or more.)

Size accounts for only half of the sycamore's charisma, however; the other half emanates from its bark. Especially in winter, when there is no foliage to hide it, the bright, white bark of a sycamore can light the sky like a strobe. Sycamores vary in their bark color—some are more gray, green, tan, or white than others—but all the old ones have mottled, patchy bark that pops off like thin cardboard as their trunks expand. Most everyone who observes sycamores will tell you that sycamore bark is its whitest in winter, but explanations for that phenomenon are hard to come by. Like the bark of some trees of arid regions, sycamore bark contains chlorophyll, and some have suggested sycamores may "pull back" some chlorophyll in their bark tissue in winter, making them more white than green, but this is by no means a unanimous opinion. What is agreed upon is that sycamores have very

thin bark, making them extremely vulnerable to fire, so they must have evolved in areas where fire was infrequent.

As you might expect, because they grow best in the loamy, well-drained soil in bottomlands, many if not most of Virginia's largest sycamores grow along rivers and streams, where they often hang out over the water at gravity-defying angles. Virginia's largest sycamore doesn't hang, it sits squarely on the shore of the Cowpasture River in Bath County, but it does seem to be defying something (maybe death itself) by persisting with a core large and hollow enough to set a card table up inside. (Huge, hollow sycamores are common, and stories of people and livestock sheltering in them are quite believable.) Virginia's second and third largest sycamores, in Montgomery and Rockbridge counties respectively, also grow in floodplains, as does the sycamore dubbed "The Dancing Tree" in Albemarle. That sycamore, beloved for its bright, balletic branches, grows near the Moormans River, where it is a frequent subject for artists.

Sycamores are much more adaptable than their association with riverbanks would suggest. They will tolerate most soils and survive even in difficult city conditions where they "shrug off" pollutants. "It's a tough, tough tree," commented forest researcher Tom Dierauf, explaining why the sycamore, given adequate sunlight, can survive most anywhere. Sycamore is also relatively fast-growing and long-lived, a combination you don't find too often in trees.

No one knows where the oldest sycamores in Virginia grow (the old ones

The third largest of its species in Virginia, this American sycamore grows along the James River at Natural Bridge Station in Rockbridge County.

are often hollow and impossible to core), but we do have a candidate for the most beautiful sycamore in Virginia. It's a street tree in the town of Accomac in the county of Accomack on Virginia's Eastern Shore. "This place has an old feel," John Hugo commented as he strolled Accomac's Back Street looking at the antebellum and Victorian houses, but it was the sycamore in front of the house called The Tannery (built in 1793) that stopped him in his tracks. This tree, huge and healthy, has already partially grown over the plaque placed at this base in 1986, a plaque reading "Sycamore, Bicentennial Tree, circa 1776" and seems quite capable of surviving another century. Who knows what other brushes with catastrophe it has survived (think hurricanes, among others), but in one modern stroke of good fortune, it grows on the side of the street where the power lines aren't.

As a street tree, it doesn't have the drama of some riverside sycamores (their impact is doubled by reflecting water), but, unlike many old town trees that have been stripped of the companions they grew up with, it does have the honor of residing among old homes and other old trees. This sycamore is also as white as any sycamore you'll ever see, and it somehow seems bigger for growing in a residential area (it LOOMS by a sidewalk) than it would if it were growing in a more rural setting.

Is it really the most beautiful sycamore in Virginia? Those who nominated it to the Remarkable Trees of Virginia Project claimed only that it was "the most beautiful street tree in eastern Virginia," but if there are other sycamores more deserving of the title "most beautiful sycamore in Virginia," let their advocates weigh in. We can think of lots of competitions less worthwhile.

This American sycamore, which has been called the most beautiful street tree in eastern Virginia, grows in front of The Tannery, an historic home in the town of Accomac. Parts of The Tannery were built in 1793, and a resident who lived in the house in 1865 told a local historian the sycamore was a large, impressive tree at that time.

Southern Magnolia, Surry and Gloucester Counties

"Yankees would kill to be able to grow this tree," writes horticulturist Michael Dirr in one of his woody plant manuals, describing the southern magnolia as "an indispensable part of the southern garden heritage." In truth, the southern magnolia is more southern than Virginia. Its native range extends only from southeast North Carolina to Florida and Texas, but it is planted over a much wider area, and modern cultivars, more cold-hardy than their predecessors, can be grown farther and farther north. In Virginia, it is considered the quintessential ornamental tree and its glossy, evergreen leaves and huge, fragrant white flowers grace many a Virginia yard, cemetery, campus, and park.

No wonder there were so many fine southern magnolias nominated to the Remarkable Trees of Virginia Project, making selection of the "best" southern magnolia difficult. Anyone who wants to appreciate how beloved and beautiful Virginia's southern magnolias are should visit the project website and peruse the photos and tree descriptions there. Included are a monumental magnolia on Magnolia Avenue in Norfolk, magnolias grown from cuttings taken from the grounds of the White House during the administration of President McKinley (a groundskeeper at the White House planted them in Farmville, where they still grow), and magnolias that have hosted generations of climbing children. One photo illustrates an entire kindergarten class cavorting in the branches of a magnolia in the city of Richmond, and a nomination from Mecklenberg describes "countless hours" spent by children in the Owen family who used their grandparents' magnolia as hotel, hobby horse, and lookout tower. Every one of these trees, and countless others, deserved to be featured.

We selected two magnolias that seemed to best illustrate the impressive forms this tree can take. The first, a massive magnolia in Surry County near Chippokes Plantation State Park, is a dense, low-branching tree with massive trunk (over 5.5 feet in diameter) and sinuous, gray-barked branches that reach out like massive tentacles in all directions. When the tree is loaded with blooms, as it is in early summer, the fragrance under and around it is overpowering.

The second (pictured on pages 132 and 133) is a magnolia that illustrates, in the extreme, the proclivity of southern magnolias to take root where their lowest branches touch the ground. We saw this over and over in our "magnolia travels," but the southern magnolia at Elmington in Gloucester is unparalleled in this regard. If you were to walk around the perimeter of this tree (or trees, if you consider each rooted branch a new tree), you'd be walking almost 400 feet. From the outside, this tree looks like an impenetrable mass of green that sits, like a jolly green giant, on open lawn overlooking the Ware River.

Underneath—or "inside," which seems the better preposition in this case—the tree is entirely different. There, the atmosphere is sort of spooky, enclosed as you are by an evergreen ceiling (the tree canopy) above and by evergreen walls (the tips of the outermost branches) around. The space feels like an enormous room in which trees are growing, because it is filled with, not the one trunk you expect, but a forest of trunks, some of them no thicker than your forearm, others 18 to 24 inches in diameter. You can pick your way through them, but even this is a little unnerving, because the ground is so deep in magnolia leaves (which decompose slowly at best and seem to have been accumulating here for decades) that it feels like you're walking on a mattress stuffed with paper.

Southern magnolias, it seems, create habitats within habitats, and this may be one of the reasons we treasure them so.

Flowers like those of the magnolia were among the first flower types to appear on earth. Evidence of this ancient lineage can be found in the structure of their reproductive parts and in their large size and shape, designed to attract beetles and flies rather than bees and butterflies, which evolved later.

This southern magnolia (Magnolia grandiflora) near Chippokes Plantation State Park is the larger of two old magnolias growing on this property across the James River from Jamestown. Standing under it when it is in full bloom is like standing in a perfume factory.

On the banks of the Ware River in Gloucester County, this southern magnolia (Magnolia grandiflora) has morphed from a single-trunked tree into a great expanse of rooted branches, leading one to wonder whether to call it a tree or a sprawling super-shrub. From the outside, it looks like one huge tree. From the inside (right), it looks like a forest.

FLOWERING DOGWOOD, CLARKE COUNTY

I s it the angle of light, the weather, or the surrounding vegetation that makes dogwood blossoms seem whiter in Virginia than elsewhere? Surely there's some physical explanation for this phenomenon, and for the associated pride Virginians take in their dogwoods. According to many, the flowering dogwood (*Cornus florida*) is *the* most valuable ornamental tree in the state, and despite the tree's disease problems, it continues to be both widely planted and beloved in the wild. Part of the dogwood's charm comes from repetition—the more of it there is, the more impressive it seems—but the tree has beauty in isolation, too.

Among its other assets, this native tree, Virginia's state floral emblem, has great fall color (varying from muted maroon to brilliant red), shiny red fruit (food for over one hundred species of birds, including Virginia's state bird, the cardinal) and interesting form (horizontal branches creating a graceful, tiered effect). Even in winter, the dogwood's fat, rounded buds and upturned twigs, often cradling the remnants of a bird's nest, provide texture and interest in the landscape.

At the State Arboretum of Virginia, a double line of dogwoods, growing in proximity to dry-stacked stone walls, showcases the intricate architecture of these trees, but equally picturesque scenes can be found throughout the state, where, as naturalist Donald Culross Peattie once put it, dogwoods are "stepping delicately out of the dark woods." An understory species, dogwoods in the wild are typically found growing on the edges of woodlands, leaning out from under the higher canopy of other trees, but in western parts of Virginia, these scenes are becoming less common. A deadly fungus—dogwood anthracnose—threatens dogwoods growing in cool, moist, shady environments, like those in mountainous parts of the state. In the coastal

plain, where temperatures rise in the 90s, the disease doesn't seem to be a threat, but in the mountains and, to a lesser extent, in the Piedmont, the problem is serious. In a 1998 survey of 2,000 dogwoods growing around the State Arboretum, Dr. David Carr found that every dogwood sampled had anthracnose, and two years later, a third of those dogwoods were dead.

In 1933, Dr. Orland White, first director of Blandy Farm (now the State Arboretum), planted dogwoods along the lane pictured here. About half of those dogwoods survive, partly because the Arboretum uses an anti-fungal spray to control dogwood anthracnose. The lane was also rejuvenated in 2000, when, with the help of the Winchester-Clarke chapter of the Garden Club of Virginia, new dogwoods were planted to replace dead or diseased ones. New dogwoods along the eastern half of the lane are native dogwoods; new dogwoods along the western half are cultivated varieties, and Arboretum staff monitors the relative health of each. In general, regardless of whether they are native or cultivated, dogwoods seem to resist anthracnose best when growing where they have good air circulation, plenty of light (at least one half day of sunlight per day), and well-drained soil.

In Virginia, dogwoods usually bloom between March and June (in the Richmond area they usually peak around April 15, at the State Arboretum around mid-May). The blossoms (actually petal-like bracts surrounding a yellow-green cluster of true flowers) are typically white, but vary from white to pink to wine red. In Mecklenburg, a noteworthy pink dogwood blooms in front of the old South Hill Elementary School, where, according to its nominators, it blooms around Easter and "lets the world know that spring and new life are upon us."

Bright red fruits called drupes brighten dogwood trees in fall and winter.

Along Dogwood Lane at the State Arboretum of Virginia, Clarke County, the flowering dogwood blossoms seem to create their own light.

GINKGO, CITIES OF RICHMOND AND CHARLOTTESVILLE

You'd think you wouldn't need to hurry to photograph a tree—trees are stationary after all—but if you want to photograph a particular ginkgo before it drops its yellow leaves, timing is crucial. We had "spotters" all over the state on the lookout for when our favorite ginkgoes turned the glowing yellow for which they are famous ("they are like lights switched on," one observer commented), but ginkgo lights don't stay on very long, and these trees often drop their leaves all at once. Leave for work one November morning with your ginkgo tree covered in yellow leaves; come home that afternoon to find them all on the ground. Complicating this scenario further was the fact that in 2007, the ginkgo we had most hoped to capture in its full autumnal glory, a fine specimen at Oatlands in Loudoun County, dropped its leaves while many of them were still green.

Photographer Robert Llewellyn crisscrossed the state photographing ginkgoes, some of which he found in leaf, some of which he didn't. (The apron of yellow leaves under a ginkgo can be almost as compelling as the leaves on the tree.) The trees we thought captured "ginkgo quality" best were the Pratt ginkgo on the UVA campus in Charlottesville and the allée of ginkgoes along Massie Road in the city of Richmond. The Pratt ginkgo grows northwest of UVA's Rotunda, where it is believed to have been planted around 1860 by the University's first superintendent of buildings and grounds, William Pratt. The trees along Richmond's Massie Road are much younger— the oldest of them were probably planted in the 1950s—but they illustrate how impressive a street tree the ginkgo can be—especially when lit with yellow leaves.

The ginkgo is a strange and wonderful tree. Sometimes called a "living fossil," it is primitive in the sense that it has come to us relatively unchanged since the Triassic Period 200 million years ago and has a primitive method of reproduction. (Swimming sperm are involved, and fertilization can actually take place after immature ginkgo seeds have fallen to the ground.) The ginkgo's fan-shaped leaves are also unique, and on older trees the leaves emerge from spurs (woody stacks of leaf scars up to 3 inches long) that give the tree a prehistoric look. (That "look" is no illusion; ginkgoes were an ancient group of trees before the first dinosaurs came along.)

The first western European discovery of this ancient tree probably occurred in 1691 when the German physician Engelbert Kaempfer discovered *Ginkgo* growing in Nagasaki, Japan. (Although native to China, many believe the ginkgo grew not in the wild but only in temple gardens of China and Japan at the time of this "discovery.") Soon ginkgo seeds were being shipped all over the world, and to own a ginkgo was to own a rare botanical treasure. The first ginkgo tree is said to have been planted in a U.S. garden in 1784 (William Hamilton's Philadelphia garden), and there is a record of Hamilton's having written Thomas Jefferson in 1806 saying he intended to send him "Ginkgo biloba or China Maidenhair tree." (There is no record of that tree's arrival or planting at Monticello, however.)

One early ginkgo arrival in Virginia was the tree that is now Virginia's state champion, a beautiful tree on the grounds of White Marsh Plantation in Gloucester County. Believed to have been planted around 1820, a photograph shows it taller than the three-story manor house around 1900. Other old Virginia ginkgoes whose sources are known include two huge ginkgoes on the Hickory Hill plantation in Hanover. They were planted around 1854 when Williams Carter Wickham received them from Commodore Matthew Perry, who had received them as gifts from the Emperor of Japan. Another fine Virginia ginkgo, believed to have been brought back from China by missionaries in the 1890s, towers over the Fellowship Hall of St. Theresa's Roman Catholic Church in Tazewell.

Today, the ginkgo, which is remarkably disease and pest free, is often used as an urban street tree, partly because of its beauty and partly because it can tolerate very difficult growing conditions. (Four ginkgo trees reportedly survived the bombing of Hiroshima, making the insults a ginkgo experiences

No one is certain when the ginkgoes along Richmond's Massie Road were planted, but Susan Overton, who lives on Massie Road, believes the effort to plant them was spearheaded by her mother-in-law in the early 1950s. The ginkgo's golden glow is magnified by repetition.

in urban America seem benign.) Urban foresters try to plant male ginkgoes to avoid the smelly "fruits" (technically seeds) of the females, but sometimes a female sneaks in, creating an unpleasant situation, because the ginkgo's seed coat has an offensive odor that some accurately compare to vomit or feces. A mushy mess of ginkgo slush is no fun on your tires or shoes.

The same ginkgo that grows as a street tree is also the source of the *Ginkgo biloba* extracts many people buy for memory enhancement and other medicinal purposes (and that has been used in Chinese medicines

for thousands of years). Unfortunately, according to studies reported by the National Institutes of Health, ginkgo may not be the memory enhancer we'd like it to be. Whatever the properties of its chemical constituents, however, ginkgo has the power to engage our imaginations and to appeal to what one paleobotanist has called "the historic soul." "We see it as an emblem of changelessness, a heritage from worlds too remote for our human intelligence to grasp," wrote Sir Albert Seward in 1938. It is a tree, he continued, "which has in its keeping the secrets of the immeasurable past."

"The tree's crown is a magnificent yellow and then suddenly it's as if a squirrel had yanked a lever and all the leaves are on the ground," says one ginkgo admirer, who might have been describing this tree, called the Pratt ginkgo, at the University of Virginia.

American Holly, Amherst County and Alexandria

You won't find many native, broadleaved evergreens in Virginia—most of our evergreen trees have needles—but the American holly is an exception. So valued were the leaves and red berries of this tree in the 1940s and 1950s that conservationists railed against the "depredations of Christmas-greens pickers" and promoted all sorts of strategies to prevent the gathering of American holly boughs for decoration. This is one case where plastic may have benefited a tree, because the popularity of artificial Christmas greens, and the introduction of hybrid hollies and other evergreens, seem to have taken some of the collecting pressure off American holly.

A beautiful tree both in the wild and in cultivation, American holly (*Ilex opaca*) grows slowly, making a large tree all the more to be valued. Unlike taller and faster growing trees, a 40-foot-tall American holly can be an heirloom and should be appreciated as such. American hollies have an appealing pyramidal shape that gets more interesting as the tree ages—its branches growing more open, sometimes swooping, and horizontally layered—and its smooth, gray bark suggests something enduring and ancient. The tree's leathery leaves have prickly edges with upper sides that can range from deep green to yellowish green, and the leaves' undersides are a paler green. Growing American hollies in full to part sun and the acid, well-drained soil they like usually makes for greener (as opposed to yellowish) trees.

As the Remarkable Tree team traveled, we saw fine American hollies in graveyards, on old home sites, in backyards, in parks, and in many a wild setting, but we never agreed on the best specimen. Of Virginia's three largest American hollies, two are multi-trunked, and one, in Hampton, has been pruned in a way that diminishes its former glory. We settled on the trees pictured here because the Alexandria holly seemed representative of the many

American hollies that have been allowed to reach maturity in the sanctuary of a graveyard, and because the pair of American hollies we chose in Amherst, a male and female, seemed like an exemplary old married couple. (You do, by the way, need both a male and a female holly in order for the females to bear fruit.)

Long gone, it seems, are the American hollies George Washington planted at Mount Vernon (a bubble-bursting dendrochronologist declared the oldest hollies there, dating to 1806 and 1812, too young to have been planted by Washington), but it's interesting to note just how valuable our first president found this tree, and how much trouble he went to in order to grow it at Mount Vernon. This tree that most Virginians take for granted is one that Washington mentioned often in his diaries and one that he not only tried to grow from saplings but from seeds. In an April 6, 1785 entry he wrote: "Sowed the semicircle North of the front gate with Holly berries sent me by my brother John—three drills of them—the middle one of Berries which had been got about Christmas and put in Sand—the other two of Berries which had been got earlier in the year gently dried, & packed in Shavings." And on March 30, 1786 he wrote, "Planted in the holly clumps, in my shrubberies, a number of small holly trees which some months ago Colo. Lee of Stratford sent me in a box with earth...I also planted several holly trees which had been sent to me the day before by a Neighbor Mr. Thos. Allison."

A favorite of Colonial gardeners, American holly is also a favorite of birds: mockingbirds, thrushes, robins, bluebirds, and other birds relish its red fruit, and the tree's dense growth habit and prickly evergreen foliage provide year-round cover and nesting sites. Small wonder, then, that conservationists shuddered to see this tree stripped for holiday decorations and all the more reason to appreciate it in the landscape today.

This old, multi-trunked American holly grows in the historic Christ Church Cemetery in Old Town Alexandria. The tombstones surrounding the tree date from the early 1800s, and vestry records show nearby burials as early as 1766. American hollies seldom live longer than 150 years, so it's unlikely this tree is as old as the oldest nearby gravesites, but it is certainly among the oldest living residents of Alexandria. This American holly, and another multi-trunked American holly in Arlington, are among the three largest American hollies in the nation.

These two fine old American hollies, a male on the right and a female on the left, grow on Holly Lane in Madison Heights, Amherst County. The street was named for the trees.

PIGNUT HICKORY, FLOYD COUNTY

Hickory is among those beloved Virginia trees that no one plants—which means that in landscapes that have been cleared for development it is losing ground. You'd have to search hard to find a pignut, or mockernut, or shagbark, or shellbark hickory in a nursery, but Virginia woodlands, especially in November, would be bereft without this tree. It's the source of the warm amber light that colors the countryside after the brilliant maples have gone out.

Warm light isn't the only heat hickory provides. It is one of the best kinds of firewood and fuels many a woodstove. According to naturalist Donald Culross Peattie, hickory wood is higher in fuel value than any other American tree except locust, and a cord of hickory is almost equivalent in thermal units to a ton of anthracite. Because its wood is so strong and flexible, hickory was one of the trees sought out by pioneers for use in making wagon wheels, and it's still used to make things that can take violent strains—like tool handles, skis, and baseball bats. It was because he was tough as hickory wood on the battlefield that Andrew Jackson was nicknamed Old Hickory.

For its history, its fall color, its tolerance of poor soils, and the heat value of its wood (not to mention the food value of its nuts, a staple in the diets of American Indians), hickory is one of those native trees we should all value in

the wild. It's also one of those trees to mark for saving in areas slated for development, because, like redbud, it is a tree whose impact is vastly increased by repetition.

Deciding which specific hickory, or even which hickory species, to highlight in this chapter was a challenge. Among the fine hickories nominated to the project were a former state champion mockernut hickory in a Charlottesville front yard, an old mockernut hickory in front of Arlington House at Arlington National Cemetery, a gorgeous shellbark hickory visible just off the deck of a home in Culpeper, and the state champion pignut hickory in Campbell County. The legendary Old Guard Tree at VMI—a hickory that served as the cadet guard post from 1839 to 1900 and is commemorated by a monument on the campus—also seemed to deserve recognition.

In the end, we chose the striking hickory pictured here because not only was it growing on protected land (along the Blue Ridge Parkway), it had the potential to be seen by the millions of motorists traveling the Parkway every year, and it seemed the healthiest, most photogenic, and accessible representative of its species we could find. This pignut hickory (*Carya glabra*) also serves as a U.S. Geological Survey benchmark (a label on the tree marks the elevation as 3,089 feet), so the curious who are drawn to the label get to experience this beautifully proportioned tree up close.

Posing beside the Blue Ridge Parkway near Tuggle Gap, this fine pignut hickory turns shades of amber and yellow-gold in the fall. Pignut hickory is a slow-growing species, but, like many slow-growing species, it has the potential for long life. A pignut hickory's typical maximum age is around 200 years, but some live 300 years.

White Pine, Augusta County

Ramsey's Draft

Most trees aren't 100 feet tall even including their crowns, but the tallest tree in Virginia, an eastern white pine growing in Ramsey's Draft in Augusta County, doesn't even begin to branch until it is almost 100 feet tall. Here in this canyon-like environment, trees compete intensely and grow extra tall just to get the sunlight they need. The top of this giant, approaching 170 feet above the ground, seems to occupy a climate zone different from that of its lower trunk, and its canopy waves like a flag in response to winds imperceptible on the forest floor. A nearby white pine, the state champion, is 166 feet tall with a girth of 139 inches (its larger girth earns it champion status over the taller pine).

Tall as they are, these extraordinary white pines are small by historical standards. Often referred to as "the monarchs of the forest," white pines that greeted settlers in parts of New England and the Great Lakes states grew 250 feet tall and 6 feet in diameter. According to legend, it took Paul Bunyan and companions seven days of sawing to fell a white pine in Michigan, and in New England the tall, straight trunks of white pines were so highly valued for ships' masts they were sometimes referred to as "New England gold." It was, in fact, competition for white pines—the British crown wanted to reserve the best ones for the Royal Navy—that helped precipitate the Revolutionary War.

Native to eastern North America, eastern white pine (*Pinus strobus*) is actually a northern species, but it grows as far south as Georgia, primarily in the mountains. In Virginia, it grows wild in the Piedmont and the western part of the state, and rarely (unless planted) in eastern Virginia. Because of our intense ice and wind storms, white pines probably never got as tall in Virginia as they did in parts of New England and the Great Lakes states; nevertheless, even today, white pine is the most commercially important pine in the mountains of southwest Virginia. Its wood, strong in proportion to its weight, is harvested for furniture manufacture and for logs sold to make log cabins; there is also a thriving market for the white pine boughs used as Christmas greenery and roping. Of the white pine acreage in Virginia, about half of it is in white pine plantations and half in natural stands. Most of the big white pines left in the state are scattered in hollows, where they were missed or left by loggers. According to naturalist Donald Culross Peattie, three hundred years of lumbering had wiped out most of the virgin white pine areas in northern forests by 1900 and in the southern Appalachians by 1915.

In Ramsey's Draft, white pines may be poised to make a comeback. The area around the white pines featured here is part of the 6,518-acre Ramsey's Draft wilderness area, an area that would appear ramshackle to the casual observer partly because the draft, or stream, for which the area is named was fragmented by hurricane Juan in 1985 and partly because it is littered with debris from dead and dying hemlocks (victims of the woolly adelgid). But in this "disarray" may be an opening for the white pine. According to Forest Service timber management assistant Mark Healey, white pine is well-suited to fill the niche left by dead hemlocks, not only because parent trees are present to serve as a seed source, but also because mature white pines have bark thick enough to withstand the fires likely to sweep through the area as dead hemlock wood accumulates. No one knows exactly how this dynamic ecosystem will respond to the insults it has received, but white pine may be one of the beneficiaries.

The tallest tree in Virginia, this nearly 170-foot white pine (Pinus strobus) grows in Ramsey's Draft, a wilderness area in Augusta County. A fast-growing species, white pine can grow up to 3 feet a year. It can be differentiated from yellow pine by the number of needles in its leaf bundles. White pines have five needles per bundle; yellow pines have two or three.

LOBLOLLY PINE, DINWIDDIE AND CAROLINE COUNTIES

When James Coleburn visited Dinwiddie County's big loblolly pine in 1967, he didn't know he was seeing Waverly Burruss's kitchen table, Judge Richard Lewis's courtroom bench, Dudley Allen's coffee table, Inez Winn's mantel, Billy Gravvatt's bed, and the gavel that calls the Ford-Hebron-Wilson Ruritan Club to order every first Thursday night. The only thing Coleburn, editor of the Blackstone *Courier Record*, knew was that he was seeing a monumental tree. "I wondered how I could have lived in Dinwiddie for twenty or thirty years without seeing it," he reported. "And I thought it was criminal that all our school children hadn't seen it." Soon, by helping to spread the word about the tree and create a nature trail to it, Coleburn and others had turned the tree, which turned out to be the world's largest loblolly pine, into something of a local attraction. Its fame was short-lived, however, because a 1976 lightning strike, coupled with pine bark beetle damage, killed the tree, and it was cut down in 1976.

Thus began this legendary tree's second, also illustrious, life as furniture, paneling, beams, pen holders, jewelry boxes, pipe boxes, gavels, and more. The tree, 199 feet tall and 17 feet 3 inches in circumference, yielded 9,000 board feet of lumber—enough, some said, to build an entire house with one tree. (An ordinary loblolly pine yields about 500 to 600 board feet of lumber.) Perhaps the most striking of the products created from the world champion Dinwiddie pine, however, were the "cookies"—cross-cut rounds—still on display in forestry offices across the state—showing that, based on tree rings, the tree was between 220 to 230 years old when it was cut down.

The Dinwiddie loblolly pine was exceptional, but the tree exemplifies (in exaggerated form) qualities that make loblolly pine (*Pinus taeda*) one of

Virginia's most valuable trees. This tall, fast-growing species is often the first tree to colonize open land, earning it the common name "old field pine," and, because of its rapid growth, straight trunk, and strong wood, it is the pine of choice for most Virginia pine plantations managed for commercial lumber and other wood products. Virginia has approximately 3 million acres of pine forest (a decline from the 6.2 million acres in 1940), and more than half of that acreage consists of loblolly pines growing in a "crop-like" arrangement. How pine plantations are managed varies, but a pine plantation managed on a 40- to 50-year cycle (like the one illustrated on the right), might be thinned for the first time 10 to 20 years after planting (taking out inferior trees, which are used to make pulp and paper), thinned again about 10 years later (taking out more valuable timber used to make small saw logs, pallets, and packaging), and finally, after 40 to 50 years, cleared of the highest quality pines used to make products like large saw timber, veneer, plywood, furniture, flooring, and trim.

In Virginia, no native tree contributes as much to human housing as the loblolly pine, and the tree is essential to other species as well. In the Nature Conservancy's Piney Grove Preserve in Sussex, for example, loblolly pines over 80 years old provide habitat for the state's last viable population of the red cockaded woodpecker—an endangered species that requires pines with heartwood deep and soft enough to accommodate their nesting chambers. Virginia's pine forests also provide nesting sites for ospreys and bald eagles, as well as prime habitat for pine warblers and brown-headed nuthatches.

In the landscape, loblolly pine is a tree that creates stately columns of soaring trunks and establishes the "cathedral feeling" in many yards. As a valuable timber tree, it also reminds us that trees can be as important after their lifetimes as during them.

The world's largest loblolly pine grew in Dinwiddie until 1976. Photo (taken in the 1950s) courtesy of the Virginia Forestry Association.

Slightly more than half of Virginia's pines now grow in pine plantations like this one, Burke Woodland, in Caroline County.

chapter eight MIGHTY OAKS

From the day our first tree nominations began rolling in, it became clear oaks would far surpass all other trees in numbers nominated and that the enthusiasm expressed for them would be enormous. We shouldn't have been surprised. There's an interesting database maintained by the U.S. Forest Service that lists the total biomass of all live trees on forest land in Virginia, and five of the top ten species on that list are oaks. In fact, although yellow poplar tops the list, and loblolly pine is second, if you add together the biomass of the top five oaks (chestnut oak, white oak, northern red oak, scarlet oak, and black oak, in that order), you find that the estimated biomass of those oaks taken together is 450,000,000 tons, compared with the 221,000,000 tons for tulip-poplar. That's a lot of tree weight and a lot of oaks to make their way into the lives, hearts, homes, and hearths of Virginians.

So we added this chapter devoted exclusively to oaks—and, although we tried hard to choose a representative sample of native oak species (there are about 28 in Virginia), white oaks, which live the longest and therefore have the longest connections to Virginia's people and landscapes, hogged the spotlight. "White oaks are Virginia's finest tree, period," one arborist told us, and if the number of white oaks we encountered over 6 feet in diameter with wide-spreading crowns is any indication, they are also the trees that most often achieve the classic form, shape, and size people expect of a remarkable tree (at least when they are grown in the open, as opposed to a forest setting, as most of our featured oaks are).

In our section describing the Powhatan post oak (page 162), you will find a description of the difference between the two broad groups of oaks, the red oaks and the white oaks, but something the oaks have in common is more relevant here: the acorn. Our appreciation of oaks, their size and longevity, is tied up with our knowledge of their humble beginnings in that small fruit. That the greatest things come from the smallest (*de minimis maxima*) is nowhere better illustrated than in the oak, and the acorn-to-oak miracle is more impressive than most people even realize. Not only do more than 180 different kinds of birds and mammals want to eat the nutritious little capped nuts oaks produce, but acorns have other reasons to fear for their safety. In one study cited by Richard Ketchum in *The Secret Life of the Forest*, scientists tracked the fates of the 15,000 acorns produced by one oak in one year. Eighty-three percent were eaten by deer and other animals, 6 percent were attacked by weevils and insect larvae, and most of the remaining acorns were naturally imperfect. Of the less than 1 percent that actually sprouted, half died as seedlings. You wouldn't want to bet on the survival of an acorn, much less on its growth into an oak several centuries old.

And yet look at the tree on the left. In a world where people seem hungry for inspiration (and get a steady diet of confusing information and conflicting opinions instead), here is something irrefutable: this oak from an acorn grew.

White oak (Quercus alba), Cumberland County

White Oak, Cumberland County

The country roads narrow to tractor paths before reaching the Cumberland white oak, not too far from Columbia, in central Virginia, but this humble approach seems to intensify, rather than diminish, the majesty of the tree. Over 7 feet in diameter with a thick, rounded crown and limbs that spread horizontally to cover an area 120 feet wide, the tree has been known to Cumberland County residents for decades but unknown to all but a few tree aficionados in other parts of the state. Its current owner, Ryne Johnson, is the great grandson of G. A. Richardson, who reported in 1976 (to the *Farmville Herald*), that the tree hadn't changed much since the time he bought the property in 1941, except that its limbs had gotten longer and lower.

According to Richardson, when he moved into the home behind the tree in 1941, he was able to drive under its limbs in "an old high wheel wagon" to unload furniture at the front door of his home, but by the 1970s he was having to stoop to walk under limbs as "big as any tree in the woods." According to Johnson, his great grandfather gave him rides on a 75-foot limb that almost touched the ground. "He would put me on the limb and then pull on the lower branches and I would ride it like a horse," says Johnson. That limb has been removed, but another massive, low-slung limb now stretches westward from the trunk over 60 feet and reaches down at the tip to invite climbers aboard.

When Ryne Johnson bought the property in 2000, the area under the white oak had grown up in weeds and pioneer species. "You could hardly see the trunk of the tree, the land was so overgrown. Everything under the canopy was covered with 6- to 7-foot cedars, dogwoods, locusts, poison oak," he says. Johnson set about clearing

out under the tree (and clearing away the remnants of his great grandfather's house), but he did most of the work slowly, and by hand, because he didn't want to bring in heavy equipment that might damage the tree. The result is a tree that seems unbothered without being neglected in a landscape that seems managed without being fussed over.

How old the tree is no one knows. Local tree lovers believe it to be 800 to 900 years old, but this is a stretch, given the fact that the maximum life span typically reported for a white oak is 400 to 600 years, with the oldest scientifically dated white oak listed as 464 years old. There is evidence, however, that the area around the tree may, in fact, have once been an Indian campground, as family lore holds, because, according to Ryne Johnson, "my great-grandfather had a jar full of arrowheads he found in the field around the tree."

For its size and seeming age, the tree seems to be in remarkably good shape—a lost limb here, a rotting knothole there, but still staunch and sturdy. This tree, in fact, may be following the career course typical of many white oaks, which are "200 years growing, 200 years living, and 200 years dying." The importance of those last 200 years can't be overestimated, since some naturalists believe the most productive years of a tree's life are those in which it begins to senesce and its decaying wood becomes home to invertebrates, small animals, and cavity-nesting birds. What is certainly true about this tree is that, in its above-ground root architecture alone—a warren of knobs, woody ridges and moldy cavities—it provides homes for insects and animals galore, and any child visiting this tree in the twenty-first century will be thrilled not just with its potential as a climbing tree but with the fence lizards in its craggy roots.

With a spread of 120 feet, the canopy of the Cumberland white oak (Quercus alba) covers almost half an acre, and its crown has the massive presence of a thunder cloud.

WHITE OAK, ALBEMARLE COUNTY

The Earlysville Oak

It was tempting to illustrate the Earlysville white oak only in its protective cloak of fog. That way, the viewer wouldn't see the heavy equipment and construction fencing that surrounded it. But the story of the Earlysville white oak includes a section on "how to survive heavy construction," and it seemed important to include it.

This imposing tree, the second largest white oak in Virginia, once grew behind the tiny Rivanna Post Office and General Store, where it was a familiar neighborhood feature. Earlier, it may have witnessed General Custer passing through this area (burning the nearby bridge over the Rivanna River after he crossed it). But it is neither foot nor equestrian traffic that passes the tree now: it is air traffic at the nearby Charlottesville-Albemarle Airport, and it is the proximity of the airport that accounts for this new chapter in the tree's life story.

Both the relocation of the highway around the airport and the extension of a runway safety area resulted in heavy construction that might have doomed this tree. Fortunately, not only was there strong community support for the tree but arborists took the steps necessary to protect it.

Because construction damage is the most common cause of tree decline in urban areas, the Earlysville oak's experience can serve as a case study in how to protect trees during construction. A tree protection zone—fencing or other barrier defining the area into which people, vehicles, or materials should not intrude—is crucial. To protect tree roots (the majority of which are in the top 12 to 24 inches of soil under the tree and often extend into an area well beyond the drip line of the canopy), the protection zone of an open-grown tree (which usually has a wide canopy) should extend at least to the tree's drip line and preferably beyond.

One rule of thumb for determining how big a tree's root protection zone should be is this: it should cover an area with a radius equal in feet to the diameter of the tree trunk in inches. For example, the root protection zone

around a tree with a trunk 36 inches in diameter would have a radius of at least 36 feet. According to Virginia Tech forest researcher Susan Day, for a very large, very sensitive, or very special tree, the typical tree protection zone is generally increased by a factor of 50 percent or more, and even if a tree's root protection zone is respected during construction, the tree will need special care and attention during periods of drought.

Among the insults trees experience from nearby construction are soil compaction, grade changes (both lowering and raising the grade can damage a tree), trenching for utilities (which severs roots), and chemical spills. The latter doesn't have to be a toxic waste spill; it can be something as seemingly innocuous as washing out a concrete truck (which raises soil pH), dumping paint thinner, or applying weed-and-feed fertilizer (which contains herbicide). Storing heavy materials on tree roots (as well as driving or parking on them) damages trees because it compresses the soil, reducing the "pore space" that is necessary for air, water, and roots to move through the soil.

To appreciate the value of tree protection zones, one need look no further than to the contrast between the areas inside and outside the Earlysville oak's construction fence. Inside the fence, the area encompassing the Earlysville oak looked like a scene from *The Wind in the Willows*—with the tree's massive trunk, craggy roots, crannies, and hidey holes suggesting an environment as inviting to forest creatures as it had always been. Outside the fence, by contrast, was all savaged subsoil, stacked building materials, and heavy equipment. Although tree damage from construction often doesn't show up until many years after it was inflicted, the Earlysville oak seems to have survived its brush with road widening and airport expanding. According to Bryan Elliott, Executive Director of the airport, the only threat to the tree now, other than the vicissitudes of old age, is the unlikely chance that it would grow tall enough to penetrate navigable air space.

It took a wide root protection zone to save the Earlysville oak from nearby construction.

Poetic in the fog, this white oak (Quercus alba) *grows near the Charlottesville-Albemarle Airport.*

Southern Red Oak, Sussex County

There was a day in the evolution of the Remarkable Tree Project when it seemed two remarkable oaks grew in Grizzard, Virginia. One tree enthusiast was singing the praises of a gigantic southern red oak in this rural Sussex County community; another was equally enthusiastic about a startling cherrybark oak. How likely could it be that two oaks of such stature (112 feet tall with a diameter of 7.5 feet and spread of 96 feet) grew in Grizzard? Not very likely, as it turned out, because, as a conversation between the two enthusiasts revealed, both trees grew in a cotton field near Rt. 612. Same tree, different identifications.

Botanists at Virginia Tech finally settled the dispute, coming down on the side of southern red oak (*Quercus falcata*), but, as this mix-up illustrates, oak species are notoriously hard to identify, and southern red oak and cherrybark oak (once considered varieties of the same species) are particularly easy to confuse. Not only are southern red oak leaves more variable than those of most other oaks, but oaks in general are hard to identify by leaf shape alone. This is because the trees hybridize (producing leaves intermediate between the two parents) and because leaves on the same tree can vary depending on the age of the tree, where the leaf appears on the tree (high or low, in sun or shade), and how stressed the tree is. Southern red oak, for example, sometimes has leaves of one shape in the crown of the tree (leaves with the curved terminal lobe referred to in the tree's Latin name from "falcatus" or "scythe") and leaves

of a different shape (less deeply cut and more bell-shaped) on its lower branches.

One of Virginia's most common oaks, particularly in the Piedmont, southern red oak is valued as a street tree, a lawn tree, a forest tree, and a timber tree. Although it is not considered prime timber, southern red oak wood is hard and strong and is often used for rough lumber, railroad ties, tools, furniture, flooring, and fuel. Southern red oak is also one of the fastest growing of the oaks in the red oak group, adding to its value as a timber tree.

Unlike the wide-spreading, open-grown oak pictured here, southern red oaks grown under forest conditions typically have long, straight trunks and relatively high, rounded crowns, reflecting the competition for sunlight and space they have faced from other trees. They are also usually much smaller (with mature heights of 70 to 80 feet and diameters of 24 to 36 inches) than the champion pictured here, but many an imposing southern red oak grows in Virginia. One towering specimen, on Hull Springs Farm, overlooking tributaries of the Potomac in Westmoreland County, was cored in 1995 by a Longwood professor who estimated its age, based on tree rings, to be 350 to 400 years. The typical longevity of southern red oak (the typical age of the older trees in an old-growth stand) is reportedly 200 years, and the southern red oak's maximum longevity (the upper known maximum above which very few trees are found) is estimated to be 275 years.

This southern red oak in Sussex County is the largest of its species in the state. Its leaves (with a curved terminal lobe and two shorter lobes on the sides) resemble turkey tracks.

Chestnut Oak, Fairfax County

From a chestnut oak in Giles County used as a bear-denning tree to a chestnut oak in an Arlington urban park, nominations of chestnut oaks came in to the Remarkable Tree Project from all over Virginia. This shouldn't have been too much of a surprise, since chestnut oak is an adaptable tree and, among oaks, second only to white oak in abundance in the state, but it was a surprise to see how remarkably varied our nominations were. Chris Ludwig, Chief Biologist for the Virginia Department of Conservation and Recreation, for example, nominated a stand of chestnut oaks on Peter's Mountain in southwest Virginia. That stand, he wrote, dominates what is probably the largest (about 3,600 acres) contiguous old-growth stand remaining in Virginia. Piedmont Master Gardeners nominated a chestnut oak on a Madison County horse farm, a tree once selected as "one of the four best trees in the Piedmont." Ted, Luke, and Hannah Arrington, school-age tree enthusiasts from Bedford, nominated a yard tree that "was already a large tree on our great grandpa's dairy farm when the house was built in the early 1900s."

The chestnut oak that surprised us most, however, was the new state champion chestnut oak in Centreville (Fairfax County). Nominated by tree enthusiasts Rod Royse and Jessica Strother, this is a tree that Royse encountered in 2007 while doing church work in Centreville. "I was saying I liked trees and someone said, 'If you like trees, you've gotta see our great oak.'" Royse expected to be shown a nice tree, but he didn't expect to be shown a chestnut oak almost 6 feet in diameter, 110 feet tall, with a crown spread of 88 feet. Encountering such a tree anywhere would be a

surprise, but encountering such a tree in a subdivision is like finding a U.S. president in the supermarket line—it just doesn't happen very often. A multi-trunked tree that branches within 10 feet of the ground, the Centreville chestnut oak was reportedly carefully protected when the Little Rocky Run subdivision was developed in the 1980s, and today, although surrounded by townhouses, roads, and parking lots, it grows on a grassy knoll about four times broader than its crown. "It looks healthy and protected enough to outlive us all," says Royse.

Chestnut oak (*Quercus montana*) is a species with leaves resembling those of an American chestnut—oval with tapering ends and scalloped edges. On the dry, rocky ridges where they often grow in the wild, they are usually short, stubby trees, but they also thrive on moist, well-drained soils, and it is there that they grow largest. Chestnut oaks are relatively long-lived (to 400 years in the wild), but, as with most trees, size isn't an indicator of age, and a stunted chestnut oak on a mountaintop can be much older than a massive chestnut oak in the Piedmont.

Although it has been called "a very lovely tree" by plantsman Michael Dirr and "a fine, soldierly sort of Oak" by naturalist Donald Culross Peattie, chestnut oak is hard to find in nurseries and seldom planted. According to one arborist, the large, sweet acorns that add to the tree's value in the wild (important not just to black bears but to deer, squirrels, and other wildlife) subtract from its value in the city, where acorns pummel parked cars. Fortunately for the Centreville chestnut oak and its neighbors, the tree has been given a growing area spacious enough to accommodate both its roots and its massive acorn crops.

Often, although street signs retain tree names, the trees for which subdivision streets were named are long gone. This chestnut oak on Giant Oak Court in Centreville is an exception. In the 1980s when the surrounding townhouses were built, great care was taken to protect this chestnut oak, now a state champion.

LIVE OAK, NORFOLK

The Willoughby Oak

Unless you have contacts within the Navy, this photo provides the closest view of the Willoughby live oak you're likely to get. Protected by a substantial fence, and looking almost like a tree in captivity, the Willoughby live oak grows on the grounds of the Norfolk Naval Station, where a gate must be unlocked to visit it.

"I've never gotten this close to it myself, so this is a treat," said Patsy Kerr, the Natural Resource Manager who managed to have the gate unlocked for the Remarkable Tree team.

The fence protects the tree from too much love (and the Navy from liability—the tree being a magnet for climbers), but it seems a shame the tree must be sequestered, because it is much more impressive up close than from a distance, and it seems to want to be climbed. One long branch reaches down to the ground like a massive arm (or ladder), and a flat area on the torso of the tree is tempting to visit. As with most large trees, this one, the second largest live oak in the state, seems to expand the closer you get to it, and its massive trunk (almost 7 feet in diameter) looks older when you're able to experience its deeply fissured bark up close. Of all the live oaks the Remarkable Tree crew

visited in Virginia, this one seemed oldest, and it is easy to believe, as its interpretive sign claims, that the tree could be 500 to 600 years old. Also easy to believe—partly because of the shape of the tree, with one branch reaching upward like a lookout tower—is the legend that Blackbeard once climbed the tree to scan the entrance to the Chesapeake Bay.

The Willoughby live oak (*Quercus virginiana*) seems symbolically suited to its site at the Norfolk Naval Station, since live oak wood, resistant to disease and decay, was once highly valued for shipbuilding. The first woodlands preserved by the U.S. government were preserved to secure the supply of live oaks for shipbuilding (1799), and the USS *Constitution* ("Old Ironsides"), got its nickname from the strength of its live-oak construction. The advent of iron and steel warships reduced the need for live oak wood, but it still seems fitting that at the Norfolk Naval Station not only is the Willoughby oak a revered presence, but new live oaks are planted each year on Arbor Day.

"If they had to give it a fence, I'm glad they gave it such a fine one," says Natural Resource Manager Patsy Kerr, referring to the protective fence that gives the Willoughby live oak the look of a caged animal.

Norfolk's oldest living resident? Believed to be over 500 years old, the Willoughby live oak has often been called "Norfolk's oldest living resident." Because there is a larger, and possibly older, live oak in Norfolk, this claim could be challenged, but the tree is certainly among the area's oldest living residents. It, and nearby Willoughby Bay, were named for Sir Thomas Willoughby, who settled Norfolk County around 1621.

WILLOW OAK, IRVINGTON

On the grounds of Chesapeake Academy, this Irvington landmark anchors the soccer field and shades graduation ceremonies, but it also stops traffic on Steamboat Road when tree-loving tourists happen by. One of the five largest willow oaks in Virginia, it has the enormous fluted trunk characteristic of old willow oaks (this one is 7.5 feet in diameter), but it is unusual in that it branches relatively close to the ground. Ten feet off the ground, this willow oak has limbs as big as most other trees' trunks, and to stand under it is to feel miniaturized.

No one knows exactly how old the tree is, but local historian Frances Chase Simmons helped us establish that it was probably planted around 1880, when James Christian Kirkmyer built a house on the property it occupies. (Kirkmyer's granddaughter, age 85, believes her grandfather planted the tree around the same time he built the house.) Mrs. Simmons also sent us a copy of a photo taken between 1905 and 1909 in which the tree is barely visible on the east side of what was then Irvington Street (now Steamboat Road), and the photo is priceless for connecting this tree to a time when the dirt road in front of it was traveled by mule-drawn carts and drays drawn by oxen. Such pictures confirm what we already know—that many human lifetimes, and their accompanying accoutrements, pass in the lifetime of an oak.

This willow oak (Quercus phellos) connects students at Chesapeake Academy to Irvington history. "I think of it as symbolic of our mission. The stronger your roots are, the broader your canopy can be," says teacher Julie Zimmerman.

White Oak, Blacksburg

"They told us it was 300 to 400 years old when we moved here, and that was 45 years ago," says Elizabeth McCann, owner of this massive white oak near the corner of Eaken Street and Preston Avenue in Blacksburg. No one has cored the tree, so its age is unknown, but when similar white oaks on the lawn of The Grove, Virginia Tech's President's house, about half a mile away, were removed between the 1970s and 1990s, growth rings on their stumps revealed they had germinated in 1452, 1518, and 1715. Those ages are particularly relevant to people in this neighborhood, because it was once a part of Draper's Meadows, site of a 1755 Indian attack that may have been witnessed by these trees.

In McCann's lifetime, the tree has witnessed events of an entirely different sort. It has sheltered neighborhood picnics, posed for Virginia Tech art students, been measured by dozens of Brownies. How many Brownies standing shoulder to shoulder does it take to surround this tree? Seventeen or eighteen. People ring the doorbell to ask for acorns and drive by slowly after storms, just to see how the old oak fared. The tree is a particular favorite of the Virginia Tech Corps of Cadets, whose members once stood under it to honor Col. James McCann (husband of Elizabeth), who helped lead the Corps for 14 years. The Cadet band, known as the "Highty-Tighties," practices each year on the street in front of the tree, and Maj. George R. McNeill offered the entire Corps of Cadets to pose with the tree the day we photographed. We decided one symbolic tuba player would be enough.

This old white oak (Quercus alba) between Draper Street and Preston Avenue in Blacksburg is over 17 feet in circumference and has a 116-foot crown spread. People are forever asking its owner, Elizabeth McCann, who has lived in its shade for 45 years, if she's not afraid it will fall on the house. She is not, partly because she's been told (correctly) that white oaks seldom fall over; when they die, they usually die standing and break up one branch at a time. To McCann, the tree is not liability, "it's my air conditioner."

WILLOW OAK, CHESTERFIELD COUNTY

"You can't miss it."

"It's easy to spot."

"You'll see it immediately."

Those were just three of the assurances various nominators of this oak provided in their directions to the tree. And they were right. With a massive trunk (over 7 feet in diameter), soaring canopy (nearly as tall as the seven-story building behind it), and incredible spread (over 60 feet in most directions from the trunk), the tree not only dominates the ground it grows on but holds its visual ground relative to the eye-catching building behind it. In fact, in a reversal of the usual fortunes of trees saved in office parks, the Boulders willow oak seems enhanced in its new surroundings. There is emphasis, it seems, in the contrast between the big, the old, and the weather-worn with the sleek, the new, and the climate-controlled.

At one time, it was thought this tree might be two trees that had grown together, but coring in the 1980s proved it was one tree—and a tree over 200 years old at that time. Because of its age, the National Arborist Association declared it a "significant tree," and in 1987 they and the International Society of Arboriculture commissioned a plaque reminding visitors that the tree would have been growing when the Constitution was signed in 1787.

According to Lee Euting, owner of the grounds maintenance company at Boulders Office Park, both the site of Boulders III (the building behind the tree) and the parkway that enters the park were adjusted to accommodate the tree. The tree was also carefully protected during construction. Euting says natural drainage patterns were maintained and the area under the tree canopy was protected from encroachment by construction equipment. The tree has also had professional tree care since the 1980s, and everyone who visits is struck not only by its size and form but also by the generous apron of mulch beneath it. Unlike the narrow mounds of mulch ill-advisedly applied to many

trees (deep collars that creep up onto the trunk and trap moisture there), this relatively shallow apron of mulch stretches all the way out to the tips of the tree canopy but leaves the trunk itself free to breathe.

The Boulders willow oak was obviously an open-grown tree—one that came up in a field or other open area where its branches could spread wide from youth—and it seems likely it has been in close proximity to human activity throughout much, if not all, of its lifetime. The Boulders property includes former agricultural land (farmed by a family that included 14 children), springs that provided mineral water (and later water for beer and soft drinks) to Richmonders, as well as the site of a once-popular picnic ground and a pony farm. Within 100 feet of the tree, Euting and his crews found half a dozen ice pits—holes once about 20 feet long, 20 feet wide, and 8 feet deep that Euting believes were used in the early 1900s to store blocks of ice cut from nearby Jahnke Lake. (The site of the ice pits is now under a parking lot; the site of Jahnke Lake, drained in 1913, is now a subdivision.)

To many local residents, the Boulders willow oak represents the last living link to neighborhood history. "When we started protecting the tree," says Euting, "people started coming by and telling us stories." Some said the last duel fought in Chesterfield was fought under the tree; others said the last hanging in Chesterfield had taken place on the tree, and still others said Union army supply forces had camped under the tree during the siege of Richmond. "Those are the three stories I heard over and over."

Neighborhood history of a different sort continues to accumulate under the tree. Tredegar Corporation, one of the occupants of Boulders III, holds its annual picnic under the tree, and scores of office workers—some of them with bird's eye views—eat their lunches while looking at the tree.

"I think it's fantastic they saved that tree," says Fran Crumpler, whose office on the third floor of Boulders III overlooks the tree. "It's like snowing leaves out there when the wind blows and the leaves are flyin'."

The weather-worn willow oak (Quercus phellos) at Boulder's Office Park in Chesterfield stands in contrast to the sleek, modern building behind it.

BLACK OAK, PRINCE GEORGE COUNTY

lack oak is usually described as a medium-sized tree only 50 to 60 feet tall, but this state champion black oak is 111 feet tall and has a crown spread of over 134 feet. Neither of those dimensions, however, is the aspect of this tree that impresses people in its presence; it's the tree's volume. This black oak is almost 23 feet around at the base, and seems even stouter 20 feet off the ground. It grows on Brandon Plantation, although not on the "cultivated" part of the plantation; it occupies an abandoned field on the banks of the James near some of the farm buildings that serve the property. "That must be the tree at the end of Point Road," Brandon gardener Kris Jones told us when we stopped to inquire about the tree. "I've actually hugged it before."

Native to the eastern and mid-western U.S. and common in Virginia, black oak is seldom mentioned in elementary school tree lists, possibly because it is hard to identify. Its shade leaves (leaves that grow in low light) resemble those of the northern red oak and its sun leaves (leaves that receive more sunlight) resemble those of southern red oak. You really need to know your oaks to recognize a black oak (which is named for the nearly black color on old trunks), but there is a clue in the tree's Latin name, *Quercus velutina.*

There is a velvety fuzz (pubescence) on the undersides of black oak leaves (a fuzz that rubs off easily, unlike that of the southern red oak), and the black oak's leaf buds are fuzzy, too. Sometimes referred to as "yellowbark oak," black oak also has orange-yellow inner bark, and this inner bark, used fresh, dried, or powdered, was once a source of yellow pigment to dye cloth, including calico prints.

Black oak, which often has a short, crooked trunk and can appear scraggly in comparison to more elegant oaks, is seldom used in landscaping, but, as naturalist Donald Culross Peattie once observed, "as a part of the hard, untamed, original silva [of North America], it has a rough, unbending grandeur of its own." To appreciate just how impressive Virginia's black oaks can be, visit the Remarkable Tree website, where extraordinary black oaks are featured in Appomattox, Augusta, Buckingham, Carroll, Charles City, Fairfax, and King William counties. The trees in Carroll, Charles City, and Fairfax counties are almost as large as the tree in Prince George, proving that black oak deserves a place in Virginia's "oak pantheon."

"Have you ever thought when you sit by a tree, maybe it's hugging you?" asked Kris Jones, gardener at Brandon Plantation, as she approached this state champion black oak in Prince George County.

White Oak, Albemarle County

Arborist Michael Abbott, who cares for the remarkable white oak at Emmanuel Episcopal Church in Greenwood, is something of an oak connoisseur. He's seen so many fine ones that he saves his highest praise for those over 50 inches in diameter. "There are lots of fine old oaks in the 30- to 40-inch diameter range," he says, "and they are often spectacular trees, but an oak with a diameter over 50 inches is worth going out of your way to see." By Abbott's logic, the white oak at Emmanuel Episcopal Church is worth traveling *way* out of your way to see, because it is 70 inches (nearly 6 feet) in diameter.

Your first impression of this tree is that you should have had to work harder to find it. Something so impressive should, it seems, require at least half a day's hike to reach, but this white oak is within a stone's throw of Rt. 250 on the grounds of historic Emmanuel Episcopal Church—an easy jaunt from Charlottesville. The tree, in fact, once grew right beside the highway, but Rt. 250 has been moved, giving the tree some breathing room. Today, it is protected not only by an arborist (who also cares for about 30 other fine trees on the property) but also by a sign warning "Thou Shalt Not Park" under the tree.

The tree's shape and setting both contribute to its charisma. Wider than it is tall, the tree seems stout and squatty—sort of a sumo wrestler of a tree. One astounding limb travels almost parallel, and only about a yard above, to the ground for over 60 feet. "I don't know how it stays up," says parish administrator Janice Fisher. According to Michael Abbott, this limb, and the overall shape of the tree, suggest it has always grown in the open and that it never needed to reach up for light. He believes the tree must have always had a dependable source of water (perhaps a nearby spring) and that favorable conditions, not age alone, account for the tree's size. Whatever its age (parishioners believe it to be 400 years old), it is remarkable not only for

its size and shape but for its setting, where one can picture decades of church-goers and many a bride walking by on the now-crumbling brick sidewalk that passes in front of the oak, and where one can view the Blue Ridge Mountains through the tree's enormous branches. Because the tree is located near the bottom of the hill leading up to the church office, one can also look down and into its canopy in a way that is seldom possible.

Janice Fisher believes the care this tree has received has prolonged its life, but she notes that much of arborist Abbott's advice has involved refraining from doing things to the tree rather than doing things to it. "You don't want to change anything," says Abbott, noting that caregivers can actually harm old trees by giving them more water or nutrients than they are accustomed to, because old trees are not adaptable. What has been particularly helpful to the tree is the "Thou Shalt Not Park" sign, because it keeps cars out of the root zone where they would compact the soil. Tree roots (and microorganisms that assist them) need the air that is squeezed out of soil when it is compressed by cars, heavy equipment, or heavy foot traffic.

Visitors will find over a dozen fine trees, all professionally cared for, on the Emmanuel Church grounds. "The churchyard is filled with gracious oaks," says parishioner Jack Scruby, who believes the white oak pictured here was probably a commanding presence on the site when the church was established in 1860. Scruby's sisters played in the branches of the tree in the early 1900s, when, says Scruby, "it looked just like it does now." That this tree has a special place in the hearts and minds of parishioners is brought home by a story Janice Fisher tells about the church's rector who once praised the property's most famous white oak as "the great Emmanuel elm." "He's a city boy," says Fisher, "so we forgave him. But we never let him forget it."

West of Charlottesville in Albemarle County, this white oak (Quercus alba) *at Emmanuel Episcopal Church provides perfect perches for children.*

WILLOW OAK, EASTVILLE

I t's one thing to find a giant tree in a national park or out-of-the-way habitat; it's another to find one, like this former champion willow oak, in a front yard. In neighborhoods, we expect the familiar—familiar sizes, shapes, patterns, and a tree that breaks the norm seems all the more startling in proximity to the familiar. The analogy isn't perfect, but the super-sized willow oak in Eastville is like a Big Gulp at a tea party—it's that out of scale.

Located on Willow Oak Road (named for the tree, of course) in Ralph and Lit Dodd's front yard, this tree was probably already growing on the site when the Dodd's house was built in 1895. How much earlier it was there, no one knows, but buildings almost around the corner from the Dodd's home date back as far as 1731, and the tree may have even been around when the Northampton Courthouse was moved to Eastville in 1677.

Today, the tree is notable not only for its size (305 inches in girth, 112 feet tall, and 136 feet in average crown spread) but also for its form and color. In winter the tracery of its tallest branches against the sky appears as intricate as lace, and the tree's trunk, like that of old willow oaks generally, is characterized by deep, vertical indentations, making it look like a fluted column. (Watching rainwater run down such channels is like seeing a stream flow perpendicular to the ground.) The tree has lost a large limb—"That limb just fell off one day. It wasn't storming, it wasn't windy. It just got tired," says Ralph Dodd—and a wound near the bottom of its trunk supports worrisome shelf fungi, but the tree seems otherwise healthy and is actually more interesting for its signs of age. Putty-colored lichen colors the tops of its branches like icing, and the lichen is so thick on the tree's lower trunk and buttressing roots it looks like someone poured leftover concrete over them. (They didn't.)

As a species, willow oak (*Quercus phellos*) grows best in the Piedmont and Coastal Plain, where it is often planted as a street tree. It makes a fine street tree because it transplants more easily than most oaks, tolerates pollution, has few disease or pest problems, and grows faster than most oaks. The only downside of the willow oak's popularity (other than potential monotony) is the danger inherent in planting too much of any one species. If a disease or insect agent moves in to target that species, entire streetscapes can be wiped out as they were when Dutch elm disease devastated the American elm. Nurserymen also grow weary of reminding homeowners and landscapers that the willow oak will eventually grow *very* large, but this photograph, or a drive down Willow Oak Road in Eastville, Virginia, should help prove that point.

This willow oak in Eastville, on the Eastern Shore, looks all the bigger in contrast to its frequent companion, Shug, the cat.

POST OAK, POWHATAN COUNTY

Margaret Christian, 96, enjoys sharing her post oak. "It's so refreshing to know that young people are interested in it," she says, noting that many have stopped by to see her tree and some have sent her photos and thank-you notes. At one time, Mrs. Christian's post oak was considered the largest in the state. That honor has now gone to a taller post oak, an impressive street tree in Arlington, but the Powhatan post oak has a broader crown spread (107 feet), is nearly as big in circumference (217 inches), and won the competition for inclusion here on "beauty points." Growing on farmland that has been in the Christian family since the 1700s, the tree may also be quite old. According to one relative, when William Christian described the tree in 1992, he said the tree looked the same then as it did over 75 years earlier, when he used to rest plow horses under it.

Native to Virginia, post oaks are slow-growing but long-lived. The average post oak lives about 250 years, and some live to be 450. They are usually stout trees, characterized by broad, dense, rounded crowns and spreading branches that are often somewhat gnarled or twisted. Post oak wood is extremely durable in contact with soil (hence the tree's use for fence posts and its common name), and post oak leaves are recognizable for their leathery texture and unusual shape. The leaves have a broad upper portion (defined by rounded lobes) and narrow lower portion, suggestive of a cross.

Post oaks belong to what naturalists describe as "the white oak group," a confusing label that nevertheless provides one way of differentiating among oaks. This descriptive system places all oaks into two broad groups, the white oak group and the red oak group, which are defined by, among other things, the shapes of the trees' leaves and the length of time it takes their acorns to mature. Oaks in the white oak group (which includes white oak, post oak, chestnut oak, swamp white oak, overcup oak, chinquapin oak, and bur oak, among others) have leaves that are smooth-lobed (meaning their edges are rounded, not bristle-tipped), and their acorns mature in one year. Oaks in the red oak group (which includes northern and southern red oak, scarlet oak, black oak, pin oak, and willow oak, among others), have bristle-tipped leaves and acorns that take two years to mature. Anyone hopelessly confused should take comfort in the fact that even experts find oaks notoriously hard to identify.

Adding to the confusion is the fact that oaks sometimes hybridize, producing leaves intermediate between parents of different species, and the fact that leaves on even the same tree can vary in shape and size based on the tree's age, its condition (how stressed it is), and how much sun its leaves receive (shaded leaves are often larger than "sun leaves"). The good news is that some oaks *are* fairly easy to identify, and, because the post oak is one of them, it's one of the first oaks you might want to add to your repertoire.

Near the end of a long lane in Powhatan County, this fine, spreading post oak (Quercus stellata) has been shading the Christian farm for as long as anyone in the family can remember.

Northern Red Oak, Washington County

"At first I didn't know how, but now I'm gettin' to be a whiz at it," says Jacob Heath, 9, describing how he's learned to measure trees. Jacob knows his local trees and their dimensions the way some kids do their baseball statistics, and his interest in champions led to the November 2007 "discovery" of this co-champion northern red oak in Washington County. Jacob and other members of his 4-H club participated in a Big Tree contest, complete with awards ceremony, which honored 20 children for the trees they had found and measured in their county. Jacob's was the biggest, his local extension agent nominated it to Virginia's Big Tree Program, and it turned out to be a state co-champion. (A similar-sized northern red oak grows at Bull Run Park in Fairfax.)

This tree, which has branches larger than the trunks of most red oaks, would be impressive in any setting, but the countryside surrounding this one contributes to its grandeur. Surrounded by hundreds of acres of cattle fields, one sees mountains through its canopy, rolling vistas from every angle. The area seems remote and accessible only to farm vehicles, but Jacob and his father know the trees on this land near Lodi (population "fifty people and several thousand cows") well. Jacob's father grew up about a mile from this farm and "walked through its fields all the time," hunting groundhogs, looking for arrowheads, heading to the South Fork of the Holston River to fish. "My dad saw it as a teenager and he showed me," Jacob explains proudly.

Northern red oaks are most abundant (and most comfortable) in Virginia's mountains, but the tree grows in almost every Virginia county. At high elevations, the tree will grow even on poor soils, but in the eastern part of the state and at lower elevations, it needs more fertile soil and a relatively cool aspect (like a north-facing slope). Northern red

This co-champion northern red oak (Quercus rubra) was nominated to Virginia's big tree program by 9-year-old Jacob Heath. It is over 7.5 feet in diameter and 108 feet tall.

oak was devastated by the gypsy moth in the 1980s and 1990s as it progressed through the mountains of northwest Virginia, and the tree, which some scientists speculate became established in Virginia during the Little Ice Age, may be particularly susceptible to these and other stresses, because it isn't perfectly suited to today's warmer climate.

Among the red oaks, northern red oak is considered the highest-quality oak. It tends to grow taller and straighter than other red oaks, and it has fewer knots in its marketable timber. Its heavy, hard, close-grained wood is exported all over the world to make furniture, cabinets, and flooring. Northern red oak is also valued as a shade tree, and landscapers like it for one of the same reasons lumbermen do—it grows relatively fast. No oak is a speed demon, but relative to many other oaks, northern red oak is more hare than turtle, sometimes averaging a growth rate of 2 feet a year over a 10-year period.

Like so many of the oaks, which have variable forms and inter-breed, northern red oak (*Quercus rubra*) is something of a challenge to accurately identify, but here are some clues. Its leaves, usually about 5 to 10 inches long, have seven to eleven bristle-tipped lobes and are less deeply cut than those of most other oaks in the red oak group. Northern red oak bark is also distinctive in that it has something often described as "ski tracks"— light-gray longitudinal lines that run down the center of its ridges. Northern red oak acorns, which take two years to mature, have caps that cover only a quarter of the acorn or less, and they are somewhat flattened, like berets. Although not so dramatic or obvious as to be of much help in identifying the tree, characteristics that help explain the "red" in the northern red oak's name include the tree's petioles (stalks that attach the leaves to the stem), reddish interior wood, and reddish to orange-brown fall foliage.

CHINQUAPIN OAK, ROCKINGHAM COUNTY

This grand old oak, the largest chinquapin oak in Virginia, grows on the west side of the South Fork of the Shenandoah River, where it is beloved by canoeists, local residents, and other visitors, some of whom have been baptized in the waters beneath its canopy. Its massive trunk (6.8 feet in diameter) leans toward the river at an angle that makes its bulk seem all the more impressive, and its wide crown (102 feet) shelters an area that includes inviting grassy shoreline and sparkling, gentle rapids. In the presence of this tree, it is easy to imagine the historic associations that owner Edward Strickler, whose Rockingham County forbears go back "five greats," has with the tree and its environs. He describes his grandfather's mill, which once operated just 150 feet downstream from the tree, the "swing bridge" that crossed nearby until a 1942 flood took it out, and a Civil War cannonball that "some older people" believe is embedded in the tree. He had not heard the story one local historian shared with us—that the tree grows where Stonewall Jackson and his troops crossed the river during the Civil War—but he believes it's quite likely.

Chinquapin oak (*Quercus muehlenbergii*) is not a common Virginia oak, but it grows in about two-thirds of Virginia's counties, where it is usually found growing on soils that range from weakly acidic to alkaline. The trees are usually relatively small (only 40 to 60 feet tall), but 160-foot specimens grew in the forests of yore, and a surprising number of large chinquapin oaks, including fine specimens in Page County, Tazewell County, and the cities of Winchester and Suffolk, were nominated to Virginia's Remarkable Tree Project. The tree has leaves similar to those of an American chestnut (oblong with shallowly notched edges), and resembles the shrubby Allegheny chinquapin, *Castanea pumila*, in that both the shrub and the tree have chestnut-like leaves. The name "chinquapin" derives from an Algonquian Indian word for chestnut, and both the nuts of the chinquapin shrub and the sweet acorns of the chinquapin oak were prized by American Indians.

Waterloo Mill Lane, a gravel, dead-end road that Edward Strickler's grandfather helped "cut in" long before it had a name, runs quite close to the champion chinquapin oak, and although visitors need to respect the rights of adjacent property owners, Strickler welcomes visitors to his property on which the tree grows. "Oh, my, no!" he says of concerns that tree lovers might prove too numerous. "We try to keep the grass cut to make it attractive to people."

Many paddlers, including students and teachers in the Chesapeake Bay Foundation's Virginia Watershed Education Program, stop to admire this state champion chinquapin oak as they travel the South Fork of the Shenandoah River. It grows near the remnants of Waterloo Mill, in McGayheysville, near Elkton.

chapter nine TREE PLACES

Trees are democratic. Given equally good growing conditions, they're as happy to grow in a poor neighborhood as a rich one, as willing to thrive in an ordinary backyard as on an estate. That's one reason searching for remarkable trees is so rewarding—it leads you into neighborhoods and niches that have nothing to do with status and income and have everything to do with soil, water, and room to grow. On the other hand, through accident or design, some neighborhoods, parks, and natural areas *are* richer in trees than others, and it is in this chapter that we want to highlight some of those.

We realized early on that there was no way we would be able to visit every great "Tree Place" in the state—there were too many of them and too few of us—but we have visited scores of them, and many more, beloved by their nominators, are described on the Remarkable Trees of Virginia website.

It is our hope that by calling attention to these tree places, not only will more people visit them, and places like them, but that people will begin to see and appreciate trees in the places they already frequent. Trees often fade into the background of our experiences, serving merely as backdrop to stores, signs, houses, highways, and other landmarks of immediate relevance to us. Sometimes seeing trees can be just a matter of bringing that background to the foreground—paying attention to the black locust trees along the interstate, for example, or looking for the hollies among the tombstones in your local cemetery, or just giving the river birches in the mall parking lot a second look. As most tree lovers know, the best places to get to know trees are usually close by. They are places where you can visit not just trees in general but *particular* trees that you can get to know in all seasons and in all kinds of weather, and for that reason, you may discover one of the best tree places is your own backyard.

Here we draw attention to some of the places where you might expect to find remarkable trees (state and national parks, for example) and some of those where you might not (urban forests). Places that have been protected for reasons unrelated to the trees that grow there—cemeteries and historic homesites—also receive attention, because they can be as effective as arboreta in protecting and showcasing trees. Virginia's love affair with famous people and their homes, for example, has been a boon to architects and antiquarians, but it has also profited trees. While protecting the land that protects historic homes, keepers of Virginia's many historic homesites have—sometimes inadvertently, sometimes with great care—also protected tree habitats that might otherwise have been destroyed. Some of those homesites have become incredible places to see trees, and, while the buildings still get all the press, one wants to shout to those waiting in line to see the mansions, "Don't forget the grounds!"

With 135 acres of rolling ground, over a thousand trees inventoried by arborists, and 50 trees designated "monarchs," Hollywood Cemetery in Richmond is one of the most remarkable "tree places" in Virginia. This collection of towering oaks and tulip-poplars grows in the historic heart of the cemetery.

CEMETERY TREES

emeteries protect more than the souls of the departed; they protect trees. Think about it. Not only are cemeteries considered hallowed ground, they are usually immune to development and other land use changes. "If people continue to die, cemeteries may turn out to be natural habitats longer than woods and prairies," the eminent Michigan botanist W. H. Wagner once asserted, and it's hard to argue.

An astonishing number of trees growing in cemeteries were nominated to the Remarkable Tree Project, and we have already featured two of them (the beautiful yellowwood in Arlington Cemetery, the historic tulip-poplars at Mount Zion Baptist Church in Gloucester). Because cemeteries provide such good tree habitat, many of Virginia's state champion trees also grow in cemeteries. Virginia's former state champion American holly towers over tombstones in Hampton National Cemetery, and the state's champion honeylocust—a perfectly beautiful tree—lends its lofty eminence to gravestones in front of Fincastle United Methodist Church.

As a ride down many a rural road will reveal, big old trees are to graveyards as unmown ditches are to wildflowers: when you find one, you usually find the other. But some cemeteries are much better than others when it comes to showcasing trees. One of the best, if not *the* best, cemetery in which to see remarkable Virginia trees is Richmond's Hollywood Cemetery. Designed in 1847, Hollywood is one of the cemeteries, like Mt. Auburn in Boston, that was designed in the "rural style"—a style designed to make cemeteries more like pleasure grounds and parks than monotonous grids of tombstones. At Hollywood, a tree lover can wander the 135 acres of rolling hills overlooking the James River and downtown Richmond in the thrall of ancient hollies, oaks, tulip-poplars, magnolias, sycamores, and other tree notables. (Notable people, like Presidents James Monroe and John Tyler, are also planted there.)

Some of the "don't miss" trees at Hollywood Cemetery include the gargantuan white oak on Cedar Avenue near the grave of Captain John C. Potts, a grand tulip-poplar on Hillside Avenue, a beautiful blackgum off

Circular Avenue, old American hollies lining Eastvale Avenue, and the ancient willow oaks lining Midvale Avenue. That line of willow oaks alone—an allée that looks like a line of Corinthian columns—is reason enough to visit Hollywood Cemetery, which is open dawn to dusk, free of charge, 365 days a year. An inexpensive Historic Tree and Rose Tour Map is available at the Cherry Street entrance.

Lynchburg's Old City Cemetery is also awash in history (founded in 1806, it is one of the oldest public cemeteries in the U.S.), but it manages to seem as lively as it is old. Accoutrements like birdhouses, beehives, and fresh flowers outside the restrooms give it the air of a place enjoyed as much by the living as the dead, and its young trees are as interesting as its old ones. In a free brochure, "Roses, Shrubs, Butterflies, Medicinal Herbs, Birds, and Trees: A Horticulture Guide," you'll find a map and tree list that will help you locate many of the cemetery's finest trees, including a fabulous old pecan in the Kids' Haven Memorial Area. Hats off to Lynchburg for giving the tree not just a label, and the 1998 Heritage Tree Award, but also a swing.

And finally, Virginia's most well-known cemetery, Arlington National Cemetery, is famous for the war heroes and other notable Americans buried there, but it should also be valued for its trees—over 8,000 of them, including many remarkable specimens, all under professional care. Because of its size and the number of visitors it receives every year (over 4 million), Arlington Cemetery is less intimate than either Hollywood or Old City Cemetery, but the grandeur of the place carries over onto its trees (and vice versa). Among the "don't-miss" trees at Arlington Cemetery are the state champion paulownia (a statuesque old specimen that grows northwest of the Spanish American War Memorial) and two enormous water oaks—at one time Virginia's co-champs—that grow in Section 18 near Clayton Drive. Another haunting tree in Arlington Cemetery is the post oak near John F. Kennedy's grave. Legend has it that two months before he was assassinated, Kennedy visited the site where this tree grows—a site that his daughter Caroline had praised—and commented, "It is so beautiful, I could stay here forever."

This water oak (Quercus nigra), a former state champion, grows in Section 18 of Arlington National Cemetery. As Stephen Van Hoven, the cemetery's urban forester points out, "A cemetery is a good place to be a tree."

Safe havens: churchyards and graveyards are among the most protected habitats for trees. This honeylocust (Gleditsia triacanthos) is believed to have been planted around the time the first Fincastle United Methodist Church was built, over 200 years ago. At 107 feet tall and nearly 6 feet in diameter, it is now the largest honeylocust in the state and the second largest honeylocust in the nation.

CAMPUS TREES

"A collection of living plants at an academic institution should be comparable to that of a collection of books in the library. They are that important." So said Dr. J. T. Baldwin, legendary biologist at the College of William and Mary, where he helped establish a fine plant collection. Some of the trees planted during Dr. Baldwin's tenure are now among the finest examples of their species, and the entire William and Mary campus, as he had hoped, is a valuable "library of trees."

In the catalog of things we expect academic institutions to offer, trees seldom appear first on anyone's short list, and yet for ecological, academic, and aesthetic reasons they should. In addition to all the biological services they render, trees provide the "ambience" we expect of a college campus, that feeling of being "embowered." In return, because college campuses are land-rich, they provide sanctuaries for trees. Some campuses also enhance their commitment to trees—and students—by using their tree resources as educational tools to increase ecological and natural history literacy.

What makes a college campus a good tree place? Certainly the number and variety of trees matters, and while exotic trees can provide great interest, a good sampling of trees native to the area seems essential to a good college campus. For example, while many of the exotics on the William and Mary campus are interesting, it is in the relatively unheralded College Woods that students will find the best examples of native trees growing in their natural habitat. Sweet Briar College, with 400 acres designated as nature sanctuaries, provides a shining example of the ways in which trees in their natural habitats can be used in research and ecological study. There, not only have trees been protected in a series of preserves, but many of them, including a 45-acre mature white oak forest, have been mapped and used by researchers around the country to study forest ecology.

For a campus to be a remarkable tree place, trees need labels and visitors need maps to significant trees. Regular walking tours led by knowledgeable faculty or staff are also a bonus. We visited lots of campuses where many of the trees were labeled— what a pleasure it is to have a tree question immediately answered by a label!—but it was amazing how few had up-to-date maps that allowed a visitor to take a self-guided

A student petition helped save these old crabapples at Sweet Briar College, Amherst County. When it seemed that repairing the wall behind the trees would require the trees' removal, students rallied to their cause. An alternate repair plan was drawn up, and the trees' "fleeting, gaudy, fragrant" flowers continue to brighten the Sweet Briar campus each spring.

tree tour. It seemed most everyone's map was in the process of being up-dated (or waiting for the funding to be re-printed).

And finally, trees on many of the campuses we visited were remarkable for their long-term connection to college life. For example, the bur oak on the drill field across from Burruss Hall at Virginia Tech is the most recognized tree on campus. It has been featured on Virginia Tech postcards since the early 1900s and has shaded thousands of cadets as they marched by. Alumni who haven't visited the campus for a while inquire about the tree as if it were a personal friend.

Similarly valued trees include the white ashes that shade first-comers on the UVA lawn at graduation, the crabapples saved by student petition at Sweet Briar, and the ancient American elm that shades bicycles outside Ewell Hall at William and Mary. Not always do students know what kinds of trees they are responding to, but they do remember experiences like walking under the same bower of leaves (a well-branched linden, say) every day on the way to sorority row. Returning years later, that spot still feels charged, and not because anything remarkable happened there, but because it is still framed by the linden tree.

With a circumference of over 21 feet and seven branches as big as trunks themselves, this black willow (Salix nigra) is a magnet to students visiting Virginia Tech's Duck Pond. Unlike weeping willows, black willows don't weep (for that reason, one wag has dubbed them "stoic willows"), but they are native to North America (the weeping willow is not) and they enjoy the same moist conditions weeping willows do.

Early engravings don't show trees on the Lawn, center of Thomas Jefferson's Academical Village at the University of Virginia, but a mixture of ashes and maples grow there today. Landscape architects, arborists, and architectural historians collaborate in decisions about tree planting on the grounds.

Not only are these dawn redwoods on the
William and Mary campus the largest
of their species in the state, they have a
remarkable history. Until 1944, this genus,
Metasequoia, was known only from fossil
records and was believed to be extinct. Then a
small stand of dawn redwoods (Metasequoia
glyptostroboides) was discovered in China.
Seeds from those trees were eventually
distributed to representatives of gardens,
arboreta, and institutions attending the
International Botanical Congress in Brussels,
Belgium in 1948. Touring Belgium that
year, William and Mary's Dr. J. T. Baldwin
obtained some seeds and shipped them back
to the College where they were germinated
and planted at the end of Sunken Garden in
1949. These stately trees, notable for their fast
growth, fluted trunks, and feathery foliage, are
now over 100 feet tall.

Hurricane Isabel felled some of the famous tulip-poplars at Westover (Charles City County), but the missing trees have been replaced, and the remaining trees still enhance the grandeur of the place.

HISTORIC HOMESITE TREES

Tourists and natives flock to Virginia's many historic homesites, but some miss the trees for the homes, and that's too bad. Many of Virginia's historic homesites are as noteworthy for their trees as for their architecture, and tree lovers might gravitate to them with as much enthusiasm as they do to parks and other natural areas.

Among the dozens of historic homesites we visited while searching for remarkable trees, several struck us as "don't miss" tree places. Among them were Mount Vernon, Monticello, Poplar Forest, Upper Brandon Plantation, and George Washington Birthplace National Monument (also known as Popes Creek Plantation). The Arlington House Woodlands (part of the Robert E. Lee Memorial near Arlington National Cemetery) also deserves mention, if only because this is an historic, 16-acre forest within earshot of Washington, D.C. Much of this upland oak forest has been overrun with invasive species, but parts of it retain landscape characteristics that would have been present when the Lees occupied the estate, and one section includes trees over 260 years old.

Two other historic homesites tree lovers should put on their itineraries are Montpelier, in Orange County, and Westover, in Charles City County. James Madison's home, Montpelier, offers an interesting mix of exotic and native trees. There you will find Virginia's state champion Spanish fir (*Abies pinsapo*), striking specimens of cedar of Lebanon (*Cedrus libani*), a collection of Atlas cedars (*Cedrus atlantica*), and a deodar cedar (*Cedrus deodara*) that is worth the price of admission to the estate. (The deodar cedar, which grows about 200 yards down the hill in front of the mansion, must be experienced up close, where the enormity of its branches can be appreciated.) Closer to the Montpelier mansion, noteworthy deciduous trees include statuesque American hollies (*Ilex opaca*), eastern red cedars (*Juniperus virginiana*), and Virginia's largest English oak (*Quercus robur*).

Montpelier is also home to what visitors call the "Big Woods," an easily accessible remnant of the old-growth forest that once blanketed the Piedmont. This 200-acre area east of the mansion includes a series of interlocking, self-guided trails along which you will find mammoth tulip-poplars, towering oaks, staunch old hickories, and an understory filled with spicebush, pawpaw, and other native shrubs (as well as some invasive exotics). Designated a National Natural Landmark in 1987, this area, also known as the James Madison Landmark Forest, is now protected by a Nature Conservancy easement.

Westover, on the James River about 25 miles east of Richmond, is usually visited for its historic home, one of the best examples of Georgian architecture in America, but tree lovers can be forgiven if they see the house as just a good backdrop for the trees. Built either by William Byrd II or William Byrd III, the house is fronted by what was, until September, 2003, a line of tulip-poplars that could have been described as one of the best ornamental plantings of tulip-poplars in North America. There were 15—some of them probably over 150 years old—on the river side of the house and they commanded the pebble path leading to the residence. Hurricane Isabel felled two of these trees (and hundreds of other trees on the property), and visitors who knew Westover before the storm feel their loss, but the lost trees have been replaced, and the corridor between Westover's tulip-poplars and historic home remains one of the most magnetic tree spaces in Virginia. Some of the magnetism comes from the shape of the trees

Tulip-poplars (Liriodendron tulipifera) *frame historic Westover on the James River.*

as they relate to the house (flat house front, with a parallel line of enormous trunks unusually close to the façade) and some relates to the trees' animation. When the leaves are on these trees, breezes off the James have lots of surface area to push against, and the sound high in their canopies, along with their quivering motion, draws eyes and spirits upward.

Other impressive trees, including striking beeches and pecans, grow at Westover, and the property is maintained in a tree-friendly sort of way (a brick wall "bumps out" to accom-modate a tree here, a pecan trunk is allowed to encroach on a smoke house there). There is also something gracious about the way visitors are allowed to enter Westover—no entrance fee, only a voluntary contribution box near the entrance. On the day we visited we had the place almost to ourselves but for the groundskeepers, who seemed to be as enthralled by the place as we were. "The rest of them are beautiful," said one house painter, referring to other plantations on the James, "but none of them feel the way this place feels."

This quiet grove of eastern red cedars at George Washington's birthplace in Westmoreland County grows on a spit of land bordered by Popes Creek, a tributary of the Potomac. Lichen-encrusted cedar benches, old rail fences, abundant wildlife, and farm animals give this eighteenth century farm a "land of plenty" sort of feeling.

Large native trees and exotic evergreens, like this cedar of Lebanon, grow near the formal gardens at Montpelier, James Madison's Orange County estate. One of them was reportedly presented to James Madison by Lafayette during an 1824 visit to the estate.

Arboreta and Botanical Gardens

"Come any time you want," says a volunteer at the State Arboretum of Virginia. "You can walk all over the place." That sums up the open-door policy at the State Arboretum of Virginia, a 175-acre "tree place" open 365 days a year, dawn to dusk, free of charge near the town of Boyce in Clarke County. A similar open-door policy applies at the city of Richmond's Maymont, where you can roam a 105-acre estate-turned-park-and-arboretum in the middle of the city, every day throughout the year at no charge and enjoy some of the best trees and tree habitats in the state.

Virginia has far too many remarkable parks, arboreta, and botanical gardens to mention them all here (you'll find a list of some of them on page 199), but the "user-friendly" atmosphere at the State Arboretum and at Maymont seemed to earn them special recognition. Both are sanctuaries for remarkable trees (we've featured the State Arboretum's Dogwood Lane on page 135, featured one of Maymont's remarkable tulip-poplars on our cover), but both sites have much more to offer. As tree places go, Maymont deserves the top honors, partly because the property's original owners (Major and Mrs. James Dooley, who purchased the property, then farmland, in the 1880s) were tree lovers who planted trees with an eye toward the future. They planted trees from all over the world (as well as native species), and they did it in a way that impresses contemporary horticulturists because it is clear the trees' future space requirements were taken into consideration when the trees were sited. "Whoever did the original tree planting was very, very knowledgeable about the way trees grow," horticulturist Robert Hebb once observed. "The original landscape architects were pretty forward-looking to suffer the barren look for our benefit."

Today, Maymont is home to 173 species of trees from five continents, many of them introduced to this country for the first time when the Dooleys planted them in the late nineteenth century. The great majority of them are labeled. Some of the best of them—including the state champion incense cedar (*Calocedrus decurrens*) and a remarkable Spanish fir (*Abies pinsapo*)—grow near the Dooley Mansion. The Spanish fir is a tree that plantsman

Across from the bear habitat at Maymont in Richmond, this American beech tree grabs a hillside with its sculptural roots and provides a playground no children worthy of their sneakers can pass up.

Michael Dirr (author of the *Manual of Woody Landscape Plants*, a bible to many a landscaper) once described as the finest specimen he had ever seen; the incense cedar is a tree kids will love—but only if you encourage them to get up under its foliage and experience its rippled reddish bark and undulating branches up close. Another wonderfully kid-friendly tree on the property is the *Persian parrotia* near the Italian Garden, which has fabulous fall color, interesting exfoliating bark, and a branching structure that may make it the best jungle gym in the state.

Oddly enough, the State Arboretum is also awash in exotic trees (as well as many fine natives). It has a noteworthy collection of pines (more than half of the world's species) and one of the largest collections of ginkgoes outside their native China. Noteworthy specimens include a spectacular weeping hemlock (*Tsuga canadensis* 'Pendula'), a fine copper beech (*Fagus sylvatica* 'Atropunicea') and a 60-foot-tall Japanese umbrella pine (*Sciadopitys verticillata*). Partly because of its quirky history (the property has had some unusual uses and languished from 1965 to 1982), the State Arboretum is more a work-in-progress than finished product, but it is a welcoming tree place— and its trees are labeled.

Although both have entrance fees, the Lewis Ginter Botanical Garden in Henrico County and Norfolk Botanical Garden are also fine places to see trees. The former is easy to reach off I-95, the latter off I-64. What may be the most breathtakingly beautiful Chinese fringe tree (*Chionanthus retusus*) in the country grows at the Norfolk Botanical Garden, as does the state champion Japanese snowbell (*Styrax japonicus*), the state champion coast redwood (*Sequoia sempervirens*), and a spring crescendo of cherries, crabapples, redbuds, and buckeyes. The Lewis Ginter Botanical Garden boasts not only a fine collection of small ornamental trees (including one of the best collections of flowering cherries in the region) but mature tulip-poplars, impressive American hollies (around the Flagler Perennial Garden), and a Woodland Walk rich in native shrubs and trees. Look for a noteworthy bigleaf magnolia (*Magnolia macrophylla*) there and for a stunning sourwood (*Oxydendrum arboreum*) and a fine old ironwood (*Carpinus caroliniana*) in woods just east and south of Bloemendaal House.

With its raspberry-red flowers and wide-spreading habit, this crabapple (Malus sp.) at the Norfolk Botanical Garden is a favorite of both visitors and staff. Garden records suggest it was planted surprisingly recently—in the 1970s. From this angle, the sinuous trunks of crape myrtles frame the crabapple.

URBAN FORESTS

Like "working vacation," the term "urban forest" sounds like a contradiction in terms, but it's not. Urban forests are not the primeval woodlands described by Longfellow, but they are tree systems of enormous value, and sometimes of grandeur, that are essential to human health, invaluable to wildlife, and crucial to urban ecology. They include much more than street trees set out to dress up downtown; they include naturalized trees along stream beds, shade trees in parks and parking lots, yard trees on private land.

In the best urban forests, trees merge to form networks of wooded greenways that cool the city, clean the air, reduce energy consumption, improve water quality, provide travel corridors for wildlife, and offer residents daily contact with trees. The latter can't be emphasized enough, because 80 percent of the U.S. population now lives in metropolitan areas and for many city-dwellers, an urban forest is the only forest they will ever see. Small wonder urban forestry has risen like a rocket in the public consciousness, and it's now possible to imagine a metropolitan area listing, among assets like good schools and reliable public transportation, an outstanding urban forest.

Cities now set tree canopy goals with the same seriousness they set revenue goals, and this emphasis on "green infrastructure" comes none too soon. That urban trees were in trouble was obvious to anyone watching bulldozers clear land for parking lots as early as the 1960s, but the extent of the problem was highlighted by a series of studies in the late 1980s that revealed, among other things, that the average city tree lives only 32 years and dies just before it reaches its ultimate potential to benefit an urban area, and that trees were disappearing from urban areas at a rate of four removals for each new tree planted. Let us count the ways urban environments do not love trees: power lines, roads, sewers, buildings, soil compaction, soil contamination, pollution, underground cables, sidewalks, gas pipelines. Geographic Information Systems (GIS) and satellite images further revealed just how significant the loss of tree cover was in some communities. In Leesburg, for example, satellite images revealed that between 1992 and 2001, the town had lost 71 percent of its tree cover—a statistic that sobered the community and helped fuel their ambitious Urban Forest Management Plan—an unusual accomplishment for a town as small as Leesburg.

Helping to fuel the enthusiasm for urban forests has been the technology to quantify their value. In the late 1990s, software became available to assess the benefits of trees to the ecosystem, and by 2006 a group of tools, free to those willing to learn the skills to use them, emerged that used scientific equations to predict the potential environmental and economic benefits of trees. Measurable benefits include things like the hourly amount of pollution removed by an urban forest of a particular size and composition, the effects of trees on the energy buildings use, the cooling effects of trees, and the amount of money saved through storm-water runoff control. Among those using these "i-tree tools" was urban forester Jay Banks of Leesburg, who quickly discovered how interested his town council became when he could report "Tree loss cost us $9 million dollars in storm water control over the last ten years."

The press also picked up reports from that ultimate urban environment, New York City, where Mayor Bloomberg had commissioned a study quantifying trees' ecological services. Among the benefits were $11 million for filtering out air pollutants, $28 million saved in energy consumption, $36 million for stemming storm-water runoff, and $53 million in aesthetic benefits, resulting in the conclusion that for every $1 spent on New York's trees, the city received $5.60 in benefits. Other systems of tree-benefit quantification (assessing a particular tree's value given its trunk size, condition, species, location) resulted in interesting signs like this one posted near a new dormitory under construction at the University of Texas: "Do not discard or pour paint, mortar, trash or any construction material or debris on this tree. The replacement value of this oak tree is $90,000."

Photo courtesy of Fairlington Historical Society

As tools for assessing tree value have improved, however, so have stresses on urban ecosystems increased, and the challenges facing urban foresters have become enormous. Discard any notion you might have that urban forestry is all about planting trees: that's the easy part. Think instead about long-term maintenance, monitoring insects and diseases, conducting inventories of existing trees, influencing land-use decisions, deciding which trees are most desirable for a particular location, removing invasive species, raising money, and educating the public. In Fairfax, for example, removing

The "before" picture on the preceding page was taken of the Fairlington development in Arlington and Alexandria in 1943. Originally built to meet WWII housing needs and consisting of 3,439 apartments, the 322-acre development now boasts mature street trees like these willow oaks.

ash trees that might attract the emerald ash borer and removing invasive progeny of the once popular Bradford pear are now as integral to the county's urban forestry program as tree planting.

So where are Virginia's most remarkable urban forests? One is tempted to say in Washington, D.C. Although not in Virginia, what Virginians call "D.C." is close enough to feel as if it belongs to us, and, at least from a visual point of view, the impact of the recently rejuvenated urban forest there is startling. The engine driving tree renewal in D.C. has been a $50 million private endowment that supports Casey Trees—and a fine engine it is. Even without such generous private philanthropy, however, many urban areas in Virginia are making tremendous strides.

Arlington, Chesapeake, Virginia Beach, Norfolk, Leesburg, and Roanoke are among the urban areas with urban forest management plans and what seems to be the political will to implement them, but Fairfax probably takes the prize for most ambitious urban forest plan, given the development pressure it faces. Fairfax's population is expected to reach 1.2 million by 2025, and it is already almost "built out," with only about 4,500 acres of public land on which it might plant additional trees, but it has set a tree canopy goal of 45 percent by 2037. (To sustain acceptable quality of life, American Forests recommends that cities east of the Mississippi set canopy goals of 40 percent overall—the equivalent of 20 large trees per acre. They suggest that central business districts strive for 15 percent coverage, urban neighborhoods and fringe business areas strive for 25 percent, and suburbs, which have more land on which to plant trees, 50 percent.)

"We'll need public-private partnerships," says Fairfax forester Doug Petersen, noting that because there is so little public land left in the county, inspiring citizens to plant "native and desirable species" will be part of the county's effort. Fairfax, and its Director of Urban Forestry, Mike Knapp, have also often been at the forefront of efforts to acquire enabling legislation that would allow municipalities to require the preservation of existing tree cover (as opposed to replacing it after it has been removed, which has been the focus of most Virginia legislation). "We've got a resource here that the community has a very legitimate interest in preserving," says

Knapp. "The intrinsic value of tree cover is so multifaceted in delivering socio-economic and ecological benefits that we can't afford to ignore it."

Sometimes the communities with the most effective and sustainable urban forests are not those with the flashiest trees. For example, it's easier to plant fast-growing, small, ornamental trees than it is to make sure your city's tree inventory includes some slow-growing trees that will persist into future generations, to select a wide variety of appropriate species (so the loss of any one species doesn't wipe out the entire urban forest), and to generate public support for ongoing maintenance, which is a "harder sell" than planting new trees.

Some of the most effective urban forestry programs in the state also have hidden resources in the form of volunteers who help with maintenance, public education, and planting. "It's the best group of people committed to actual work I've ever been in," says Herb Rinehart, a volunteer with Front Royal's Tree Steward program, which trains citizen volunteers in the basics of tree biology, physiology, tree identification, and tree maintenance in exchange for volunteer hours devoted to improving community forests. Lynchburg, Virginia Beach, Albemarle/Charlottesville, and Arlington/Alexandria also have Tree Steward programs. (For more information, visit www.treesvirginia.org). Master Gardeners, Master Naturalists, scouts, and church and civic groups also contribute to community forest projects, and volunteer members of Fairfax ReLeaf

Photo courtesy of The Library of Virginia

have been working to conserve, restore, and promote sustainable urban forests in Northern Virginia for over 20 years.

It has become commonplace to think of cities and trees as antagonists—to assume that where people congregate, trees will suffer and that people are too short-sighted to appreciate the ecological, aesthetic, and economic value of trees. There is an alternative view. Imagine people caring for the urban forest as carefully as ants tend their colonies or farmers their fields. It is true that, in urban environments, trees seem to be at the mercy of people, but people can be merciful *and* smart. They can realize their relationship to trees is mutually beneficial and that the healthier the urban forest, the healthier the community.

When unveiled in May of 1890, and for over a decade thereafter, the Lee Monument stood in an open area used as a parade ground (pictured on the left). Today, trees old and new help soften the landscape along Richmond's Monument Avenue.

State and National Parks and Forests

Hiking down the Mill Prong Trail in Shenandoah National Park, you work your way through the overgrown fields and the old orchards, past the pool under the waterfall, across the stream that bisects the trail (three times), and down into the hollow where President Hoover once vacationed. There you find the three cabins the Hoovers built (their rooflines adjusted to accommodate trees), and you find the enormous tulip-poplars you've heard grow in the area—trees that are unmarked and unheralded but as historic as the ancient stone chimneys nearby. Stopping to rest on the porch of the Hoovers' cabin, you marvel at the beauty of the site overlooking the two rushing streams that merge to form the Rapidan River, and you think, "Wouldn't it be great to own this place?" Then it occurs to you: you do! You own not only this cabin but the entire forest, and not only this forest but every state and national forest and park in Virginia.

Virginia—and every Virginian—is rich in forests. The state is about 62 percent forested, and of that approximately 16 million acres, about 2.1 million acres is on public land. (By comparison, the entire state of Delaware is only about 1.3 million acres.) This means Virginians have the opportunity to see trees where they grow best—in community with other trees and with the myriad other plants, animals, insects, and fungi, not to mention the seeps, soils, and angles of light, that make up the living thing called a forest.

Even a quick look at the state and national parks and forests nominated to the Remarkable Tree Project as "remarkable tree places" (see page 199) reveals how rich and diverse they are. As a public landowner, you own baldcypress swamps in First Landing State Park, woodlands within sight of the Washington Monument (along the George Washington Memorial Parkway), and thousands of acres of hardwoods and evergreens on Mt. Rogers, the highest mountain in Virginia. And your investments of 70 years ago—buying up worn-out tobacco lands that no one else wanted—are paying off now in state forests like the Cumberland, and the Buckingham-Appomattox, where trees grow 100 feet tall, foresters model best timber-management practices, and thousands of wooded acres are available to enjoy.

You also own "blue-chip" forests, including the vast George Washington and Jefferson National Forests and the incomparable Shenandoah National Park. These are the long swaths of green that run northeast to southwest down the western half of every Virginia map. With 1.8 million acres that spill over into West Virginia and Kentucky, the George Washington and Jefferson National Forests combined represent one of the largest areas of public land in the eastern United States. (The George Washington extends

from near Roanoke northwest into West Virginia; the Jefferson extends from near Roanoke south to North Carolina.) Shenandoah National Park, which encompasses the Blue Ridge Mountains between Waynesboro and Front Royal, comprises "only" 196,000 acres, but it is a tree-lovers paradise and includes the vista-rich 105 miles of Skyline Drive.

To appreciate how remarkable these public lands are, remember that in the 1920s, the great majority of these lands were a mess. Intense farming, livestock grazing, and the unchecked extraction of resources (iron, coal, lumber, fuel wood, bark for tanning), followed by fire and erosion, had turned much of the Appalachians into a wasteland. What you see in these forests now is the result of concerted public effort to restore a resource—and a remarkable recovery it is. Today, there are 2,000 miles of hiking trails through dozens of forest habitats in the George Washington and Jefferson National Forests, 500 miles of trails through Shenandoah National Park, and few visitors complain about the lack of trees. Shenandoah Park alone boasts 87 species of native trees and forest habitats, from rich coves to dry ridges.

There is little old growth in these forests, however, and what there is is not what most people would expect. Less than one percent of the eastern deciduous forest in the U.S. has never been cut, but there *are* small old-growth areas—and one large one—in Virginia's public forests. The largest old-growth area in Virginia is 3,600 contiguous acres on Peter's Mountain in Alleghany County in the James River Ranger District of the George Washington National Forest. It is not populated by towering giants the way a redwood forest might be. Instead, it is rimmed with relatively short, contorted chestnut oaks—trees with diameters of 2 to 4 feet—that have managed to eke out a living on the thin soils of this ridge for 175 to 300 years (more like the bristlecone pines of the desert southwest than the redwoods of the Pacific Coast). Like a similar, but smaller, old-growth area in Craig County on Brush Mountain (in the Eastern Divide Ranger District of the Jefferson National Forest), the chestnut oaks on Peter's Mountain have benefited from two things that help account for their longevity—inaccessibility and short stature—making them hardly worth harvesting but now ecologically invaluable.

In terms of their appeal to visitors, there are significant differences between Shenandoah National Park and the George Washington and Jefferson National Forests. Shenandoah National Park requires an admission fee, but it prohibits hunting and allows no commercial timber harvesting. There is no fee to enter George Washington and Jefferson National Forests (although fees are collected at some high-traffic campgrounds and day

In all of Britain there are only about 40 species of native trees; in Shenandoah National Park there are 87. This is a view of Shenandoah National Park from Skyline Drive, about 10 miles south of the Swift Run Gap entrance.

areas), but hunting is allowed, and hunting season is not the best time to wander remote areas. Thirty-nine percent of the George Washington and Jefferson National Forests is actively managed for the production of timber and wood products, and "multiple-use" is their mantra, making public input particularly important in determining how they are used and managed. If you accept the idea that you really do own these natural resources, issues you need to be concerned about include invasive insects and disease, urban and suburban sprawl, wildfire, acid rain, ozone depletion, global warming, conflicting recreational activities, land clearing, and timber and mineral extraction.

As always, the price of ownership is active and informed stewardship, but it's hard to imagine lands more worth the effort.

In addition to Virginia's large national parks and forests, which offer vast woodlands for hikers to explore, scores of smaller parks and natural areas offer tree lovers places where they can walk all day in the woods—and some of them are within easy driving distance from the state's most populous areas. Prince William Forest Park, for example, is within 35 miles of Washington, D.C., and it offers 37 miles of hiking trails through one of the few remaining Piedmont forest ecosystems in the national park system. Caledon Natural Area, about 30 miles east of Fredericksburg on the Northern Neck, is smaller (only about 2,500 acres), but it, too, is an extraordinary "tree place." Unlike most state parks, Caledon's mission has more to do with preserving plant and animal habitats (including bald eagle habitat) than it does with providing recreation, and its trails reflect that focus. The walker-friendly site is noted for its spring wildflowers and other native plants (over 500 species of them), but tree lovers will find the place as impressive in fall and winter as in spring. Visit in November, when the gray-barked beeches are hung with yellow and burnt umber leaves, and you'll not only be able to take the trail to the Potomac River (closed from April to September to protect eagle habitat), but you'll have great expanses of mature beech, oak, and tulip-poplar forest almost to yourself.

A day's journey through the Caledon Natural Area on the Northern Neck (King George County) is more like a walk in the park than a hike. Its easy trails meander through mature beech trees, towering tulip-poplars, and other native trees, including American holly and ironwood.

American beech (Fagus grandifolia) trees at Caledon Natural Area represent the climax, or mature, stage of natural forest succession. Once a beech forest has reached this stage, it can dominate its site for centuries, because beech trees are long-lived and cast deep shade in which few other tree seedlings can grow.

This vista overlooking the George Washington National Forest can be viewed from the Blue Ridge Parkway's Twenty Minute Overlook in Nelson County. The name of the overlook refers to the fact that, in June and July, the sun sets 20 minutes after the sun hits a nearby rock face, and workers in the valley used this signal to time their departure from the fields.

AFTERWORD

O n Robert Llewellyn's desk sit a collection of acorns and a pot in which several sprouting chestnut oaks grow. The acorns collected in our travels include the tiny acorn of a willow oak, the oblong acorn of a live oak, the fringed-capped acorn of a bur oak, and the nearly-enclosed-by-its-cap acorn of the overcup oak. The sprouting chestnut oak grows from an acorn collected at the base of the state champion chestnut oak in Fairfax County. Sticks of various descriptions decorate another table, because we have been smitten at one time or another by the resting buds of the cottonwood, the stacked leaf scars of the ginkgo, and the wintergreen fragrance of the black birch. And then there are the images dancing in our heads—of white oak crowns silhouetted against the sky, of deeply fissured blackgum bark, and of sycamores so white you could almost read by them.

We've had an opportunity to explore, investigate, and collect like kids, and we complete four years of visiting trees with impressions as varied as our trees. Here are some of them.

Adults aren't the only children interested in trees. Real children have been thrilled to be included in this project, and we'd argue that trees are an exciting point of entry to natural history education. In our experience, children aren't overly impressed by tree age (how could they be; they're too young to have any sense of what it means to be 40 much less 400), but they are impressed by size, and the bigger the tree the bigger the impression. We've mentioned some of the big tree searches in which children have participated, and these are a great way to get children involved in tree investigations, but there are other ways, too. Part of feeling at home in the world involves a level of nature literacy that includes recognition of common trees, their patterns and rhythms. You'll find an SOL-targeted lesson plan that involves tree

identification on the Remarkable Tree website, but here's a short test you can use to see how "tree literate" your children are: Can they recognize a red maple in flower, a river birch by its bark, a sassafras by its leaves, a walnut before it has lost its husk, and a dogwood in fruit and flower? If not, you've got some very enjoyable work to do.

Another impression (and this one involves those chestnut oaks Robert Llewellyn is growing from acorns) is that it's easy to plant trees, but it's hard to sustain them. Exciting as it is to grow an oak from an acorn, the real trick to making an oak contribution to the landscape is finding a place where it can grow, undisturbed, for more than 100 years. In Tree Places, we've described some of the places, like cemeteries, college campuses, and national parks, where trees have a good chance of growing without disturbance, but if Virginia is to remain rich in trees, more "tree places" will be required.

Our strongest impression after four years of focusing on trees and their habitats is that a

Black oak (Quercus velutina) *acorn*

194

landscape rich in trees is no longer something Virginians can take for granted. Urbanization and other pressures are too strong for us to assume we will have trees by default. If Virginia is to continue to have trees and tree places of the quality featured in our book, it will have to be by design.

We've been heartened by the efforts of tree stewards, urban foresters, and community activists of all kinds to protect and improve community tree resources, but, as many of them have pointed out, it won't be enough to protect trees on public land if Virginia is to remain "tree rich." Private property owners have got to get into the act, and not just by planting a few ornamentals. It's illuminating—and a little distressing—to travel the state looking at fine, old trees and to see that the young trees many well-meaning property owners are planting will never achieve the age and stature of the trees they are ostensibly replacing.

Here are several things to think about if we are to have trees "coming on in promise" that have the potential to grow old and large. First, if you have the space for a large tree (plenty of ground space, no overhead wires), consider planting a tree that will grow large. There are more spaces that can accommodate small trees than can accommodate large ones, and it's a shame to waste a spot that could accommodate a white oak on a crape myrtle. Also, although everyone is in a hurry to see his or her tree get big, consider a slow-growing species. Slow-growing trees are typically longer lived than fast-growing ones, and for future generations to have the kinds of legacy trees we have inherited, someone is going to have to have the foresight to plant them and the patience to nurture them.

How long a tree lives depends on many things, including where it is planted, but some species are genetically predisposed to live longer than others. Consulting an arborist and doing your research will help you choose the right tree for the right spot. What is the best legacy tree for one part of the state is not necessarily the best legacy tree in another, but some long-lived native trees to consider are these: white oak (*Q. alba*), bur oak (*Q. macrocarpa*), chestnut oak (*Q. montana*), northern red oak (*Q. rubra*), overcup oak (*Q. lyrata*), post oak (*Q. stellata*), willow oak (*Q. phellos*), baldcypress (*Taxodium distichum*), American beech (*Fagus grandifolia*), blackgum (*Nyssa sylvatica*), eastern arborvitae (*Thuja occidentalis*), shagbark hickory (*Carya ovata*), sugar maple (*Acer saccharum*), and tulip-poplar (*Liriodendron tulipifera*).

The wonderful thing about planting a long-lived tree is that, if you are committed to it, you are also committed to protecting its habitat for the long term. And its habitat includes not just the land use around it but the air above it, the water and soil beneath it, and the climate that affects it. For insightful discussions of trees, their biology and their prospects for the future, we recommend *Tree: A Life Story* by David Suzuki and Wayne Grady and *The Tree: A Natural History of What Trees Are, How They Live, and Why They Matter* by Colin Tudge, both of which deal intelligently with the ecological challenges facing trees. Tudge, for example, reminds us that trees, with long life spans, cannot adapt to changing conditions the way, say, short-lived insects can, and that every discussion of climate change—and the bewildering array of variables involved—should have trees at its heart. This is not just because the survival of trees is at stake, but because human survival and tree survival are inextricably linked.

So back to our sprouting chestnut oaks: We will plant them, of course, and we'll find the most appropriate and protected sites for them we can. We'll write down where we planted them, we'll record their source, and maybe we'll make a few notes about what the world was like when we planted them. That way, someone looking for remarkable trees years from now may find them noteworthy for knowing their history. But their survival will depend on much more than our deciding where to plant them and our watering them for the first few years; it will depend on the state of the atmosphere and the vicissitudes of the weather; it will depend on politics, personal choices, and planetary policy. Over some of that, we have no control, but for the parts we do, we'll use these words of the naturalist Aldo Leopold as a guide: "A thing is right when it tends to preserve the integrity, stability and beauty of the biotic community. It is wrong when it tends otherwise." We don't expect our decisions to be always right, and many of them certainly won't be easy, but we think they'll be better for keeping Leopold's maxim—and our young chestnut oaks—in mind.

*Chestnut oak (*Quercus montana*) seedlings*

SPONSORS

Trees Virginia. Established in 1990, Trees Virginia (Virginia Urban Forest Council) works to promote an awareness of community forests and the value of trees. Members represent a wide range of professions, organizations and volunteers who are interested in stimulating a public awareness of the role trees and forests play in the urban environment.

The Robert H. Smith Family Foundation.

The Peck Foundation. The Peck Foundation is a family foundation supporting projects that foster a sense of community.

Bartlett Tree Experts. Founded in 1907, the F. A. Bartlett Tree Expert Company is dedicated to scientific tree care. The company's mission is to improve the landscape by protecting the health, beauty, and value of trees and shrubs. Bartlett Tree Experts not only provides tree care, the scientists at the Bartlett Tree Research Laboratories educate arborists around the globe in the latest research in pruning, soil science, root system care, pest management, tree structure evaluation, and general tree care practices and techniques.

Virginia Forestry Educational Foundation. A charitable and educational foundation, the Virginia Forestry Educational Foundation advocates the conservation and wise use of forest resources for the best interest of society. It supports educational programs that speak to the benefits of forests and forest products and programs that demonstrate how sustainable forestry can protect watersheds and wildlife while preserving aesthetic and recreational values of the community.

Virginia Tech Department of Forestry. Virginia Tech's forestry program, located in the mountains of southwest Virginia, is ranked among the best in the nation. It offers studies in environmental management, outdoor recreation, and environmental education, in addition to forest management.

The Ballyshannon Fund of CACF. The Ballyshannon Fund supports educational endeavors designed to encourage greater understanding of rural living, the ethos of commercial farming and timbering, and the responsible use of natural resources, including hunting and fishing.

Other sponsors include, Gwathmey Memorial Trust; The Seay Foundation; Virginia Foundation for the Humanities; Virginia 4-H Foundation; 3North Architects; American Society of Landscape Architects, Virginia Chapter; Grace Street Residential Design Systems; Anne McCracken and Jim Rogers; Jeanette and David McKittrick; Frank Hardy, Inc., Realtors; Colesville Nursery in memory of Al Gardner; Virginia Nursery & Landscape Association; Robert Strini; Anna Lane, Ted and Sheila Weschler; Mr. and Mrs. Frederic Scott Bocock; Mid-Atlantic Chapter International Society of Arboriculture; Precision Landscaping Company; Virginia Tree Farm Committee; Virginia Horticultural Foundation; Three Chopt Garden Club; Valley Beautiful Foundation.

OTHER FRIENDS OF THE PROJECT

We like to extend special thanks to everyone who agreed to appear with trees in our photographs. To everyone we asked, this was like being asked to do something especially pleasurable, but some people had to travel long distances, get up early, or take a day off school or work to accompany us on tree trips. Thanks especially to the following children (and a few adults): Alex Andersen, Walker Antonio, Cannon Binns, Chase Binns, Eliza Binns, Damon Bradshaw, Ryan Campbell, Byron Carmean, Joshua Crabill, Giulio Degiorgis, Olivia Degiorgis, Jadah Douthett, Abbey Etheridge, Caitlin Grady, Dan Grogan, Thomas M. Harter, Jacob Heath, Victoria Herrala, Diamond Holmes, Collin Hu, Adam Hugo, David Hugo, Grace Ann Hugo, Mariah Jayne, Harold Jerrell, Cyrus Jett, Arshanique Jones, Kris Jones, Amie Kaui, Bill Keene, Sam Keessee, Austin Lambert, Daniel Larios, Gabriel Larios, Evelyn Lawrence, Parker Lee, Noel Livingston, Jenna Llewellyn, Carleigh Luck, Davis Luck, Peyton Luck, Mathias Lund, Nicolas Lund, Deanna Mangano, Katherine Martin, Maggie Mascaro, George R. McNeill, Alexus Mills, Norah E. Murray, Sylvia, Alison Murray, Evan O'Brien, Elena O'Brien, Liam O'Brien, O. E. Parker, Lahjaé C. White-Patterson, Haley Poulson, Araceli Isabel Rodriguez, Isak Edward Rodriguez, Jose Perez Sanchez, Luke Sanyour, Matthew Seawood, Kim Sorensen, Molly Vaira, Taron Ware, Angel Whitehead, Lauren Wolfang, Aiden Workman, Haley Workman and Alex Zuppoletti.

ACKNOWLEDGMENTS

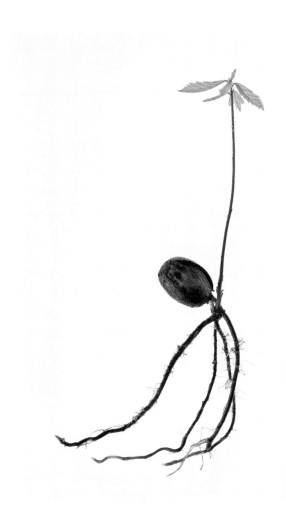

Sprouting chestnut oak (Quercus montana)

In the text of this book, we occasionally refer to the Remarkable Tree team, usually meaning Bob (our photographer), Jeff (my co-author), and me, but the team that made this book possible actually included hundreds of people. Just getting to some of the trees we've featured (and many that we visited but didn't feature) required complicated logistics and sometimes guides. For helping us reach inaccessible or hard-to-find trees, thanks to Byron Carmean, Gary Williamson, Mike Resnake, Harvey Darden, Tom Wieboldt, Mitchell Norman, Patricia Kerr, Harold Jerrell, Nick Fisichelli, Mo Stevens, Chip Morgan, and Karen Snape.

For answering questions about tree biology and ecology, thanks to Tom Dierauf, Chris Ludwig, Gary Fleming, Jay Stipes, Carolyn Copenheaver, John Peterson, John Seiler, and Tom Wieboldt. No botany or forestry class ever had better professors (or field trips!). For trolling their data bases for the statistics and "forest facts" we needed, thanks to John Pemberton and Charlie Becker. For their insights into tree care, thanks to Joel Koci, Eric Wiseman, and Susan Day. For editing, thanks to John Hayden, who kept us botanically accurate while letting us use everyday words, and to Rebecca Barns, who kept us grammatically correct.

We also had the great privilege of working with Mike Fitts on our book's design. Wednesday nights just won't be the same without our "work" sessions and their accompanying discussion of art, film, and the best new YouTube videos. For office and photographic assistance, thanks to Tina Nunez, Jon Golden, David White and Adam Litvin. For designing and managing the Remarkable Tree website, which received nearly a thousand nominations and over 20,000 visits in under two years, thanks to Tracey Sherman in the Virginia Tech Department of Forestry, and thanks to Virginia Tech student Andrew Meeks for programming the Remarkable Tree online database.

Thanks, too, to the children and adults who allowed us to photograph them with trees. Our experiences with "models" ranged from the sublime (the Luck family making an overnight trip to help us get their children into the swamp by sunup) to the ridiculous (stopping a passing car to see if a passenger might not pose for us), and never did we receive anything but an enthusiastic response to our requests for help. We wish only that we could have included every tree for which we found a willing hugger!

Some of our sources for natural history information included *Silvics of North America*, the *Atlas of the Virginia Flora*, and Virginia Tech's Forest Biology and Dendrology websites. We also used scores of primary sources to assess the accuracy of often-repeated-but-seldom-confirmed information about trees, their uses, and history. Thanks to all the state and local historians who have assisted us in our efforts as well as to the Pamunkey Regional Library and Virginia Tech's Newman Library for helping us acquire hard to find and out of print books.

A source we went to for both inspiration *and* information was Donald Culross Peattie's *A Natural History of Trees of Eastern and Central North America*. First published in the 1940s, Peattie's guide is a classic and as valued for its language (which we've often quoted) as for its information. As Robert Finch wrote in the book's introduction, you go to Peattie not just to identify trees but to identify with them.

Anyone attempting a project of this scope should also know that it can't be done without money, and we'll be forever grateful to those who supported the Project financially. All of our sponsors are listed on the preceding page, but we'd like to give special thanks to our coordinating sponsor, Trees Virginia, and to Jeanette McKittrick, who helped us keep the fundraising ball rolling.

And, finally thanks to our spouses, John Hugo, Judy Kirwan, and Bobbi Llewellyn, who kept the home fires burning (how ironic is *that*?) while we pursued our passion for trees.

N.R.H.

TREE NOMINATORS

Thank you to all the Virginians who nominated trees to the Remarkable Trees of Virginia Project. You have helped us create a record of some of Virginia's finest trees, and this book would not have been possible without you.

4-H Wild Fire Club
Kari Abbott
David Abdullah MD*
Neva Adams
Frank & Joy Albertson
Karen J. Allen*
Edna Allen-Dean
Tony Altman
John Anderson
Mark Anderson
Chris Anderson*
J.T. Anderson
Donna Anderson
Dennis Anderson*
Leon App*
Jason Applegate*
Harry N. Arey
John Armstrong
Stacey Arnold
Daniel Arnold
Ted, Luke, & Hannah Arrington
John & Tracy Atkinson
Theresa Augustin
Mike Aust
Alexander Austin

Bob Baird
Blake Baker
Cynthia A. Baldini
Stan Balducci*
Bill Bane*
Robert Barksdale
Virginia Barnes
Jane C. Barnett
Elizabeth D. Barnwell
Lisa Batchelder
Beach Colony Corporation
Wayne Beagle
Michael Bednar*
Michael Bedwell
Liz Belcher
Virgil O. Benfield
Cathy Benson
Bridget Belkacemi
Margaret Berryman
Kathy Beverage*
Peter Bihl
Eliza Binns
Chase Binns
Cannon Binns
John Blankenship*
Debbie Blanton*
Jim Blowers
Nanette Bloxom
Tim Blumenschine*
E. Raymond Boc
Fred & Roberta Bocock
Bob Boeren*

Laurel Bolton
Boy Scout Troop 700, Ashland, Va.
Wilfred Brabant
Ed Bradley*
Chris Bradshaw
Kirk Brady
Cyrus Brame*
Town of Bridgewater
Julia Bristow*
Patricia Brookman
Ellen Brown
Steven Brown
Lynn C. Brownley
Riley Bruce
Keith Brudin
Betsy Duet
Deedy Bumgardner
Scott Burger
John W. Burke III
Reuben Burton*
Jarrod Burton
Angela Butler
Marie Butler

Victor B. Calaman Jr.
Robert and Ruth Campbell
Byron and Jean Carmean*
Jack Carney
Annabel Carrington
Beth Carson
Holly Carson
Tony, Emily, and Clyde Carter
Sandra Cartwright-Brown
Lila Casati
Wendy Cass
Starke Cauthorn
Clifford B. Chambliss III
Nancy C. Chandler, PhD
Arthur Charlesworth
Susan G. Check
Children of the Sycamore Tavern
Pat Churchman
James C. Clark*
Tammy Clarke
Eva Clarke
Cathy Clary*
Lisa Clary
William and Gladys Cleary
Billy Coates
Samuel Edmund Coffey*
Russ Collier
Michael Collins
Stephen Connally
Jocelyn and Tom Connors*
Hildred Cook
Carolyn Copenhaver*
Hilda J. Cosby

William D. Cosby Jr.
Deborah Costello
Carpie Coulbourn
Tammy Coulter*
Clint Cox
Kathleen G. Crandell*
Jeff L. Crowder
Jordon Crumley

Debbie Dabney
Kimberly Lanier Dalton
Michael L. Dance
Courtnay Daniels
Nevin W. Davis
Stan Dawson
Bonnie Deahl*
Marlon Dean
Lisa Deaton
Anne Dellinger
Margaret Denham
David Deshler
Charles Dickson
Tom Dierauf
Debbie Dillion
Michael Dodd
Paul Dolinsky*
Grete Dollitz
Adam Downing*
William Drummond
Don Duckhardt
David Dunaway*
Judy Dunlap
Patricia Dunthorn

Dave Eckert
Ann Eddins
Page Edgerton*
Lois Edlund
Aaron Eichorst
Brian Eick*
Linda Eikmeier
Lizabeth Ann Elder
Tamsey Ellis*
Nancy Elliott
Catherine Ellyson
John Epling
Jesse Epperson
Moonie Etherington
Fay Eure & John Long
Joel B. Evans

Tim Farmer*
Farrcroft Homeowners Association
Sarah Farrell
Ruth Fifer
Linda S. Fink*
Kris Fischer
Musci and Fred Fisher*
Julie Flanagan
Gary Fleming*
Michael Flythe
Ellen G. Ford
Joe Foreman
Carolyn Fournier*
Nelson B. Freeman Jr.
Susan French
Friends of Historic Centerville*
Dan Frisbee
Janice Frye*

Thom R. Gallagher

Bill and Vicki Gallant
Paula Galloway
Catherine Galvin
Jerry Garrison
Cameron and Kate Gary
Curt Gaul
Chris Gensic*
John Giannico
Leah Settle Gibbs
Keith E. Gibson
Robert D. Gilges
Catharine Gilliam
David Girard
Jim and Debbie Gleason
Tiffany Glenn
Violet R. Gonzalez*
Ernest J.W. Goodrich
Ned Goodwin
Bryan Gorsira
Sarah Grant
David & Sarah Green
Wesley Greene
Rolf Gubler*
Lane Guilliams
Betty H. Gwathmey

Lucy H.
Leslie Hager-Smith
Molly Hakopian
Michael Hale
Virginia and Peter Haley
Roderick Hall
Jim Halley
Justin Hancock
Mary Ann Hansen
Anna Hardy
Ed and Sandy Harlow
Jeremy Harold*
Karl Harrelson
Atiya Harris
James Harris
Peter Hatch*
Jennifer Hauck
Joan Haverson
Ted Hayes
Billy Healy
Jacob Heath
Dr. Fred Hebard
Elizabeth H. Hefner
Gary Heiser*
David Helms*
Vicky Herrala
Michael Hill
Cathy Hill
Elizabeth H. Hefner
Beverly Bass Hines
Historic Polegreen Church Foundation
Becky Holland*
Suzanne Holland*
Kathie Hollandsworth
Mary C. Holliman
Beau Hooker
Randolph Hoover
Sharron Hopkins
Brian Hostetler
Leslie Houston
Edward Hubbard
William Huehn*
Roger Huff
Gary Huffman
Ransom Hughes

Adam Hugo
Nancy Ross Hugo*
David Hugo
Grace Ann Hugo
Linda Hunter
Robert R. Hunter Sr.*
Cedric Hurte

Peter Imhof
Mykala Ingram
Glen Isom

Phil James
Judith M. Jay
Harold Jerrell*
Catherine Jewell
Steve Johnson
Jason Johnson*
Patrick Johnson
Ryne Johnson
C. Dwayne Jones
David E. Jones
Alan Jones
Bernice Jones
Stephen Jordan*

Susan Kappel
Joan Kark
Tom & Belinda Karow
Cathy Kennan
Lynette Kessinger
Ada Marie Crenshaw Kindrick
Jeff and Judy Kirwan*
Meg Klekner
Marty Kline
Eva Kling
Sophia Kling
Dean Knight*
Charlie Knoeller
Mike Knott
Lisa E. Krajewski
Tim Kubinak
Gary Kwolek

Darwin and Eileen Lambert
John S. LaMonica*
Carolyn B. Lane
Robin K. Lanham
Terrance Lasher*
Jane Lauve
Charles C. Law
Evelyn T. Lawrence*
Rosie Le Fontaine
Alonza Lee
Debbie Lee
Shirley Lerman
Russ Lescault
Miklos Lestyan*
Sara Lewis
Morten Libarkin
Elizabeth Lieberman
Leonard Lindstrom
Robert Llewellyn
William H. Lloyd
Melissa Long
Frank Longaker
Darren Loomis
Chis Ludwig*
Lyles-Crouch Elementary School

Alexander M. Macauley
Nathan Macek

W. Mackay-Smith
Matthew Mackay-Smith*
Nate Mahanes
Dana Malone*
Tony Mangano
Margaret Beeks 4-H Club
Dorothy Marshall
The Marshall Family
Michael Martin
David Martin*
Mearis M. Martin III
Tom Martin
Brian Martin
Staci R. Martin
Joyce & Ken Martin
Jim Masters
Eleanor G. May
Sybil Mays
Fay A. Mays
Anne-Marie McCartan*
John McCormick
Anne McCracken
Travis McDonald
Jeanette McKittrick
Emma Mednikov
Andrew Meeks
Cheryl Melton
Members of Merchants Hope Church
Lucile Michaels
Dan Miles*
Tim & Christal Miller
Irene Mills
Paul Minkin
Joyce Mitchell
Alan Moeller
JoAnn Mollisee
Roseanne B. Moncure
Paula Moore
Rijk Morawe*
Brittany Moring
Cheyenne Henderson Moss
Candy Mott
Sandra Mudrinich*
Kevin Murphy
Joseph Murray*

Carol Nansel
Belinda Nash*
Elizabeth Neff
Pamela Nehls
Will & Lily Nelms
Anne D. Nelson
Janie & Newc Newcomb*
Randal A. Nixon
Dean Norton*

Jim and Lynn O'Brien
Brian O'Donnell
Tom O'Grady*
Steve O'Leary
Mary Olien
Jim Orband
Jesse Overcash
Gregory Overkamp
Kim Overstreet
Susan Overton
Sarah Owen

Page County Tree Board
Page Library History Camp
Marty Palmore

William Parker
Lloyd M. Parker
Debbie Parks
David Parrish
Audra Parson
John Pataky
Nathaniel Pate
Karen Patterson*
Tracy Pecsek
Linda Proctor Peebles
Toby Pennell
Archer D. Peppe
Carl Perdue
Steven and Joyce Peterson
Max Peterson*
Trish Downey Phipps
Robert Pickett
Piedmont Master Gardeners*
Frances Pike
Berkeley Plantation*
Kathy Poff
Blake Poindexter
Danette Poole*
Tom Priscilla
Gerail Pugh

Stuart L. Rada
Diane Rader
Jane and Tim Radford
Lynn H. Ramsey
Mike Rasnake
Mary Alice Rath
Rehan Razzag
H. M. Redman
Jonathan W. Reed
Richard Reuse
Dr. F. Turner Reuter
Luther and Sara Reynolds
Matthew Rhoads*
Suzanne Rice
Al Rice
Andrew Rich
Larry Riddick
Steve Riethmiller
Members of Roanoke
    Country Club*
Ward Robens
John Aubrey Roberts III
Leon Robertson
Chris Robichaux
Kevin L. and Katherine B. Robinson
Pam Robinson*
Jon Rockett
Gary Roisum*
Roslyn Retreat Center
Erich Rott
Rod Royse*
Robin C. Ruth*

Cathy Salgado
Richard Salzer
Ron Sanders
Paul Santay
Jacob & Hope Sayas
Carla A. Schaaf
Karl von Schmidt-Pauli*
Ted Scott
Lester O. Seal
Brandon Searcey
Tracy Sebring
Paul Segretto
Nancy Sentipal

John Settle*
Donald Shade
Austin Shepherd*
Tracey Sherman
Jim Shockley
Megan Shogren
Eunice Showalter
Karen K. Shriver*
Karl Shuford
Walter Shugart
Emily Simcox
Rod Simmons*
Timothy Sims*
Peggy Singlemann*
W. E. Singleton
Mark Skinner
Courtney Sloan
Stephanie Slocum
Vicki Slonneger
Mike Smith
Stephen A. Smith*
Amelia C. M. Smith
Brian Smith*
John Henry Smith
Arthur and Peggy Smith
Brenda Smonskey
Karen Snape
James C. Snipes
Thomas Snoddy
Georgia Anne Snyder-Falkinham
Martha Sole
Barbara and Robin Sorensen
Barbara Souders
Jo Lee Gregory Spears
Harold H. Speed Jr.
Bridget Spencer
Sarah Stacey
Dwight Stallard*
Henry B. Stamps
Karen Stark
Dave Starner
Holmes Stephenson
Rikki Sterrett
Trina Apple Stevens
Paul Stoneburner
Mary Catherine Stout
Judy Strang
Jean and Craig Stratton
Scott and Dixie Stromberg
Jessica Strother
Hal & Laura Stuart
Patricia R. Sullivan
Patti Sunko-Imhof*
Brandey Sutphin
John R. Sweet
John Swift

Carla T. Takacs*
Verdie Tate*
Fred Tate
Thomas E. Tennille
Rebecca Terrill
Dave Terwilliger
Paige E. Thacker
Terri Therrian*
Ron and Margaret Thomas
C. D. Thomas
Stephanie Sharpe Thomas
Kenneth Thompson
Kendell Thompson*
R. C. Thompson
John C. Thornton

John and Kirsten Tice
Edith Tolley
Lori Tolliver-Jones
Tiffany Tran
Najah R. Travis
Jeff Turner
Sarah E. Tweedy
William Tyler

Dennis and Gayle Unger

Dr. and Mrs. Richard S. Vacca
Kent Van Allen*
Peter Van Dyke*
Stephen Van Hoven*
Val Van Meter
Lisa Van Ravenswaay
Autumn Vaughan
Mike Vaughan
Sabastian Velilla
Robert Vickers*
Kristina Villaire

Kelley Wagner
Stan Warner
Peter Warren
Washington County 4-H
    members
Elma J. Watson
Virgil E. Watson III
Dr. Lewis Weber
Ross Weeks Jr.
Sam Welch
Dr. Carolyn Wells
John Welch
Jeana and Karl Werwath
Grady Wesson*
J. B. Wharton*
Kim Wheeler
Jane B. White
Warren A. Whitworth*
Dennis Wick
Tom Wieboldt*
Ken Wieringo
Shirley J. Wilkins
Ruth Williams
Mark Williams
Richard G. Williams Jr.*
Gary Williamson*
Eric Wiseman
Name Witheld*
Valerie Wohlleben
Crystal W Wood*
Todd Woodson*
Edgar and Betty Woodson
William & Isaac Worrell
Catherine Wray
Suzanne Wright
Sylvia Wright
John Wright
Gibson Wright

Matthew Yancey
Elizabeth Harrison Yancey
Dan Yatsko
John, David, and Lauren Yoder

Sammy Zambon*
Greg Zell*
Laurence Zensinger

*Nominated more than one tree.

Byron Carmean, pictured here on a baldcypress growing in Lake Drummond, nominated scores of trees to Virginia's Remarkable Tree and Big Tree programs. Other nominators whose efforts we particularly appreciate include Gary Williamson, Dean Norton, Greg Zell, Dennis Anderson, David Martin, Joe Murray, and the late Richard Salzer..

The following areas were nominated to the Remarkable Trees of Virginia Project as tree places of note. To learn more about them, visit the project website.

Caledon Natural Area, King George County; The Cedars, Lee County; Cumberland Gap National Park, Lee County; First Landing State Park, Virginia Beach; George Washington Birthplace National Monument, Westmoreland County; Great Falls National Park, Fairfax County; Kiptopeake State Park, Northampton County; North Side Richmond and the Lewis Ginter Botanical Garden; Maymont, city of Richmond; Montpelier, Orange County; Norfolk Botanical Garden, Norfolk; Occoneechee State Park, Mecklenburg County; Old City Cemetery, Lynchburg; Ramsey's Draft Wilderness Area, Augusta County; Ridgeview Park, Waynesboro; Sweet Briar College campus, Amherst County; Turkey Ridge Natural Area, Cumberland County; University of Mary Washington campus, Fredericksburg; Veterans Memorial Park, Abingdon; Virginia Tech campus, Montgomery County

INDEX

Note: Italicized *page numbers* indicate photographs.

Japanese maple (Acer palmatum), *Oatlands, Loudoun County*

INDEX

Osage-orange (Maclura pomifera), *Elmington, Gloucester County*

River birch (Betula nigra), Kenmore, Fredericksburg

Live oak (Quercus virginiana)*, Fort Monroe, Hampton*

Tulip-poplar (Liriodendron tulipifera), *Maymont, city of Richmond*